GOD
Meetings

*Build Healthy Leadership
and
Prevent Ministry Shipwreck*

ENDORSEMENTS

Your emphasis on ministry being to people, not building an organization, needs to be read by every pastor in ministry. I see this as the future textbook for practical theology (Christian ministry and leadership) courses in seminaries and Bible colleges!
—**Dr. Rex Johnson**, Professor in Christian Ministry & Leadership, Director Pastoral Care and Counseling, Biola University and Talbot School of Theology (ret.)

Dr. Dave Beckwith is a man on a mission to grow churches globally. Over the years, I have seen many corporate organizations transform their teams by creating cultures that rely on collaboration. I am impressed how Dave has focused this book on creating winning collaboration in churches, particularly between the pastor and the board. The goal is to grow the impact by getting everyone on the same page and moving together in a positive way! I highly recommend every church get copies of this book for their leaders and members.
—**Dr. Willie Jolley**, Hall of Fame Speaker, Nationally Syndicated Radio Host, and Best-Selling Author of *A Setback Is A Setup For A Comeback* and *An Attitude of Excellence*

Having been a coach, a Marine colonel, and a ministry CEO, I'm familiar with the challenges of effective leadership. I've always believed that it starts with relationships—those that are genuine, transparent, and trustworthy. Do you want to change the culture and overcome conflict in your church? This is the how-to book for pastors and church boards to work together and win!

—**Les Steckel**, President/CEO Fellowship of Christian Athletes (ret.), veteran NFL Coach, Colonel USMCR(ret.)

This is governance done God's way.

—**John Thune**, United States Senator

Dave addresses the elephant in the room of church leadership—the all too frequent conflicts between pastors and their church boards. He uses his own life experiences, his many years of being a pastor and caring for pastors, reliable research, and relevant Scripture to offer practical ways to create healthy church leadership. This should be required reading for all seminary students, pastors, and church board members.

—**Jim & Debbie Hogan**, Executive Director and Founders of Standing Stone Ministry and authors of *Shepherding Shepherds: The Standing Stone Story*

What a significant and essential book! There is so much pain within church leadership. Dave Beckwith's book is inspirational, encouraging, honest, and vulnerable. He shares from the heart and gives biblically-based practical wisdom. We are confident God will use this book in a huge way to bring peace and greater love into church leadership.

—**Larry Miller and Kathy Collard Miller**, speakers and authors of *God's Intriguing Questions* and over 50 other books

The most important formation in any local church is the relationship among the senior leaders who make up the church's governing board. These godly servants are seldom offered a concise workbook of biblical principles and best practices for the task they've been called to do together. Dave Beckwith comes with a deep foundation of Scripture and decades of experience as a senior pastor to provide profound wisdom for the leaders called by God to protect and encourage the church. Church boards would benefit greatly from using this training manual to ensure that their efforts will result in a healthy local congregation.

—**Bob Shank**, Founder/CEO, The Master's Program

Our churches are under relentless spiritual attack, with the enemy's primary bullseye being the church's "board room" (leadership team). Any role confusion, relational dysfunction, and unresolved conflict will ultimately ripple into the church. The body of Christ *desperately* needs a book like this to effectively help church leadership teams become relationally healthy and spiritually vibrant.

—**Lou Damiani**, Church Conflict Conciliator, Anchor Point Ministry

This book is both compelling and practical. It's a *must-read* for everyone in a leadership position in ministry. If we could turn all our meetings into God Meetings, more churches and organizations would be thriving!

—**Sam Lee**, author of *Be Free*, pastor, and field shepherd for Standing Stone Ministry

Dave masterfully shines a penetrating spotlight on the truism, "As the leadership goes, so goes the church." If the church today is weak and suffering, we need to look no further than its leaders. In my own pastoral experience, I have enjoyed the huge blessings right alongside the deep disappointments, and even despair, of working with the various boards of four different churches over the past forty years. The bottom line, as Dave rightly points out, is that the toxic fallout in the church from the dysfunctional and ungodly attitudes and actions of its leaders is enormous today! I so appreciate the practical, biblical insights Dave shares from his own journey.

—**Brad Fogal**, Senior Pastor of Anderson Island Christian Fellowship, Anderson Island, Washington

I've known the author of this book since boyhood days. Somewhere along the line, he picked up some smarts! Seriously, Dave does a great job differentiating church from business. Insightful. Enjoyable. Helpful!

—**Bob Thune**, Senior Pastor, Biola University Lifetime Achievement Award Winner

It is my privilege to wholeheartedly endorse *God Meetings* to any and all church leaders! A seasoned, wise, and gentle shepherd, Dave Beckwith addresses the elephant in the room of church meetings and then provides a way forward. Do yourself and your church a favor: Read and apply the principles of this book and watch your pastors flourish in their calling!

—**Chris Cannon**, HomeWord Center, Pastor to Pastor Director

Pastor Dave Beckwith and his wife, Joanne, have been coworkers and very dear friends for decades. I have always found them both to be compassionate and theologically sound. Their writings are practical, pointed, and very helpful.

—**Kitty Jones**, mentor, Bible teacher, and author of several studies, including *A Woman of God and a Wife*

Concise, biblical, and practical. *God Meetings* offers many helpful insights for pastors, church boards, and committees. One of the most challenging and frustrating aspects of a lead pastor's responsibilities is understanding how to lead and work with the church board effectively. This book provides senior ministry leaders with the principles and tools that can radically change the nature and interaction of those meetings. Highly recommended!

—**Dr. Gary Tangeman**, Lead Pastor of Celebration Church, Santa Ana, California

Dr. Beckwith has done it again by identifying and answering a critical need in the world of pastor and church board relationships. Do a pastor and church board desire to serve out of a biblical model while building a healthy relationship between the two? Then *God Meetings* should be required reading for both pastor and church board.

—**John Duval**, Executive Ministry Director, Standing Stone Ministry

This book is written with the wisdom of many personal experiences, and I believe it will help future leadership teams be what God calls them to be.

—**Frank Winans**, Senior Pastor, Woodbridge Community Church, Irvine, California

Many of the things that drive pastors to burnout are barely mentioned in seminary. Boring board meetings, contentious budgeting, and the endless pressure to be productive are just a few of the basics of ministry that no pastor can avoid, but few of us feel we've mastered.

That's why I'm grateful for the scholarly, wise, and proven guidance of Dr. Dave Beckwith. What they didn't cover in the classroom, we can get from a great coach. This book taught, encouraged, and inspired me!

—**Dr. Bruce Garner**, Senior Pastor at CrossPoint Church, Huntington Beach, California, and author of *The Resilient Pastor*

GOD
Meetings

Build Healthy Leadership
Prevent Ministry Shipwreck

DAVE BECKWITH
WITH
JOANNE BECKWITH

ALSO FEATURING 15 VIDEOS FROM
CHRISTIAN LEADERS

COPYRIGHT NOTICE

God Meetings: Build Healthy Leadership and Prevent Ministry Shipwreck

Third edition. Copyright © 2022, 2023 by Dave and Joanne Beckwith. The information contained in this book is the intellectual property of Dave and Joanne Beckwith and is governed by United States and International copyright laws. All rights reserved. No part of this publication, either text or image, may be used for any purpose other than personal use. Therefore, reproduction, modification, storage in a retrieval system, or retransmission, in any form or by any means, electronic, mechanical, or otherwise, for reasons other than personal use, except for brief quotations for reviews or articles and promotions, is strictly prohibited without prior written permission by the publisher.

Unless otherwise noted, all Scripture is from the *New Living Translation* (NLT) Copyright © 1996, 2004, 2007, 2013 by Tyndale House Foundation. Used by permission of Tyndale House Publishers Inc., Carol Stream, Illinois 60188. All rights reserved.

Other translations include:
—*New American Standard Bible* (NASB) Copyright © 1960, 1971, 1977, 1995, 2020 by The Lockman Foundation. Used by permission. All rights reserved. www.lockman.org.

—*The Living Bible* (TLB) Copyright © 1971 by Tyndale House Foundation. Used by permission of Tyndale House Publishers Inc., Carol Stream, Illinois 60188. All rights reserved.

—*The Message* (MSG) Copyright © 1993, 1994, 1995, 1996, 2000, 2001, 2002 by Eugene H. Peterson. Used by permission of NavPress Publishing Group.

Cover and graphics design: Derinda Babcock
Editors: Carrie Del Pizzo, Judy Hagey, Deb Haggerty

Authors represented by WordWise Media Services

PUBLISHED BY: Elk Lake Publishing, Inc., 35 Dogwood Drive, Plymouth, MA 02360, 2022

LIBRARY CATALOGING DATA

Names: Beckwith, Dave and Joanne (Dave and Joanne Beckwith)
God Meetings: Build Healthy Leadership and Prevent Ministry Shipwreck / Dave and Joanne Beckwith

420 p. 23cm × 15cm (9in × 6 in.)

ISBN-13: 9798891342170 (paperback) | 9798891342187 (trade hardcover) | 9798891342194 (trade paperback) | 9798891342200 (e-book)

Key Words: Church Boards; Dissension in the Church; Leadership; Pastoral Duties; Handling Difficult Situations; Building Harmony in the Church; Effective Team Building

Library of Congress Control Number: 2022931008 Nonfiction

DEDICATED TO THE GLORY OF GOD

Every morning
you'll hear me at it again.
Every morning
I lay out the pieces of my life
on your altar
and watch for fire to descend.
(Ps. 5:3 MSG)

WITH RECOGNITION AND APPRECIATION FOR:

Jim and Debbie Hogan

Visionaries to Shepherd the Shepherds

and the

Team of Shepherds with Standing Stone Ministry

TABLE OF CONTENTS

FOREWORD by Dr. Ken Eichler xv

ACKNOWLEDGMENTS xix

INTRODUCTION
The Fireplace to Ignite the Flames for Revival xxi

SECTION ONE—PURSUING GOD
The Almighty Awaits 1

1—FRUSTRATION IN THE BOARD ROOM
Why the Spiritual Life of Leaders Is Spiraling Downward and Pastors Are Exiting 3

2—WHO'S IN CHARGE?
Who Tells Who What to Do and Why It's Not Working. 17

3—TEAMWORK
Overcoming the Dark Side of Leadership and Discovering the Biblical Ideal of Team Ministry 37

4—BIBLICAL MEETINGS WITH GOD
Centuries Before Board Meetings, Leaders Met with the Almighty 55

5—BOARD MEETINGS OR GOD MEETINGS
What's the Difference? Why Is the Outcome So Different? 75

6—A MEETING WITH GOD
A Powerful Purpose and a Pattern to Follow 93

7—HOTHEADS AND BULLIES NEED NOT APPLY
Choosing Leaders God's Way 111

8—PURSUING DREAMS TOGETHER
Leaders Listening to God and Each Other 137

9—PREVENTING A BUDGET BLOW-UP

Avoiding the Pitfalls of a Play-It-Safe or Presumptuous Budget 155

10—GOD MEETING WITH THE PEOPLE
Engaging the Congregation to Catch the Vision and Transforming Business Meetings to Sacred Assemblies 177

SECTION TWO—PREVENTING PROBLEMS
Safeguarding the Ministry from Shipwreck 199

11—STORM NO. 1: UNREALISTIC EXPECTATIONS
Preventing Misunderstanding and Discouragement.. 201

12—STORM NO. 2: UNREALISTIC SCHEDULE
Preventing Burnout and Family Breakdown 225

13—STORM NO. 3: UNREALISTIC PRESSURE TO SUCCEED
Preventing Feelings of Failure in a Success-Saturated Culture 255

14—STORM SURVIVAL GUIDE: A PLAYBOOK FOR THE TEAM
Preventing Problems and Resolving Conflict 283

15—STORMS AND STANDING STRONG
Preventing Disaster by Developing Deep Roots and Authentic Relationships 309

ABOUT THE AUTHORS 323

APPENDICES:

1. God Meeting 325
2. Biblical Qualifications for Leadership 327
3. A Cheerful Giver 329
4. Three Simple Steps to New Life 331
5. Sr. Pastor Ministry Position Description 333
6. Core Values 337
7. Charting the Course Ministry Planner 339

TABLE OF CONTENTS

8. Commitment to Ministry Integrity 341
9. Staff Review and Excellence Planner 343
10. Ministry of Restoration 349
11. My Commitment to the Team 351
12. Playbook for God's Team 353

ENDNOTES 355

SCRIPTURE INDEX 371

SUBJECT INDEX 385

GOD MEETING VIDEO SERIES 397

FOREWORD

Written from the trenches of ministry, *God Meetings* is a gold mine of biblical insight to help pastors and board members walk in unity and partnership—a critical component for the health and success of our churches today.

Years ago, when pursuing my master's degree in theology, my professor pulled me aside to ask my perception of the course he taught regarding practical ministry for church leaders. He wanted to know if I (an older student who had served in pastoral ministry for a couple of decades) felt the strategies he taught were "relevant for ministry success" in today's culture.

Taking the risk of hurting his feelings, I expressed that some of his strategies wouldn't work well in ministry. He responded, "I knew it!" He explained that his longevity in academia kept him from experiencing hands-on ministry. He thanked me for my honesty, gracious response, and willingness to interact. Below the surface, I heard his heart's cry to be relevant in equipping and encouraging ministry leaders.

Dave and Joanne Beckwith have given their lives to equip and encourage ministry leaders (and their spouses) for biblically faithful success. I have enjoyed working with them for years. I can assure you they are wise and seasoned servants of God who peel away the façades church leaders build for appearances and carefully encourage them to deal with the truthful realities.

As I read each chapter in this book, I found myself repeatedly nodding, identifying with the stories shared. They brought up past feelings of frustration, discouragement, anger, disappointment, and betrayal. It was like Dave and Joanne were in the same meetings with me. My church leadership team needed and desired a God Meeting, but it often seemed impossible to experience. Differences in personalities and approaches to issues caused significant problems and hurt feelings. I didn't want to see a board member approaching me in the parking lot with an agenda-driven sidebar conversation.

God Meetings highlights everyday needs among ministry leaders. Pastors need to feel supported by their church board members, and those members need to feel heard and valued by their pastors. It's also critical for board members to feel mutually respected and valued as ministry partners. Too often, big and loud personality types hinder others from expressing their thoughts and ideas. This book helps board members recognize and practice the dynamics and strategies leading to a successful ministry team.

As the former Director of Ministry for an organization caring for thousands of ministry leaders and their spouses throughout the United States and different parts of the world, I have worked closely with pastors around the country and found church board meetings to be one of the most significant areas of stress. Whether elder boards, deacon boards, or other church governance boards, the vast majority are not functioning efficiently or successfully.

I love the humor in this book. Many authors try to be clever and funny but fall short of the mark. Dave does this effortlessly and satisfies my "humor buds," much like my wife's homemade mango-pineapple-jalapeno salsa. Enjoyable going down—with a kick at the end.

As a pastor/minister or board member, you will find Dave's writing style to be engaging and surprisingly unbiased. His honest portrayal of different members on leadership teams demonstrates his high regard for people making sacrificial contributions while serving their churches and communities.

Dave does not write from a theoretical approach but one forged in years of experience. His insight into the unique composition of church boards (personality types, leadership styles, etc.) is highly beneficial for understanding the makeup of your current leadership team. Whether you're a lead pastor/minister or a volunteer serving on a church board, knowing your teammates will prove valuable in the process when making wise and God-honoring decisions for the sake of your congregants and community.

As you read this book, I pray you will grasp the power available to your church when board members walk in unity and partnership. We will never experience that kind of power until God Meetings become common in our churches.

I suggest pastors and board members use this book as a template to help them get on the same page. It could also greatly benefit their churches in identifying, selecting, and preparing new board members to join their teams.

God Meetings is a gold mine for leadership—a game-changer!

—Dr. Ken Eichler

ACKNOWLEDGMENTS

I am grateful for the leadership and encouragement of Jim and Debbie Hogan, founders of Standing Stone Ministry. Their passion and commitment to the well-being of spiritual leaders is the backbone of this work.

I appreciate and applaud the work of Dr. Ken Eichler, who spent long hours reviewing the content of this book and offering helpful perspectives. Thanks, Ken.

Best-selling authors and professional editors Dr. Jeramy and Jerusha Clark invested long hours working on the manuscript. The book wouldn't be what it is without the insights and valuable editing of Jeramy and Jerusha. Their fingerprints are throughout the book. Thanks to both of you.

Working with the Elk Lake Publishing Team has been a delight. They are professionals with a passion for excellence and communicating spiritual truth. My appreciation to Deb Haggerty, Publisher and Editor-in-Chief, Derinda Babcock, Carrie Del Pizzo, and Judy Hagey. An enormous thank you for your patience and wise counsel.

My literary agent, Steve Hutson, has been a great help with advice, assistance, and encouragement. Thanks Steve.

I also appreciate those who reviewed the content or contributed stories. These include an exceptional group of pastors, leaders, and writers: Lou Damiani, Bob Thune, Rex Johnson, Gary Tangeman, Fred Chambers, Sam Lee, Larry Shelton, Willie Jolley, Les Steckel, Bob Shank, John Thune,

Frank Winans, John Duval, Al Yamashita, Chris and Anne Cannon, Bob Neu, Brad Fogal, and Bruce Garner.

My wife, Joanne, and I partnered together to write this book. While I am the primary writer, Joanne's insight and perspective are reflected in every paragraph. For over fifty years, we have weathered the storms of ministry plus the challenges and incredible joys of marriage. I admire and love her more than any person on earth. Thanks, sweetie, for the journey together.

INTRODUCTION

THE FIREPLACE TO IGNITE THE FLAMES FOR REVIVAL

The inside workings of too many Christian organizations stink to high heaven—horrific infighting, backstabbing, jealousy, and jostling for power damage the ministry and turn people away from Christianity.

In these dark days, the church needs a fresh awakening. So, what stands in the way? One of the major obstacles is the behavior of leaders in board meetings. In too many cases, the Holy Spirit has little influence as the elected leaders assume power and authority, muscling their way to get what they want. Aside from a prayer at the beginning and the end, board meetings are not much different from what goes on at city hall or a corporate board meeting. Board meetings are not mentioned in the Bible.

There is a better way.

For more than twenty years, I have been telling disillusioned, frustrated boards and pastors to cancel board meetings. Then, after they recover from the shock, I introduce them to a transformational way of working together. Petty jealousies, infighting, and politicking go by the wayside. Arm twisting and power plays are out. Rather than pressure to perform, rejoicing and mutual encouragement bolster the team. God is in control. A thirst for the Almighty becomes the norm as leaders seek a deepening relationship with God. Teamwork begins to flourish. Leaders awaken to an entirely new way of discerning God's direction and imparting vision.

Jesus told his disciples that leaders in the world throw their weight around and flaunt their authority, but "among you it will be different" (Matt. 20:26). Jesus is saying, "Discard the world's methodology and discover a distinctly new way of teaming together."

As you read, you'll discover several things in my approach.

1. **The governing group is sometimes referred to as the "leadership team."**

   This is a general term for elders, trustees, directors, boards, sessions, councils, deacons, or other designations. The name of the group is less important than how they function.

2. **Gender issues in leadership roles are intentionally avoided.**

   While the subject is important, it is beyond the scope of this work. Each organization needs to study this topic and reach a biblical decision.

3. **This is written to a broad spectrum of churches and Christian organizations.**

   From Baptists to Presbyterians, Quakers to Episcopalians, charismatics to conservatives, summer camps to outreach ministries, this book fits. Rather than recommending structural change, this book teaches governing groups of churches, schools, camps, mission organizations, and parachurch ministries about heart change resulting in relational change—regardless of the historical structure of the organization. Whether the body consists of 50, 500, or 5,000 people, surrendering to God's sovereign control in God Meetings, rather than board meetings, will deliver astounding results.

4. **Preventative solutions are offered for the explosive problems that can destroy ministries.**
Unhealthy conflicts, budget blow-ups, bullies and hotheads taking control, moral failures, destructive narcissistic leaders, contentious congregational meetings, and the unnecessary and premature exit of pastors are among the issues discussed.

God wants to bring revival to the church—beginning with leaders who humbly seek God, confess sinful behavior, and rely on the Holy Spirit to direct their work. God Meetings ignite the flames for revival. As the Psalmist said, "Revive us so we can call on your name once more" (Ps. 80:18).

May the fire of revival begin in God Meetings all around the world.

SECTION ONE

PURSUING GOD

THE ALMIGHTY AWAITS

Seek the LORD while you can find him.
Call on him now while he is near.
"My thoughts are nothing like your thoughts," says the LORD.
"And my ways are far beyond anything you could imagine.
For just as the heavens are higher than the earth,
so my ways are higher than your ways
and my thoughts higher than your thoughts."

(Is. 55:6, 8–9)

Leaders gather for one transcending purpose: to meet with God. It's that simple ... and I can't think of anything more important. Leaders stand on holy ground, lift up holy hands, listen to the Word of God, and discern God's marching orders. Leaders gather in the throne room of heaven, God's living room. This section will discuss how to accomplish the following goals:

- Prevent power struggles and questions of "Who's in charge?"
- Prevent the wrong people from occupying positions of power.
- Prevent a fiscal fiasco with a prayer and faith budget.
- Replace contentious congregational business meetings with spiritual renewal in a sacred assembly.
- Come together in team ministry with Jesus as the coach and owner of the team.
- Seek God's direction in every facet of church life.

The Almighty waits to meet with you!

> **Each chapter has a featured video by a Christian leader. See pages 399-400 to access the code for free access to the video series.**

—1—
FRUSTRATION IN THE BOARD ROOM

WHY THE SPIRITUAL LIFE OF LEADERS IS SPIRALING DOWNWARD AND PASTORS ARE EXITING

"I hate going to board meetings," I blurted out to a friend, who was shocked to hear this from his pastor. It was an honest admission but probably not a wise one to share with a church member.

It hadn't always been this way. During my thirty-plus years as a lead or senior pastor, I'd generally enjoyed good relationships and affirming friendships with board members. Yet, there had been a few tough times, and this was one of the most difficult. Every month in the board meeting, I listened to a couple who were long-time members attack my leadership and slice open my wife's ministry. They seemed intent on running us out of the church. I tamped down my desire to retaliate and jotted notes of what they said.

Perhaps if they perceived I was listening and addressing their concerns, the attacks would subside. I was wrong.

I remained determined to respond in a godly manner, but trying to sleep after a board meeting was futile. I didn't want to burden my wife with my hurt since she was in pain herself. Without someone to talk to—a safe place to share my pain—I sank, wounded and bleeding, into a deep depression. *How did things get to this point?*

When I first arrived as pastor, I discovered a dozen families had put their homes up as collateral to secure the church mortgage. The church carried excessive debt, and people were uptight about every expenditure. So we launched a campaign to eliminate the mortgage and add staff. For two years, the church thrived—healthy relationships, decisions for Christ, and an influx of new people. With the church nearly doubling in size and the loan paid off, we felt we'd found our church family and place of ministry for many years to come. But Joanne and I had poured ourselves into the work while ignoring our stress levels and lack of personal balance. We'd fed off the good feelings of ministry to the detriment of our own emotional and physical reserves. And then the bottom fell out.

Easter Sunday was planned as a major outreach to the community. When Joanne, the administrative secretary for the church, noticed on Good Friday the nursery was not yet set up for Sunday, she jumped in to help. Later that afternoon, friends joined us for a festive lunch at our home.[1] As the food was placed on the table, Joanne took a phone call in the office and motioned for the group to go ahead and eat. About thirty minutes later, she returned to the table with tears running down her cheeks—an awkward moment for everyone. I put my arm around her and asked, "Who was that on the phone? What happened?" Joanne wiped her tears and explained that a leading woman in the church verbally ripped into her, accusing her of meddling in her husband's responsibility. Joanne had quickly and profusely apologized, hoping to put the matter to rest, but this woman's words hurt deeply. Her unwillingness to accept Joanne's apology hurt even worse.

The Easter services were packed with record attendance and many decisions for Christ, but our joy was clouded by what had occurred. As the conflict intensified, Joanne drove her car to a quiet spot to be alone and cry out to God. She'd done nothing with ill will. Her efforts were intended to help a ministry, and now she was being attacked for her hard work. It didn't make sense.

A misunderstanding that should have been quickly resolved and forgotten, instead festered and escalated as this couple used their significant power base to cause a bitter distrust of our leadership to develop. They wanted an austere atmosphere in the services and felt everyone should enter the sanctuary and sit in silence before the worship service began. Any outburst of laughter or spontaneous applause in the worship service was, in their way of thinking, disgraceful. On their own initiative, they visited all the adult classes to lecture them on the proper way to enter a worship service. When worship participants, for the most part, ignored their chiding, the couple felt I should support them in their worship-in-silence crusade. I disagreed. I encouraged warm interaction, humor, and spontaneous clapping when appropriate. The couple used the monthly board meeting to present their list of what I was doing wrong as senior pastor. I protested to the board that this was wrong and hurtful to me, but they said, "We have to let people have their say."

Though the ministry continued to grow, Joanne and I were in pain. Bitterness weakened our effectiveness. The joy of ministry drained. Even with the assistance of a veteran pastor, attempts at reconciliation failed, and bitter resentment took root in our lives like a crop of weeds in a beautiful garden. I assumed I was the cause of the board dysfunction in that church. I blamed myself—if I had been emotionally stronger, prayed more, took a firmer stand, confronted the couple, built a stronger team to face the negativity—things would have been different. Erroneously, I also assumed most pastors and church boards worked together harmoniously. Not so!

Frustration and Friction

In the years that followed, I discovered many churches have dysfunctional relationships among their leaders. The inner workings—the crucial relationships that drive the ministry—are often fraught with antagonism, distrust, in-fighting, jealousies, hidden or spewed anger, and high levels of exasperation and disappointment. Why is this happening? What is the root of the problem?

For Volunteer Leaders

When meeting privately or in a group with volunteer board members—leaders who love the Lord and want God's work to advance—I have heard comments like these:

- I can't wait until my term of service is over. I'll never sign up for this again.
- I thought there would be a great sense of working together. I'm disappointed with the conflict and squabbling that goes on.

- I feel farther from God now than when I began serving on the board.
- I'm confused about who's in charge. Is the pastor the leader, or should the board take control?
- Board meetings are more like what goes on at city hall than a Christian gathering.

Dr. Robert Munger, professor at Fuller Theological Seminary and author of the best-selling booklet, *My Heart—Christ's Home*, surveyed those serving on church boards. One question asked, "Since serving on a church board, do you feel your spiritual life has improved or declined?" A shocking 80 percent of board members said their spiritual life had declined.[2] Eighty percent? If this were 30 percent, I would be deeply concerned. Eighty percent is tragic.

This is a flashing red light on the church health dashboard. Something is seriously wrong! How can people do God's work while growing more distant in their relationship with him? We can't serve God when our spiritual lives are in a tailspin. How can an unwatered and neglected tree bear good fruit? A pastor friend from years ago, Chuck Miller, often used a phrase that has stuck with me: "To *do* the work of God, we must first *be* the people of God." Jesus said, "Yes, I am the vine; you are the branches. Those who remain in me, and I in them, will produce much fruit. For apart from me you can do nothing" (John 15:5). Spiritual fruit comes from healthy spiritual roots: "The root of the righteous yields fruit" (Prov. 12:12 NASB). Withered spiritual roots can't produce fruitful trees. Paul said, "Let your roots grow down into him, and let your lives be built on him. Then your faith will grow strong in the truth you were taught, and you will overflow with thankfulness" (Col. 2:7).

Serving the Lord as a leader should be a spiritual growth catalyst—not a spiritual catastrophe. I allow that some may discover serving on the church board isn't their calling. I also acknowledge adding the busyness and responsibility of being on the board may hinder spiritual life. However, I think the inner workings of church boards are, in too many cases, not conducive to spiritual growth. The work of being on a board should not be more business-like than spiritually uplifting.

Sometimes there is a gradual drift. In the early days of a church, the pastor and leaders often have a strong sense of community—sharing personal needs, praying together, and growing in faith. They know if God doesn't show up, the whole thing will collapse. In humility, they're driven to their knees. Redemptive life flows freely. Friendships flourish. But as the church grows, a subtle shift takes place. Strategizing, analyzing statistics, developing policy and procedure, hashing out issues—all important things—become predominant, leaving less and less time for God-dependent prayer and deeper growth in the Word. A dangerous assumption prevails—surely spiritual leaders are mature and thriving in their walk with God—so there's little time spent on spiritual growth. The busyness of leading chokes the inner spiritual life, which becomes dry and malnourished—much like the shriveled roots of a once fruitful tree.

For Pastoral Leaders

What is it like for pastors working with the board?

Pastoral ministry is a difficult task. Along with the many joys, there are hidden landmines. Surviving brutal attacks is one thing when surrounded by a supportive team but nearly impossible when alone. Unfortunately, many pastors don't have a strong support team. Isolation is one of the primary indicators of pastoral danger.

As I care for leaders, I frequently talk with pastors on edge and at odds with their governance board—elders, deacons, trustees, etc. Governance issues are often high on their list of frustrations. Some have felt betrayed, stymied in their vision, misunderstood in their motives. They may feel more criticized than encouraged, more micro-managed than trusted.

Other pastors—perhaps in reaction to this—choose to "take the board by the horns." They become dictators who run roughshod over anyone who disagrees with them. Don't you dare trample on their vision! They get their orders from God Almighty. If you oppose them, you are fighting G-O-D (spoken with a thunderous voice). This leadership style often causes an explosive reaction.

This internal rub and friction fracture the work of God. Let's not assume the pastor is right and the volunteer leaders wrong or vice versa. It goes deeper to something systemic, something toxic in the inner workings. Are we using methods of the world to do spiritual work? Is God really in charge of the work? Or is Jesus merely a figurehead? In too many churches, there is little difference between a corporate board and a church board—other than a prayer at the beginning and the end.

The Francis A. Schaeffer Institute of Church Leadership Development found that 52 percent of pastors identified organization control issues as the number one reason they left the church they were serving. In other words, a conflict arose that forced them out based on who would lead—pastor, elders, deacons, a power-wielding church member, or a faction. In addition, 14 percent of pastors stated the number one reason for leaving was resistance to their leadership, vision, teaching, or change.[3] The research was from a sample of 1,050 pastors at a conference (not intended as a controlled statistical study). This identifies a significant sore point that leads to disruption and upheaval. Combining these two statistics, approximately 66 percent of pastors identify control issues and resistance to their leadership as the number one reason they left the church they were serving.

In a study of Church of Christ pastors who left the ministry, 60 percent pointed to an unsatisfactory relationship with church board members as the reason. The root problem, according to one denominational leader, was the authoritarian role assumed by the elders.[4] And a survey of over 35,000 churches by LeaderCare, a ministry of LifeWay Christian Resources, indicated "the top reason for firing pastors is still one of control—who is going to run the church."[5]

There are times when a change of leadership is appropriate and needed. But when disruption occurs over preventable, unresolved issues among leadership, the cost to the church and the ministry is staggering. Strictly from a dollar standpoint, personnel change is very costly. In the business world, the cost of replacing a top-level executive is estimated somewhere between $100,000 and $250,000. A church leader's stormy departure seriously disrupts the congregation as well. When the pastor leaves, some people leave. When the new pastor arrives, more people leave. When the new pastor makes some changes, additional people leave. It's a moving experience!

I firmly believe if churches and Christian non-profit organizations functioned in harmonious, spiritually uplifting ways and pursued kingdom goals, the course of Christianity would march forward rather than limping from one resignation to the next.

Pursuing Peace

Paul reminded all believers, "If possible, so far as it depends on you, be at peace with all men" (Rom. 12:18 NASB). Peter chimed in, "Search for peace, and work to maintain it" (1 Pet. 3:11). Chuck Swindoll commented on this verse, "We're a people who love to argue and fight. We jump to our feet when wronged, dig in our heels when challenged, and clench our fists when crossed. Whether it's over minor doctrinal differences or carpet color, Christians can quickly rob each other of peace. Instead of seeking and pursuing peace, we often pursue controversy or engage in open conflict."[6] What a contrast to these refreshing words from the Psalmist, "How wonderful and pleasant it is when brothers live together in harmony!" (Ps. 133:1).

Is the Holy Spirit prompting you to pursue peace with a brother or sister in the family of God? Maybe it's with the pastor. Or pastor, it may be with a board member or a church attendee. Do you need to take a step toward reconciliation by acknowledging a rift between you and someone else and asking forgiveness for your contribution to the problem? Don't let pride stand in the way. Pride and peace are like oil and water—they don't mix. This phrase from Romans 12:18 is crucial: "so far as it depends on you, be at peace." The ball is in your court—initiate the action, make the appointment, and do your part to pursue peace. Reconciliation may occur immediately. Wonderful. It may be years before you experience reconciliation with that person. Or it may not take place at all. That's okay as long as you did your part to pursue peace.

The Rest of the Story

To continue the story from the start of this chapter, my wife and I pursued peace with the antagonistic couple, but nothing changed. No reconciliation. Three years later, we moved to another church ministry and began the hard work of forgiveness—for our own health and peace of mind.

Fast-forward seventeen years. A Sunday was proclaimed "World Reconciliation Sunday." Believers around the world were encouraged to make restitution, apologize for hurts, and seek peace with one another. Globally, pastors were encouraged to speak on reconciliation, and I prepared a message on the topic.

As I stood up to speak that Sunday, I was stunned to see the couple who'd inflicted such pain in our lives sitting in the fourth row. What were they doing here? They lived nearly five hundred miles away, and I couldn't imagine why they'd be in the congregation that day. I certainly didn't want to see them. Strong feelings of hurt and resentment surged through my emotions, making it difficult to continue speaking. Old wounds and painful memories from the past were triggered, overwhelming me. Silently I protested, "Lord, this isn't fair putting *them* in the audience while I'm trying to speak on this topic." Meanwhile, Joanne was in pain, as this couple was sitting in her row, a few seats away.

I struggled to continue. How could I speak of reconciliation while simultaneously fighting a fierce battle with the issue? This was too close for comfort—too personal. Finally, while delivering the message, I prayed silently, "Lord, I'm willing for reconciliation." Immediately, I had the freedom to continue with the message.

Following the service, Joanne and I talked with the couple and discovered they were visiting Southern California and randomly chose a church. They were as shocked as we were when they walked in and saw I was the pastor of the church and the speaker for the morning.

Who but God could have arranged this miraculous meeting on World Reconciliation Sunday more than seventeen years after the conflict?

Reconciliation may take years, but pursuing peace today is not optional.

> Work at living in peace with everyone, and work at living a holy life, for those who are not holy will not see the Lord. Look after each other so that none of you fails to receive the grace of God. Watch out that no poisonous root of bitterness grows up to trouble you, corrupting many. (Heb. 12:14-15)

REFLECTION AND DISCUSSION

Quick Recall

- Chuck Miller said, "To do the work of God, we must first _____."
- According to the survey by Dr. Robert Munger, _____ percent of board members said their spiritual life declined while serving on a church board.
- According to the Francis A. Schaeffer Institute of Church Leadership Development, _____ percent of pastors identified organization control issues—who would lead the church—as the number one reason they left the church they were serving. In addition, _____ percent of pastors stated the number one reason for leaving was resistance to their leadership, vision, teaching, or change.

Thinking It Through

1. Why do you think such a large number report their spiritual life declined while serving on the church board?

2. Why is the following assumption dangerous? Spiritual leaders are mature and thriving in their walk with God, so there's little need to spend time on spiritual growth. Describe the type of leadership team you'd like to be part of. How would that team help you grow spiritually?

3. Is there someone you need to contact to pursue peace and forgiveness?

> Let your roots grow down into him, and let your lives be built on him. Then your faith will grow strong in the truth you were taught, and you will overflow with thankfulness. (Col. 2:7)

—2—

WHO'S IN CHARGE?

WHO TELLS WHO WHAT TO DO AND WHY IT'S NOT WORKING

"Who's in charge?" is not a theoretical question. It hits the core of the most important working relationship in the church. Does the board tell the pastor what to do, or does the pastor tell the board what to do? Sometimes it simmers under the surface, creating occasional friction and irritation without turning into a significant problem. Other times a major crisis causes this below-the-surface issue to burst into flame, bringing contention and a potentially ugly showdown.

This issue came to a head at the worst possible time in a church I served decades earlier. The church had experienced rapid growth, increasing from several hundred in attendance to several thousand. With the numerical growth, the church launched into a massive building program incurring millions in debt. The senior pastor was a likable leader with a dictatorial style. He decided the church should buy a strip mall nearby for additional space. The elders pushed back, questioning the wisdom of the decision and refusing to back the pastor's plan. So the pastor fired the elders—all of them. He did not have the constitutional right to fire the elected elders, but he felt he could get away with it. After several attempts to reconcile the situation, but without success, the elders and conference leaders took the appropriate steps. They fired the senior pastor (which they had a constitutional right to do).

The senior pastor left to start a new church in town, taking hundreds of people with him. His departure left behind a bewildered congregation with an enormous crisis on their hands. Construction on a new worship center seating thousands was already in progress. Should they halt construction? The building program was in jeopardy, and the ability to make payments on the debt was in question.

Fortunately, God brought a wise and courageous pastor who stepped into the lead pastor position. He worked with the elders, rallied the remaining church to move forward, completed the building campaign, and the church continues today with a vital, healthy ministry. The "who's in charge" issue nearly destroyed this church, but God brought clarity out of confusion.

Confusion and Chaos

As I meet with pastors, I frequently discover confusion regarding their role with the board. "I tried to take the lead, but the board shot me down. In essence, they've told me, 'You preach and teach and visit the sick. We handle the direction and administration of the church.'" On the other hand, I find board members equally confused. "Why do I serve on the board? All the pastor wants is yes-people around him. My opinion matters little. When the pastor brings something to the board, he has already decided the course of action. All he wants is a unanimous vote so he can proceed."

One senior pastor who led a sizeable congregation for decades acted as a dictator under the guise of "board approval." He would bring a course of action to the board, and with little discussion, announce, "I know you're all in favor of this. The Bible says dissension is a sin. All in favor say, 'Amen.'" No one dared oppose the pastor who used the board as a rubber stamp. What a façade!

The ins and outs of leading and decision-making in the church can feel like this description of baseball from the Minnesota Twins program a few years ago.

- You have two sides, one out in the field and one in.
- Each man that's on the side that's in goes out, and when he's out, he comes in, and the next man goes in until he's out.
- When three men are out, the side that's out comes in, and the side that's been in goes out and tries to get those coming in out.
- Sometimes you get men still in and not out.
- When both sides have been in and out nine times, including the not outs, that's the end of the game.[1]

Confusion in baseball may lead to errors or a team loss, but chaos in church leadership has much higher stakes. A clouded decision-making process threatens the spiritual well-being of all involved. What are the roles of the pastor, the board, and the congregation? Who's in and who's out? Churches need biblical clarity *before* a big crisis hits the fan. Constitutions and bylaws establish the formal organizational and legal structure, but this is not about changing these documents. While these may need revision and biblical alignment, my concern is fine-tuning the week-to-week and month-to-month decision-making processes and working relationships involving the pastor, staff, and representative leadership.

THREE MODELS

Your decision-making style and board expectations are usually shaped by past experience and personal preference. If you're a small business owner, you may assume a one-person decision-making model works best. If you're coming from the corporate world, the board-led church with a subservient pastor and staff is likely your model of choice. If you're a blue-collar laborer, you may expect a foreman-like pastor to give you directions without much discussion—just do it and ask questions later or not at all. If your background is military, you probably expect a top-down authority structure where the general barks orders and everyone falls in line. If you played sports, your ideal might be a team approach that rallies everyone together for a big win.

Several pastors told me they had to change their leadership style when they moved to a new church. In a blue-collar working community, the board expected the pastor to develop the plan and tell them what needed doing. Church leaders who were executives in the business world felt insulted if shut out from making a decision. They didn't appreciate the pastor telling them what to do, and more likely, they preferred telling the pastor what to do.

In addition, the pastor's style is strongly influenced by past training or giftedness. If mentored by a successful, autocratic leader, the pastor will likely follow the same pattern. The pastor with a strong leadership gift will feel shut down and frustrated if denied the opportunity to cast vision and lead the charge. The people-loving, compassionate pastor who feels uncomfortable as a "general issuing marching orders" will favor the board taking the lead.

Dr. Michael Anthony, former Chairman of Christian Education at Talbot School of Theology, served as my associate pastor, ministry partner, and friend for many years during my two decades of ministry at Woodbridge Church. He wrote *The Effective Church Board*, and I contributed to some of the sections in his excellent work. In his chapter on "Organizational Structure in the Church," Michael includes content from my original training materials, "Keys for Team Ministry," regarding the following three models of church government.[2]

Corporate Model

Many assume the corporate model is the biblical model, but it's not. The corporate model with a board of directors is a relatively recent development in history. The concept of a board of directors originated in seventeenth-century Europe with companies of considerable size.[3] More recently, the church, as a non-profit corporation, began to follow the pattern below:

Corporate Model

Board of Directors

President, CEO, or Sr. Pastor

The board of directors establishes direction and policy, and the president, chief executive officer, or senior pastor carry out the board's directives.

In identifying faulty models of leadership, Pastor Robert H. Thune wrote, "In this model, which closely mirrors corporate governance, the pastor functions as the CEO or 'point leader' of the church. The elders are not seen as pastors but rather as a sort of 'governing board' whose job is to keep the pastors in check and provide a system of checks and balances (lest the ministry staff or pastors have too much power). ... Churches that practice this model are not following the Bible's teaching on church leadership."[4]

While this is not the biblical model, it's worth identifying some of the advantages and dangers inherent in the corporate model. Major decisions for the corporation are deliberated by a plurality of individuals who presumably have a wealth of knowledge and experience. The corporate board has the advantage of seeing a larger picture than the CEO involved in managing the day-to-day operation.

The CEO or other officers are held responsible for carrying out the directives of the board, and the board has the liberty to hire or fire the CEO and other officers. If the corporation is a publicly-traded company, the board of directors may focus to a large extent on keeping the stockholders happy. In the corporate world, boards of directors often have power skirmishes. Controlling interests may be vested with a voting block of directors, and the voice of the stockholders may cast a foreboding shadow over decisions. Directors may seek majority stock ownership to take control of the corporation.

When the corporate model is applied in the church, the board (elders, deacons, trustees, council, session, etc.) are the directors, the pastor is the CEO, and the congregation functions somewhat like stockholders. Many decisions are based on the concerns of the church members. Board meetings may open with a quick prayer followed by the latest complaints circulating among the congregation, setting a negative tone for the meeting. Elected board members are likely to focus more on pleasing the congregation than pleasing God.

Like the corporate world, too many church governance meetings are marred by power skirmishes and heated disagreements. Dominant personalities may exert dictatorial control—seeking to establish voting blocks. James rebuked this kind of behavior: "If you have bitter jealousy and selfish ambition in your heart, do not be arrogant and so lie against the truth. This wisdom is not that which comes down from above, but is earthly, natural, demonic. For where jealousy and selfish ambition exist, there is disorder and every evil thing" (James 3:14-16 NASB). Demonic influence in the board room? Yes. Demons kicking up their heels in delight over disorder and ego skirmishes? Absolutely. James doesn't mince words: this behavior is *earthly* (the world's way of operating), *natural* (self-seeking, rooted in the sin nature), and *demonic* (inspired and instigated by the prince of the darkness).

I know a pastor who took his shoe off and banged it on the conference table because he didn't get his way. I'm well acquainted with another pastor who frequently went into a tirade. He would climb up on the conference room table and shout to force the issue and get his plan approved. A board member I served with blew his top when the other members of the board wouldn't change the dollar amount in the line item for his favorite project. He promptly resigned from the board and every position he held in the church.

A church leader threatened Pastor Charles Stanley, "If you don't watch what you're doing, you're going to get hurt." And then he hit Charles Stanley in the face. A former boxer jumped up to defend his pastor while another friend intervened.[5] It was quite a showdown at the carnal corral.

Chuck Swindoll tells about an individual who opposed him by threatening him with a gun.

Many years ago, in another place and at another time in my life, I went through a dreadful experience with a person who decided to make me his enemy. I still don't know why. It remains a mystery. Nevertheless, it occurred. This individual decided to make my life miserable. He watched my every move. He questioned my decisions. He cast doubts on my ministry. This person applied pressure, sometimes to the point where I thought I would scream. I don't know how much he said to others. I never asked. But he said enough to me and was bullying and intimidating enough that I became frightened, especially when I realized he carried a gun. Eventually, on one occasion, he threatened me with it.[6]

What despicable behavior while supposedly serving God. James asks, "What is the source of quarrels and conflicts among you? Is not the source your pleasures that wage war in your members?" (James 4:1 NASB). The corporate model doesn't cause these ugly behaviors—they come from the evil and self-centered desires that wage war within.

Presidential Model

On the other end of the spectrum is a second model, the presidential model.

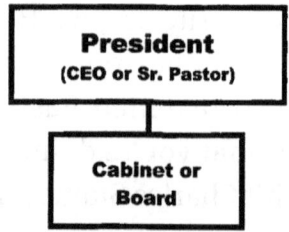

The cabinet or board gives advice, but the president, chief executive officer, or senior pastor set the direction and make decisions.

A flip from the corporate model is the presidential model. In this model, the corporate president or chief executive functions in a similar fashion to the president of the United States. Of course, the president doesn't have absolute power because of the legislative and judicial branches. However, the president has total control over cabinet decisions regardless of their opinions.

For example, when Abraham Lincoln presented the Emancipation Proclamation to his cabinet, they opposed it, feeling it would unnecessarily block peaceful reconciliation with the Confederacy. Following the discussion, all cabinet members voted "nay," and Lincoln voted "aye." President Lincoln announced, "The ayes have it." This story may be part folklore, but we know several of Lincoln's cabinet members opposed the Emancipation Proclamation—one of the greatest documents in history, ending human slavery in the United States.

The role of the president's cabinet is advisory only. They are selected by the president (subject to approval by the senate), and they serve at the wishes of the president. As we often see in the headlines, the president can fire cabinet members on a whim.

The presidential model has advantages. The cabinet may offer competent counsel to the president if the president is willing to accept it. Things get done much more quickly with the presidential model than the corporate model. If the president is a good and benevolent leader, the best interests of the people are served. If the leader is corrupt and dishonest, disaster is ahead. As Proverbs says, "When the godly are in authority, the people rejoice. But when the wicked are in power, they groan" (29:2).

Perhaps in reaction to some of the board-led corporate model abuses, I'm finding a growing number of pastors following the presidential model. They believe God appointed them to lead the church up the mountain. They are visionary, passionate, and impatient with the status quo. They may achieve much, and if the pastor is godly and compassionate, kingdom work advances. However, this model is open to misuse and abuse, sometimes fostering leaders with an exaggerated sense of self-importance who are prone to use their power to manipulate and control others. In their drive to succeed, they may resist wise counsel and approvals. "Without consultation, plans are frustrated, but with many counselors they succeed" (Prov. 15:22 NASB).

Advocates of the pastor-presidential model often cite the presidential-like style of Moses, who received his orders directly from God. Moses had his inner-circle of assistants, Aaron, Miriam, and Joshua, plus the seventy elders (Num.11:16-25), and another group of appointed leaders of thousands, hundreds, fifties, and tens who settled disputes before they came to Moses (Exod. 18:25-26).

Did the seventy elders tell Moses what to do and threaten to remove him if he didn't get them to the Promised Land in thirty days or less? Hardly. Those who opposed the leadership of Moses were dealt with by God—the rebellion of the sons of Korah (Num. 16:1-40) and Miriam and Aaron speaking against Moses (Num. 12:1-15) are prime examples. Moses was in charge—no question about it.

Should a leader today assume the Moses mantle of leadership style, leading via direct communication with God? I don't think so because of one fundamental difference. Moses received explicit, infallible, word-for-word instructions from God. I acknowledge I am suspect of any leader today claiming God gives them infallible, not-to-be-questioned, do-it-or-die directions. God has never left a voice mail on my phone or sent me a registered letter

(I do receive text messages from God—text messages from the biblical text!). Since we have the written Word of God, we seek to discern the leading and will of God through the Bible, the leading of the Holy Spirit, and the wise counsel of others. I confess that some of the ideas I thought were from God turned out to be pretty whacko. Seeking the counsel of others has prevented me from proceeding with some very crazy ideas.

Leaders need to set an example of being subject to one another (Eph. 5:21). Erwin W. Lutzer, who served as senior pastor of the Moody Memorial Church in Chicago, commented, "I wince when I hear a pastor teach his congregation to submit to authority when he believes he is an exception to the rule. 'I'm accountable to God alone' sounds pious, but it can be poisonous. The New Testament teaches that a congregation is to have a plurality of godly leaders with no one person assuming the role of dictator."[7] This is quite different than the presidential model.

Team Ministry Model

Though often overlooked, there is a third model of ministry that aligns with the teaching in the New Testament.

Many churches are discovering a team approach to ministry, a pattern that has been around for centuries and is rooted in biblical teaching. In the New Testament, Jesus was head of the church (Col. 1:15-18), and a plurality of elders led the individual churches (Acts 14:23). This was a safeguard preventing any single individual from playing God or being a self-appointed dictator. The team ministry model is not the same as the corporate model since pastors have equal status with the elders—pastors are elders. "Certainly, the biblical model of eldership in principle authorizes at least an equal status for the pastor with his board."[8]

Jesus Christ, as head of the church, directs the ministry through a plurality of surrendered servant-leaders who seek to know and do the will of God.

Team ministry allows for shared decision-making and mutual accountability. The team approach also works with a variety of existing structures, whether the pastor is teaming up with elders, deacons, trustees, or lay ministers. Chapter 3 is devoted to a broader discussion of teamwork.

WHO IS *REALLY* IN CHARGE?

Whether it's the corporate, presidential, or team ministry model, the question of "Who's in charge?" *must* be answered. The answer to this question will ultimately determine the health and vitality of an organization or its ultimate schism and demise.

Politics and Power Plays

One of the pet topics of the disciples was to argue about who was the greatest (Luke 9:46; 22:24). It would have been fascinating to eavesdrop on their pride parade. Proverbs 27:2 (NASB) says, "Let another praise you, and not your own mouth." When someone sings their own praises, they usually get the pitch painfully out of tune. One day, Mama Zebedee came to Jesus and asked that her two darling sons, James and John, be given the privilege of sitting on his right and left in his kingdom. The other disciples were fuming mad. Of all the nerve—send your mama to worm your way to the top.

Jesus used the occasion to teach the nature of genuine greatness and authentic leadership—an entirely new concept called "servant-leaders." In this power struggle, Jesus called the disciples together and said, "You know that the rulers in this world lord it over their people, and officials flaunt their authority over those under them. But among you it will be different. Whoever wants to be a leader among you must be your servant, and whoever wants to be first among you must become your slave" (Matt. 20:25-27).

Notice the phrase, "among you it will be different." Distinctly different. Radically different! Not a dressed-up, warmed-over Christian version of the world's system, but a uniquely powerful way of doing things that is quite contrary to the world's idea of leadership. Too many church board meetings are more political than spiritual. Jostling and positioning for personal preferences and plans is common fare. Individuals huddle in advance to plan a strategy to get their proposal approved and scheme to sideline the opposition. Voting blocks form to control the direction of the organization. This is how the world operates. But "among you it will be different," Jesus said.

One definition of the word *politic* means "to look out for one's interests; to scheme; to be crafty." This is fairly typical behavior in corporate board meetings and legislative halls, but should church leaders be playing politics? Should board members or pastors look out for their own interests, scheme, be crafty, and pursue what they want? By no means!

Politicking poisons churches. Numerous surveys of pastors and volunteer leaders identify board relationships as one of the most painful and disappointing parts of their church relationship. I ache for pastors who have been stabbed or betrayed by the church leaders. And I spend a lot of my time coming alongside wounded and discarded pastors. It's sad to see those who volunteer their time to serve on a church board but depart disillusioned and discouraged with the infighting and politics. I mourn, knowing there have been times when I contributed to the problem.

Jesus Is in Charge!

Jesus is not a figurehead, a beloved but absent leader who exercises little or no actual authority. Jesus is the absolute, sovereign head of the church. He is present whether we acknowledge his lordship or not. "Not my will, but your will be done" must be the mindset for every servant-leader. Like the mountain God called Moses and the elders to climb to meet with him (Exod. 24:9-11), the board room should be a sacred meeting place with servant-leaders gathered around the throne of God. "So let us come boldly to the throne of our gracious God. There we will receive his mercy, and we will find grace to help us when we need it most" (Heb. 4:16). In weakness, we come knowing "nothing in all creation is hidden from God. Everything is naked and exposed before his eyes, and he is the one to whom we are accountable" (Heb. 4:13). Tremble with awe when you enter a God Meeting, humbled by the privilege and overwhelmed with how little you know.

As servant-leaders, this awareness should change how we treat each other. How can we discover his will, his plans, his directives without complete surrender in our lives? We need to set aside our arrogance, our pompous self-will, our pushy, nasty narcissism. Let no unwholesome word—cutting, critical, conniving, condemning word—proceed from your mouth (Eph. 4:29). Because God is present in this holy meeting room—present in the lives of each team member—we ought to bow before him and let grace and kindness flow freely. This is a radically different way of working together. If the meeting isn't fundamentally different from the last corporate or city hall meeting you attended, Jesus probably is not in charge.

Jesus Christ is the head of the church worldwide and every local church and ministry. The lead pastor, chairman, executive officers, and all team members surrender before Jesus.

> Christ is the visible image of the invisible God. He existed before anything was created and is supreme over all creation, for through him God created everything in the heavenly realms and on earth. He made the things we can see and the things we can't see—such as thrones, kingdoms, rulers, and authorities in the unseen world. Everything was created through him and for him. He existed before anything else, and he holds all creation together. Christ is also the head of the church, which is his body. He is the beginning, supreme over all who rise from the dead. So he is first in everything. (Col. 1:15-18)

The Bible proclaims Jesus Christ as the absolute sovereign over all creation and the supreme head of the church. Yes, there may be a chairman, senior or lead pastor, chief financial officer, etc., but the headship of the organization is vested in Jesus Christ alone. Theologically, this is rock solid truth. All who affirm God's Word hold to this, but relatively few practice it. So how do we recognize Jesus Christ as the head of the church? I admit A. W. Tozer gets under my skin. He speaks with a probing prophetic voice as he opens his heart of concern regarding the authority of Christ in the church today.

> Here is the burden of my heart, and while I claim for myself no special inspiration, I feel that this is also the burden of the Spirit. If I know my own heart, it is love alone that moves me to write this. My grief is simply the result of a condition which I believe to be almost universally prevalent among the churches. I should acknowledge that I am myself very much involved in the situation I here deplore. This is written with the hope that we all may turn unto the Lord our God and sin no more against Him.
>
> Let me state the cause of my burden: Jesus Christ has today almost no authority at all among the groups that call themselves by His name. And I include those that protest the loudest that they are in spiritual descent from our Lord and His apostles, namely, the evangelicals.
>
> The present position of Christ in the gospel churches may be likened to that of a king in a limited, constitutional monarchy: no more than a traditional rallying point, a pleasant symbol of unity and loyalty, much like a flag or a national anthem. He is lauded, feted and supported, but his real authority is small.
>
> The idea that Christ Jesus has absolute and final authority over the whole church and over its members in every detail of their lives is simply not now accepted as true by the rank and file of evangelical Christians. What church board consults our Lord's words to decide matters under discussion? What Sunday school committee goes to the Word for directions? Who remembers when a conference chairman brought his Bible to the table with him for the purpose of using it? Minutes, regulations, rules of order, yes. The sacred commandments of the Lord, no.[9]

We come running into a meeting after a busy day, say a quick prayer asking that God will see our view as his view, and then make decisions assuming our will is his will. We are agenda-driven, hurried to rush on with life, rather than God-directed. But there should be no higher priority for us as spiritual leaders than to seek the mind of God and the clear authority and direction of Jesus Christ. Is that possible if we don't spend time with him listening to his Word? God may want to reveal a plan we haven't even thought about ... that is if he can get on the agenda. What if he wants us to take a step of faith that seems humanly impossible? What if he wants us to bury a sacred cow—something that has been around so long it's begun to stink? It takes prayer and study of the Word of God to discern his thoughts and plans. How sad to think we can know the mind of God without spending time listening and waiting before him. His thoughts are often contrary to our thoughts. "'My thoughts are nothing like your thoughts,' says the LORD. 'And my ways are far beyond anything you could imagine. For just as the heavens are higher than the earth, so my ways are higher than your ways and my thoughts higher than your thoughts'" (Isa. 55:8–9).

Who's in charge? Surrendered, we affirm, "Lord Jesus, this church or Christian ministry belongs to you. Take charge!"

All in favor, say aye ... or better, amen.

Reflection and Discussion

Quick Recall

- What are the three models of board governance mentioned in this chapter?

- Politicking _____ churches.
- Describe the observation of A. W. Tozer in your own words. The present position of Christ in the gospel churches is...

Thinking It Through

1. What or who provided a model for you regarding leadership and decision-making?

2. What is your church's leadership structure? What are its strengths? Weaknesses?

3. What steps would you suggest to acknowledge the lordship of Jesus Christ when servant-leaders meet?

4. What do you purpose to do before entering a leadership meeting if you're harboring sin or animosity in your heart?

> You know that the rulers in this world lord it over their people, and officials flaunt their authority over those under them. But among you, it will be different. Whoever wants to be a leader among you must be your servant, and whoever wants to be first among you must become your slave. (Matt. 20:25-27)

—3—
TEAMWORK

OVERCOMING THE DARK SIDE OF LEADERSHIP AND DISCOVERING THE BIBLICAL IDEAL OF TEAM MINISTRY

Year after year, the Super Bowl, NBA Championship, World Series, Stanley Cup, World Cup, Rose Bowl, and many other events are won not by individuals but by teams. Interviews after championships frequently show team members giving credit to coaches and other team members and coaches giving credit to players. Teams who finish second, third, or lower may have greater talent, but often they failed to win the championship because individual players who were more concerned about their personal stats or divisiveness hurt the team.

TEAM MINISTRY
The Biblical Ideal

Championship teams have a secret sauce—an elusive, shared energy that flows in the veins of the players, inspiring them to higher levels of performance until they stand clutching the trophy. The secret sauce for teams that win championships is *synergy* (from Grk. *synergos* "working together"). Synergy is the impact of working together and cooperating such that the total effect is greater than the sum of the individual abilities. Teaming together captures the potential to perform at a higher level than individually possible. Infect a group with synergy, and the results are inspiring and rewarding. Team ministry is both spiritual synergy and the biblical ideal.

Teams in the Bible

In the New Testament, the work of God was accomplished through teams. Jesus did his work surrounded by the twelve disciples. Paul traveled with Barnabas, Timothy, Luke, Silas, and others less well known—Sopater, Aristarchus, Secundus, Gaius, Tychicus, and Trophimus (Acts 20:4). Once a church was established, a plurality of leaders were selected. Note the use of the plural in the following verses (emphasis supplied).

> When they had appointed *elders* for them in every church, having prayed with fasting, they commended them to the Lord in whom they had believed. (Acts 14:23 NASB)
>
> *Elders* who do their work well should be respected and paid well, especially those who work hard at both preaching and teaching. (1 Tim. 5:17)
>
> Set in order what remains and appoint *elders* in every city as I directed you. (Titus 1:5 NASB)

Teamwork in the Bible

The word *teamwork* does not appear in the Bible ... but it's everywhere. Teamwork and an attitude of working together radiate from the pages of Holy Writ.

Solomon cautioned that plans are frustrated and fail without a wise team of advisers—but with counselors, plans succeed (Prov. 15:22; 24:6). He further cautions that going it alone leaves you unprotected and affirms there is strength in two or three teaming together (Eccl. 4:12). According to King David, it's wonderful and pleasant when brothers work together in harmony (Ps. 133:1-3). Zephaniah adds three keys for team ministry: purified lips, praying together, and serving the Lord shoulder to shoulder (Zeph. 3:9 NASB).

Paul championed the attitude for teamwork in this delightful paraphrase, "If you've gotten anything at all out of following Christ, if his love has made any difference in your life, if being in a community of the Spirit means anything to you, if you have a heart, if you *care*—then do me a favor: Agree with each other, love each other, be deep-spirited friends. Don't push your way to the front; don't sweet-talk your way to the top. Put yourself aside, and help others get ahead. Don't be obsessed with getting your own advantage. Forget yourselves long enough to lend a helping hand" (Phil. 2:1-4 MSG).

Teamwork is the modus operandi for a magnifico ministry.

Shaping a Group into a Team

A group of leaders is not necessarily a team. Individuals may be pursuing their own agenda, going in their own direction. Team ministry doesn't just happen. It takes hard work to form a team with synergy. Developing a winning team requires seven essential steps:

1. **Choose the right people.**

You can't develop a winning lineup with the wrong people. Jesus spent an entire night in prayer before selecting his team

(Luke 6:12). Fasting and prayer accompanied choosing elders in the churches (Acts 14:23). Biblical leaders don't just fill vacancies. Because character counts, they choose godly team players. They ask whether potential teammates are unselfish or self-seeking, pushy or patient, intent on pleasing people or pleasing God. Biblical qualifications warn against putting quarrelsome people into leadership (1 Tim. 3:1-7), so don't choose a hot head for leadership, no matter how talented or successful. Look for those who have "a heart of compassion, kindness, humility, gentleness, and patience; bearing with one another, and forgiving each other" (Col. 3:12-13 NASB). I'll discuss the selection process and how to choose the right people in chapter 7, "Hotheads and Bullies Need Not Apply."

2. **Establish a clear, compelling mission and vision for the team.**

Where are you going, and how do you plan on getting there? What do you hope to accomplish in the next year? The next three years? To cultivate spiritual synergy, the church and its leaders need a written statement of purpose and specific goals relating to the purpose statement.

3. **Identify the gifts and motivational drive of team members.**

If you're assembling a hundred-piece orchestra, you don't want fifty people playing the flute. A football team doesn't need twenty quarterbacks. You need some linemen, running backs, and receivers. Each of these positions requires a unique skill set. Discuss with each team member what their spiritual gift is. Ask what brings them joy and satisfaction in serving, then capitalize on their unique giftedness and abilities.

To develop a synergistic team, I use and recommend a tool called CoreStrengths, which has been tested for over fifty years and is now available for the faith community at a reasonable cost. Unlike traditional personality tests, this tool provides insight into the motivational drive in each person—their God-given internal desire for doing God's work. Primary motivations fall into three areas—people, performance, and process—and the results provide four beneficial insights:

- The primary motivation of their soul when things are going well.
- The motivational changes when things aren't going well.
- The behaviors they are most likely to employ when things are going well.
- The behaviors (or strengths) they are most likely to overdo when things aren't going well.

Research by CoreStrengths indicates up to 80 percent of conflicts are rooted in the misunderstanding of the other person's motivational drive, so helping your team members better understand one another will reduce conflict when differing views emerge. To access this tool, go to consentiagroup.com.

4. **Communicate the value of each team member.**

"We can't do this without you."

"God brought you on this team for a great purpose." Sometimes people feel like they're selected to the church board just to fill a vacancy. If they left, there'd be an empty chair and a little more coffee to go around, but not much else. To combat this, regularly communicate their importance to the team. "You are gifted by God and play a crucial, indispensable role." The Corinthian church was a divided, squabbling bunch. In response, Paul writes 1 Corinthians 12—a profound chapter on biblical teamwork which identifies valuing one another as a crucial component for maintaining team synergy.

5. **Appreciate individual achievement and applaud the work of team members.**

Each person needs to know their effort is making a difference. Speak highly of the team. Read the last chapter of Romans for an example of how enthusiastically Paul commended his fellow workers. On President Ronald Reagan's desk in the Oval Office, a plaque read, "There is no limit to what a man can do or where he can go if he does not mind who gets the credit." Next to this was a sign with the words, "It CAN Be Done."[1] Anyone visiting the President would see these two mottos—reminders that in America, anything was possible.

6. **Spend time together growing spiritually and relationally.**

Read the Word of God together and pray for each other. Get to know each other's families, including their children's names, so you can pray for them effectively. Ministry is about caring for people.

7. **Have fun together.**

Plan fun activities to do together. Golf anyone? Try ping pong, basketball, or boating. Maybe enjoy dinner out and include the spouses. After the wedding in Cana and before cleansing the temple, Jesus hung out for a few days with his mother, brothers, and disciples (John 2:12). What did they do? We don't know, but I'm confident it was relaxing and fun. They enjoyed being together. Amid the pressures of ministry, take time out to be together, tell funny stories, and enjoy side-splitting laughter. It's a great way to lower the stress level.

Team Ministry
and the Leadership Gift

Team ministry often includes God choosing and directing a single visionary leader or multiple leaders who set the pace, cast a vision, and mobilize others to action. This is the leadership gift. The Bible is filled with God-appointed and anointed individuals with the gift of leadership—Moses, Joshua, Caleb, Esther, Deborah, Nehemiah, Ezra, David, Paul, Peter, John, and James, to name a few. Paul clearly was the leader of the teams that worked with him to establish churches. James was the lead pastor of the Jerusalem Church. Nehemiah was a take-charge leader who mobilized others to rebuild the wall around Jerusalem. Moses, in my opinion, was one of the top leaders in history—without a doubt, the greatest camp director of all time. Imagine ... two to three million campers and no facilities!

How do you identify a person with the gift of leadership? Spiritually gifted leaders have a restlessness in their spirit for bold new ideas and innovative ways to do things. Romantics sing in the shower. Leaders dream dreams in the shower. Before they're dried off and dressed, the adrenaline is pumping with a new idea—a fresh passion for something that advances the kingdom of God. While the vision grows in their mind and heart, they start telling everyone about it. Spiritual leaders are bold in communicating their new idea and often mystified by anyone who doesn't share their enthusiasm.

Churches do not intentionally attempt to stifle the spiritual gift of leadership, but unfortunately, this often occurs. "Churches undermine the leadership gift by implementing church governance systems that frustrate gifted leaders into oblivion. Leaders need a certain amount of room to operate, a certain amount of trust from the church or the organization in order to express their skill or gift. ... Pastors and staff and lay leaders with leadership gifts must be given real challenges, real hills to take, real problems to solve."[2] In a rare bright spot in the book of Judges, we find this verse: "The leaders led, ... the people volunteered, bless the LORD!" (Judg. 5:2 NASB). That's how it's supposed to happen. When God is at work and the organization is healthy, you will always see three things taking place:

- Leaders lead
- People follow and volunteer
- God receives the glory

Accountability and Team Ministry

While Jesus Christ is the leader and head of the team, this does not eliminate human accountability. To say, "I answer to God alone" is a giant cop-out and a distortion of servant-leadership. Be wary of any leader who has not learned surrender in their relationship with Christ and submission to the authority God has placed in their life. "You who are younger must accept the authority of the elders. And all of you, dress yourselves in humility as you relate to one another, for 'God opposes the proud but gives grace to the humble'" (1 Pet. 5:5). The word "submit" is the Greek word, *hupotasso,* from *hupo* meaning "under" and *tasso* meaning "to arrange in an orderly manner." Far from being a negative word, I define submission as a powerful humility of spirit as a result of choosing to trust God to perform his will through flawed human beings that he has placed in a position of authority and responsibility over me.

As a senior pastor, I considered myself accountable to the leadership team, and I reported to them and listened carefully to their advice. They also looked to me to be visionary, lead them, and hold them accountable. In this sense, we shared mutual accountability. If the leadership team gave me a directive I felt was not wise, I wouldn't hesitate to discuss this with them and explain my reasoning. However, if they insisted I follow their directive, I would take their instruction as being from the Lord. Even if their input turned out to be wrong, God's blessing would be on me for humility and obedience. Leaders need others who will speak the truth and confront them before making a potentially disastrous decision.

The Dark Side of Leadership

There was a leader who played dictator in the early church, "Dictator Diotrephes." John the Apostle strongly condemned his actions and warned the church: "Diotrephes, who loves to be first among them, does not accept what we say. For this reason, if I come, I will call attention to his deeds which he does, unjustly accusing us with wicked words; and not satisfied with this, he himself does not receive the brethren, either, and he forbids those who desire to do so and puts them out of the church" (3 John 9-10 NASB).

What motivated Diotrephes? He loved to be first—a classic narcissistic leader. A story from ancient Greek mythology regarding narcissism provides insight into this highly destructive behavior.

> As one fable goes, Narcissus was a beautiful hunter. As a boy his face looked as if it were chiseled from the purest marble. His beauty attracted others to him, but he could never let anyone get close even though they tried to extend their love to him. He resisted because he had found another love.
>
> One day at age 16, as he walked along the mythical river Styx, he stopped to sip water from a calm pool. As he knelt, the image he saw in the pool transfixed him. He immediately discovered his new love, the image of himself. His obsession with his own image kept him

from giving or receiving love from others. The story says that because he could not bear to leave his reflection, he lay down by the pool and pined away for himself. Eventually the earth absorbed him, and he became the flower narcissus. Thus, the word narcissist came to mean a person who has a fixation with himself.[3]

Such was the sickness displayed by Diotrephes—he was fixated on himself. He probably clouded the issue with spiritual-sounding, intimidating rhetoric. "God has directed me to decide what goes on around here. I take my orders from the God Almighty. Get in line or leave." Belligerent, bullying behavior that is disrespectful and dismissive of others does not come from the heart of a servant—it is not godly leadership. This driving, me-first motivation displayed itself in Diotrephes in five destructive ways:

- Didn't listen to others
- Rejected authority
- Maligned others
- Attempted to control others
- Rejected others, putting them out of the church

Let's be honest. Most of us have some unhealthy desires—lurking narcissism in the heart—to be recognized and applauded above what is healthy. Remember the argument of the disciples over who would be the greatest (Luke 9:46)? Blooming, narcissistic, flower children, every one of them. Later, when they gathered in the upper room after the death and resurrection of Jesus, I think they acknowledged and confessed their arrogance and self-centeredness. It's just my assumption, but I also think there were tears of apology for things they did to hurt each other. And a miracle occurred—they became of "one mind" (Acts 1:12-14).

Meeting and working with a leader who exhibits genuine humility is a delight, but I'll let you in on a secret. *Pride is an issue for every spiritual leader.* It will rear its ugly head in a flash. Defensiveness when someone questions our plans, a gnawing need to be recognized and applauded, feeling intimidated by the gifts of others, resisting advice, selfish desires—these issues must be dealt with at the cross daily. The servant-leader must continually surrender the need to be first, to be the top dog, to be lauded as a spiritual hero. We have one hero—Jesus, who died and rose again.

Did you know narcissism contributes to clergy sexual affairs? "Peter Steinki, a prolific author and church ministry consultant, has been working with hundreds of churches and pastors in the last forty years. He once worked with sixty-five pastors who had affairs and found that narcissism lay at the root of most of those failures. These pastors' need for others to value them and their need to feel important led them to sexualize their desires. Their narcissistic tendencies led them to moral failure."[4]

Diotrephes is a prime example of the destructive results of a dictator in the local church. As Proverbs 18:1 (NASB) says, "He who separates himself seeks his own desire, he quarrels against all sound wisdom." Dictators may push things through in a hurry and seemingly get a lot done, but the end result is usually destructive, both to themselves and those who get trampled. Churches have split, pastors have left the ministry, and devoted followers of Christ have been deeply hurt and disillusioned over the fallout from dictatorial leaders.

Narcissistic, self-serving, destructive behavior is flat-out wrong. What do you do when dealing with a narcissist in full bloom? Confront them head-on, and if they don't change their behavior, remove them. Be prepared for a tough fight. John didn't go light on Diotrephes. He promised to deal with him when he arrived, and he wrote for all future generations about the destructive ways of Diotrephes.

Decision Making

Rather than the oppressive ways of a Diotrephes, it is better to make decisions as a team. Is unanimity required for all decisions? Some believe that all decisions must be unanimous, while others feel a simple majority is sufficient. Generally, the unity of the congregation will be reflected in the oneness of the team. Because a divided leadership is often the prelude to a divided congregation, I believe it is best to pursue oneness and cohesiveness on major decisions. No decision should be coerced, and the open expression of all viewpoints is essential.

What was the decision-making process for the early church? Ray Stedman explains it.

> In the day-to-day church decisions, elders are to find the mind of the Lord through an uncoerced unanimity, reached after thorough, biblical discussion. Thus, ultimate authority, even in practical matters, is vested in the Lord and in no one else.
>
> The Book of Acts describes how the Holy Spirit planned and ordered the evangelizing strategy of the early church. The elders sought the mind of the Spirit. When it was made clear to them, they acted with unity. "For it has seemed good to the Holy Spirit and to us to lay upon you no greater burden ..." (Acts 15:28). The authority, therefore, was not the authority of men but of God. It was expressed not through individuals but through the united agreement of men whom the Spirit had led to eldership (Acts 20:28).[5]

Chapter 5, "Board Meetings or God Meetings," further discusses how God directs the final decision through a Spirit-led consensus.

Lonely Quarterbacks

Can you imagine the insanity of a football quarterback taking the field without a team around him? He might be multi-talented and have a great throwing arm, but without a team, he will be eating a lot of turf. I have often thought of the role of the senior or lead pastor somewhat like a quarterback. The pastor-quarterback is not the coach nor the owner of the team. Jesus Christ is both. The pastor, like a quarterback, serves a crucial role—calling plays, throwing passes, and sometimes running the ball. But too often, committed pastors are trying to move the ball down the field with a weak line or opposition from their own team members. No wonder the church fails to move forward.

I visualize a quarterback standing with the coach during a time-out. The game is on the line, the crowd is screaming, tension fills the air. The coach points to a diagram on his clipboard, and the quarterback nods affirmatively. "All right, let's go get 'em," the coach shouts. Imagine yourself as a pastor during a time-out standing next to your coach, Jesus. He is correcting you, directing you, reminding you of the next move. You charge onto the field to follow the play outlined by the coach, leading your team to fulfill God's vision.

Ministry thrives on teamwork, and each person's gifts and energy are crucial to the success of the team (Rom. 12:4-5; 1 Cor. 12:15-18). In football, plays are established during practice. When the quarterback calls a play during the game, the running back can't protest, "I don't like that play. I want to run a 'thirty-four' where I carry the ball. If you don't do it my way, I'm going to quit." Unthinkable. Can you imagine the left guard turning and tackling his own quarterback in the middle of a play? Absurd.

If you see your role on the board is to oppose the pastor, to be a pain in his side, resign. I can't imagine a lineman saying to the quarterback, "Look, I'm here to make certain you don't get too cocky, so I'll see to it that you get sacked regularly." As ridiculous as this sounds, I've seen it done. The pastor is making a crucial presentation, and a member of his team stands and opposes it. Team members *must* roll together and support one another when the game is on—they work out their differences in private.

Healthy leaders need a few very close friends—relationships where they can be real regarding their inner life and feel accepted as a person. Many relational-style pastors have large circles of fifty, one hundred, or one hundred fifty people they know on a first-name basis, but these relationships are mostly one-way: pastor to people. While rewarding, these relationships also tend to be draining. Relational pastors are perceived as warm, friendly, and caring—others call them "people pastors." How can they be lonely when surrounded by so many people? But truth be told, many of these pastors lack the close confidants necessary to sustain a healthy ministry. Surrounded by people, they may still suffer relational loneliness. Justin Barrett stated, "Relational-style pastors and missionaries average fewer personal relationships than the typical adult, and an alarming number have too few close confidants to support them in their life and calling."[6] Barrett recommends a leader have thirteen good friends and family members and four to six best friends. Healthy and intimate friendships are non-negotiable for healthy servant-leaders.

Pastors need caring team members. It's easy for a pastor to think, *I'm a shepherd of the sheep, so I'm no longer a sheep.* Though shepherds, all pastors are still sheep needing care, nurturing, encouragement, and friendships. Isolation and invincibility are predictors of a potential fall. In Standing Stone Ministry, we shepherd the shepherds, providing confidential relationships where a pastor can bare his soul. Every pastor needs a shepherd.

The famous line from the *Rhyme of the Ancient Mariner*, "Water, water, everywhere; nor any drop to drink," is the lament of the sailor on a becalmed ship surrounded by saltwater that he cannot drink. For pastors, it may be, "People, people everywhere, but not a single relationship that waters my soul." Solomon said, "By yourself you're unprotected. With a friend you can face the worst" (Eccl. 4:12 MSG). We all need someone who speaks into our life, a person we can confide in. A close-knit team of godly leaders can provide caring relationships, so essential to a healthy ministry. Paul paraphrased, said, "Agree with each other, love each other, be deep-spirited friends" (Phil. 2:2 MSG).

The rush is on, move the ball down the field, ... and don't let your pastor get sacked by the opposition.

REFLECTION AND DISCUSSION

Quick Recall

- The plaque on the desk of President Ronald Reagan read, "There is no limit to what a man can do or where he can go if he _____ _____."
- The driving me-first motivation of Diotrephes displayed itself in these five destructive ways:
  1. Didn't _____ to others
  2. Rejected _____
  3. Maligned _____
  4. Attempted to _____ others
  5. Rejected others, putting them _____ _____
- Research has shown that a healthy pastor needs _____ to _____ very close friends—relationships where the pastor can be real regarding his inner life and feel accepted as a person.

Thinking It Through

1. What are your thoughts about this statement, "Pride is an issue for every spiritual leader"? In what ways does pride rear its ugly head? What's the solution?

2. Have you served on a board where each person had their own agenda, and they didn't work as a team? What was this like? If you were given the opportunity to turn this situation around, what would you do and why?

3. Do you think the decisions of a biblical team should be unanimous? Why or why not?

4. For fun, have someone bring a football to the meeting. Everyone takes a position forming the line (center, guards, tackles, ends), and two people line up like half-backs. As your senior pastor lines up behind the center like a quarterback, he shouts, "Down, ready, set, Jesus is coming soon." With the snap, the center turns around and does an imaginary tackle of the quarterback. Have fun (but don't get hurt). This is a vivid reminder of what not to do. You may also want to have someone take a picture to post in the board room or share it with the congregation.

Since God chose you to be the holy people he loves, you must clothe yourselves with tenderhearted mercy, kindness, humility, gentleness, and patience. Make allowance for each other's faults, and forgive anyone who offends you. Remember, the Lord forgave you, so you must forgive others. Above all, clothe yourselves with love, which binds us all together in perfect harmony. And let the peace that comes from Christ rule in your hearts. For as members of one body you are called to live in peace. And always be thankful. (Col. 3:12–15)

—4—

BIBLICAL MEETINGS WITH GOD

CENTURIES BEFORE BOARD MEETINGS, LEADERS MET WITH THE ALMIGHTY

When interacting with church leaders, I frequently hear their disillusionment and frustration with board meetings.

"Seems like we just spin our wheels."

"The pastor tells us his plan, expecting us to rubber-stamp it. Why do I waste my time going to a meeting?"

"I get tired of the conflict and nitpicking over trivial issues."

"We sometimes have heated arguments and hurt feelings."

After listening to their woes for a while, the room grows quiet. I see them searching for an answer, so I suggest a solution: "Why don't you cancel board meetings?"

"What?" Stunned, they don't know whether to cheer or choke. Some like the idea. Others ask, "Are you serious?"

My reply, "Yes, the board meetings seem to be a waste of time, so why not cancel them?"

Then someone—usually a duty-bound, die-hard loyalist—pipes up, "If we cancel board meetings, how are we going to get the work done?" By now, they usually assume I think board meetings are of the devil. Not so! Let's look at the historical and relational board dynamics before deciding to cancel the next meeting.

History of Board Meetings

Are board meetings biblical? If you check your Bible, you won't find the phrase "board meeting," nor do you find the word "board" referring to people meeting together. Biblically, a board was a plank of wood (we might say Noah was chairman of the boards, and he and his family went on board the ark). The meeting in Acts 15 may resemble a corporate board meeting in some respects, but I will discuss unique differences later in this chapter.

If board meetings aren't in the Bible, when and how did this practice get started? In the sixteenth century, boarders were house guests who typically ate together and hobnobbed around a table made of boards. By the early seventeenth century, boarders deliberating and discussing issues while sitting around a wooden table made of boards came to be called "the board." This led to the expressions "above board" or honest, in contrast to "under the table" or dishonest.[1]

John Morrish wrote in *Management Today*, "If you find yourself thinking there's a lot of dead wood at board level, remind yourself that it's only natural. A board is dead wood. Historically, from the sixteenth century, a board was a table around which important meetings took place. The name then shifted from the furniture to the important people who sat around it. 'Board of directors' is first recorded in 1712."[2] Other sources confirm 1712 as the earliest reference to a board of directors. Today, a board meeting has become a common designation for deliberating groups around the world.

A board meeting is not necessarily a bad thing. Much of the progress in this world happens at board meetings, a central piece in corporate decision-making. During my undergraduate work at Biola University, I majored in business administration and seriously considered going into the business world. Instead God directed me to devote my life to pastoral ministry, but I have been thankful for my business training. It helped me relate to those in the congregation working in the business world. In addition, many business practices are helpful when applied in a church setting. I am not opposed to a godly board meeting.

Why, then, the concern about board meetings? To start with, interpersonal dysfunction too often accompanies these meetings. Board meetings that mirror the world's way of operating—in-fighting, jealousy, lording it over others, self-centeredness, using and discarding people in destructive ways—dishonor God and damage the ministry. Some churches are plagued with a board bully who takes a position of power and runs over people. To paraphrase the words of Jesus, "You've observed how godless rulers throw their weight around, how quickly a little power goes to their heads. It's not going to be that way with you. Whoever wants to be great must become a servant" (Matt. 20:25-26 MSG).

I meet regularly with pastors, called and gifted by God, who have been beaten up by the board and run out of the church. Some of them never return to the ministry. Unlike a dismissal in the business world, when a pastor is fired, their family is cut off from many of their friendships and their place of worship. The hurt runs deep, and sometimes their children turn their backs on God and the church for years to come. On the other hand, I also meet with volunteer board members who have been injured and wounded by pastors who manipulated and misused them. Too many say they'll never serve on a church board again, and some leave the church with bitter feelings.

The church can't move forward with this kind of toxic behavior among the leadership. There is a better way: *God Meetings*.

GOD MEETINGS IN THE BIBLE

Centuries before they discussed matters leaning over tables made of boards and called it a board meeting, God called leaders to a different type of meeting. God was the focus and directed these meetings—thus, a God Meeting. Let's visit five God Meetings in the Bible.

1. A God Meeting to Share the Load

Three days after leaving Mt. Sinai (Num. 10:33), where the Israelites had spent a year, Moses faced an enormous crisis. This massive crowd in the millions was moaning for meat—steaks and fish topped with onions and garlic plus cucumbers and melons on the side. One of the greatest leaders of all time was having a major meltdown. Moses submitted his letter of resignation to God with a take-my-life request attached. "Where am I supposed to get meat for all these people? They keep whining to me, saying, 'Give us meat to eat!' I can't carry all these people by myself! The load is far too heavy! If this is how you intend to treat me, just go ahead and kill me. Do me a favor and spare me this misery!" (Num 11:13–15). Moses is brimming with four types of resentment:

- resentment about circumstances ("Where am I supposed to get meat for all these people?),
- resentment about griping, moaning people ("They keep whining to me."),
- resentment about the workload ("The load is far too heavy!"), and ultimately,

- resentment against God for putting him in this impossible job ("If this is how you intend to treat me, just go ahead and kill me.").

Moses is burned out on ministry, and the Hebrews are on the verge of a riot.

With this crisis fast becoming a catastrophe, God graciously supplied Moses with what every leader must have—a team of people to share the load. God told Moses, "Gather before me seventy men who are recognized as elders and leaders of Israel. Bring them to the Tabernacle to stand there with you. I will come down and talk to you there. I will take some of the Spirit that is upon you, and I will put the Spirit upon them also. They will bear the burden of the people along with you, so you will not have to carry it alone" (Num. 11:16–17).

Moses hand-picked the seventy elders based on their maturity and the respect they commanded among the Israelites. You've probably heard of a "standing committee," but this is different. They were told to stand while God spoke, an indicator of respect and honor. For example, the Bible teaches, "Stand up in the presence of the elderly and show respect for the aged" (Lev. 19:32). When I preach, I often say, "Let's stand as we read the Word of God. You may be seated while I'm speaking." I want to make it clear there is a difference between God speaking and me speaking. In the excellent book entitled *The Council*, the authors suggest, based on Scripture, that "overseers of Christ-centered churches and ministries prioritize time for standing and listening to the reading of Scripture. Allot margin for times of silence as well, to attune to the still, small voice of the Holy Spirit."[3]

Selected by Moses, the elders presented themselves before God for their first meeting—and what a meeting it was. "He [Moses] gathered the seventy elders and stationed them around the Tabernacle. And the LORD came down in the cloud and spoke to Moses. Then he gave the seventy elders the same Spirit that was upon Moses. And when the Spirit rested upon them, they prophesied. But this never happened again" (Num. 11:24-25). The power and presence of God gripped them as they stood in reverence and awe, listening to the Lord speak. And then the Spirit of God rested on each of them, confirming their calling to serve. In this first meeting, the seventy elders prophesied, giving praise and glory to God in spontaneous expressions of worship. Why it never happened again mystifies me.

In verse 29, Moses expresses his desire and anticipation of the day when all believers would have the Holy Spirit. In the Old Testament, the Holy Spirit came upon a person for a special task. In the New Testament, the believer is given the Holy Spirit at the moment of salvation, and the Spirit indwells them permanently (Rom. 8:9; 1 Cor. 12:13; 2 Cor. 5:5; Eph. 1:13-14; 4:30). When surrendered, the Holy Spirit fills you with his presence. In a God Meeting, you acknowledge his presence, surrender to his will, and offer praise and worship.

The Sanhedrin who condemned Jesus to death (Matt. 26:59; Mark 14:55) thought of themselves as the successors to Moses and the seventy elders. They were a ruling body of seventy-one with the High Priest presiding. I see a warning here: *biblical structure without godliness is an empty shell, a sham.* Rather than surrender under God's authority, the Sanhedrin became a corrupt ruling council. Traditions took precedence over God's Word, and they thought nothing of conjuring up false evidence and plotting murder. They were a den of vipers intent on preserving their positions of power and authority no matter the cost.

2. A God Meeting to Confront a Rebellion

In Numbers 16, we see another meeting of leaders at the tabernacle (also called the tent of meeting). This one goes down in infamy! Two hundred and fifty prominent leaders of the people incited a rebellion against Moses, and their argument sounded compelling: "You have gone too far! The whole community of Israel has been set apart by the LORD, and he is with all of us. What right do you have to act as though you are greater than the rest of the LORD's people?" (Num. 16:3). Moses met this crisis with humility (literally falling on the ground). The rabble refused an invite from Moses to meet personally—always a tipoff when people are not interested in a resolution. When it was time for the God Meeting, they "stirred up the entire community against Moses and Aaron, and they all gathered at the Tabernacle entrance. Then the glorious presence of the LORD appeared to the whole community" (Num. 16:19). God instructed Moses and Aaron to get away from the tents of the rebels. "He had hardly finished speaking the words when the ground suddenly split open beneath them. The earth opened its mouth and swallowed the men, along with their households and all their followers who were standing with them, and everything they owned" (Num. 16:31-32).

The motion to dismiss Moses was grounded. Meeting over.

The timeless lesson from Numbers 16 is straightforward and simple: *Don't go to a God Meeting with a pompous attitude or a spirit of rebellion.*

3. A God Meeting of Fellowship and Feasting with God

This meeting, a leadership retreat on the mountain, sends chills up and down my spine. I would love to have been there. "Then Moses, Aaron, Nadab, Abihu, and the seventy elders of Israel climbed up the mountain again.

There they saw the God of Israel. Under his feet there seemed to be a surface of brilliant blue lapis lazuli, as clear as the sky itself. And though these nobles of Israel gazed upon God, he did not destroy them. In fact, they ate a covenant meal, eating and drinking in his presence!" (Exod. 24:9-11).

At this awesome God Meeting, the leaders saw the manifest presence of the Almighty. This was not the face of God. Scripture teaches that no man can see God the Father and live in the human body (Exod. 33:20). This may have been a theophany or a preincarnate appearance of Christ the Lord Jehovah, which occurred on other occasions (Gen. 32:29-31; Josh. 5:14; Judg. 6:11-14; 13:2-24). They gazed upon God, eating and drinking in his presence. This was a covenant meal celebrating the sealing of the promise described in verses 3-8. "It foreshadows the Lord's Supper, which celebrates the new covenant sealed by Christ's death."[4] Today's servant-leaders do well to share a meal highlighted by observing the Lord's death and resurrection in Communion—a celebration of his glorious presence.

Wouldn't it be something to come home after the evening leadership meeting knowing you've been in the presence of God? In the morning, your spouse asks, "So how was the meeting last night?"

"Honey, it's hard to describe, but we had an experience with God that I'll treasure for years to come. The sense of God's presence in the room gripped us all."

4. A God Meeting to Prepare for the Future

> When they had entered the city, they went up to the upper room where they were staying; that is, Peter and John and James and Andrew, Philip and Thomas, Bartholomew and Matthew, James the son of Alphaeus, and Simon the Zealot, and Judas the son of James. These all with one mind were continually devoting

> themselves to prayer. ... At this time Peter stood up in the midst of the brethren (a gathering of about one hundred and twenty persons was there together), and said, "Brethren, the scripture had to be fulfilled, which the Holy Spirit foretold by the mouth of David concerning Judas, who became a guide to those who arrested Jesus." (Acts 1:13-16 NASB)

Something amazing happened in this meeting of a hundred twenty men and women gathered in the upper room. This may have been the very room where Jesus celebrated the Last Supper with his disciples (Mark 14:15) and where the Lord appeared to the apostles after the resurrection (Luke 24:33-36; John 20:19). If so, the room was filled with fresh memories. So much had happened in such a short time.

Before ascending into heaven, Jesus had told his followers not to leave Jerusalem but to wait for the coming of the Holy Spirit (Acts 1:4-5). Wait? How long? They didn't know. So they waited. Jesus ascended into heaven forty days after his resurrection (Acts 1:3). The disciples waited from the ascension of Jesus until the Feast of Weeks or Pentecost (fifty days after Passover). Therefore, it was ten days since Christ ascended into heaven—ten days of waiting in the upper room.

I think this meeting had the earmarks of potential disaster. No one likes meetings without an ending time ... let alone an ending date. Typically, people get on each other's nerves in close quarters. Put a hundred twenty people in a room to wait for who knows how long—someone's going to go bonkers with being cooped up so long. Or somebody is going to make a rude statement and tempers will flare. It says they "were staying there." This sounds like a ten-day sleepover. What do you think? Did they have separate sleeping quarters, or was it a hundred twenty people sleeping in one large room? I'm sure there would be ten or more hardcore snorers in the group. Happy campers, one and all?

Other factors could have turned this meeting into a catastrophe. With Jesus absent, the leadership vacuum could have led to a power struggle. The eleven remaining disciples could have resumed their argument about who would be the greatest. After all, this group Jesus assembled was beyond diverse—they had political opposites in the group. Before following Jesus, Simon the Zealot had been part of the radical group intent on overthrowing the Romans. Matthew had worked for the Romans, collecting taxes to keep them in power. That's like putting a far-right, get-government-off-my-back nationalist with a left-wing, government-is-the-solution liberal. Now add to the mix James and John, nicknamed by Jesus "sons of thunder" for their testy tempers. Among other things, these firebrand disciples wanted to call down fire from heaven to burn up the Samaritans for their lack of hospitality (Luke 9:54). I picture James and John with sticks of dynamite poking out of their travel bags, had it been available. There was no problem annihilation couldn't solve.

Why didn't this meeting turn into a disaster? Prayer. They devoted themselves to prayer. Simple as that. Something transforming happens when people pray together. I believe a tender breaking took place in all one hundred twenty hearts in that upper room. Rather than accusing each other of disloyalty (all the disciples had left Jesus and run away according to Mark 14:50), they acknowledged their own unfaithfulness. I believe there was confession of sin, releasing of resentments, apologies for wrongs done. And something as beautiful and amazing as the Day of Pentecost itself occurred—they all shared one mind. There was no division. Prior political party loyalty or previous cultural bias didn't matter. They were intent on one purpose. It was the miracle before the miracle that birthed the church.

5. A God Meeting to Resolve an Explosive Issue

Over a decade after the birth of the church, there was a crucial leadership meeting in Jerusalem to address a grievous issue—a thorny question about the law and grace. It was an issue that could split any church wide open.

> When they arrived in Jerusalem, Barnabas and Paul were welcomed by the whole church, including the apostles and elders. They reported everything God had done through them. But then some of the believers who belonged to the sect of the Pharisees stood up and insisted, "The Gentile converts must be circumcised and required to follow the law of Moses."
>
> So the apostles and elders met together to resolve this issue. At the meeting, after a long discussion, Peter stood and addressed them as follows: "Brothers, you all know that God chose me from among you some time ago to preach to the Gentiles so that they could hear the Good News and believe. God knows people's hearts, and he confirmed that he accepts Gentiles by giving them the Holy Spirit, just as he did to us. He made no distinction between us and them, for he cleansed their hearts through faith. So why are you now challenging God by burdening the Gentile believers with a yoke that neither we nor our ancestors were able to bear? We believe that we are all saved the same way, by the undeserved grace of the Lord Jesus."
>
> Everyone listened quietly as Barnabas and Paul told about the miraculous signs and wonders God had done through them among the Gentiles.
>
> When they had finished, James stood and said, "Brothers, listen to me. Peter has told you about the

time God first visited the Gentiles to take from them a people for himself. And this conversion of Gentiles is exactly what the prophets predicted. As it is written:

'Afterward I will return and restore the fallen house of David. I will rebuild its ruins and restore it, so that the rest of humanity might seek the LORD, including the Gentiles—all those I have called to be mine. The LORD has spoken—he who made these things known so long ago.'

"And so my judgment is that we should not make it difficult for the Gentiles who are turning to God. Instead, we should write and tell them to abstain from eating food offered to idols, from sexual immorality, from eating the meat of strangled animals, and from consuming blood. For these laws of Moses have been preached in Jewish synagogues in every city on every Sabbath for many generations."

Then the apostles and elders together with the whole church in Jerusalem chose delegates, and they sent them to Antioch of Syria with Paul and Barnabas to report on this decision. The men chosen were two of the church leaders—Judas (also called Barsabbas) and Silas. This is the letter they took with them:

"This letter is from the apostles and elders, your brothers in Jerusalem. It is written to the Gentile believers in Antioch, Syria, and Cilicia. Greetings!

"We understand that some men from here have troubled you and upset you with their teaching, but we did not send them! So we decided, having come to complete agreement, to send you official representatives, along with our beloved Barnabas and Paul, who have risked their lives for the name of our Lord Jesus Christ. We are sending Judas and Silas to confirm what we have decided concerning your question.

"For it seemed good to the Holy Spirit and to us to lay no greater burden on you than these few requirements:

You must abstain from eating food offered to idols, from consuming blood or the meat of strangled animals, and from sexual immorality. If you do this, you will do well. Farewell."

The messengers went at once to Antioch, where they called a general meeting of the believers and delivered the letter. And there was great joy throughout the church that day as they read this encouraging message. (Acts 15:4-31)

Here are seven observations about this meeting.

- **There was potential for deep division (15:1-2, 5).**
  What was the issue at hand? The believing Pharisees were sharpening their words and their blades. "Let's get out the knife and get these Gentiles circumcised. Make 'em bleed if they want to be believers," they insisted. Paul and Barnabas were intent on stopping the bleeding before it started. The believing Pharisees were concerned about the externals of religiosity, while Paul and Barnabas were focused on issues of the heart. The new movement could have split into two groups—something like the "All Saints, All Circumcised Church" and the "Jews and Gentiles: Come-As-You-Are to Jesus Church."

- **There was vigorous debate (15:7).**
  There is nothing wrong with an animated discussion of two opposing viewpoints. After a lengthy discussion, Peter made a passionate presentation of salvation by grace, not dependent on human works.

- **There was a period of silence and listening (15:12).**
  This was very important. Everyone needed space to ponder the arguments and the ramifications. After considerable debate and discussion, there needs to be a time when the room grows quiet. Let things settle down, carefully consider what has been said, and calm the emotions.

- **They reported what God was doing (15:12).**
  Barnabas and Paul gave a first-hand account of the miracles God had performed among the Gentiles. There was no denying this was the hand of God.

- **They listened to Scripture (15:15-18).**
  Rather than tossing around opinions and feeding on conjecture, they went to the clear teaching of the Word of God. To paraphrase Amos 9:11-12, it was clear the Gentiles were part of God's plan of salvation. In Acts 15, Scripture won the day.

- **They responded to the leadership of James (15:13-21).**
  James, the pastor of the Jerusalem church, brother of Jesus, and writer of the book of James, took the lead, encouraging believers not to make it difficult for Gentiles to turn to God (15:19). After the discussion, reports, and Scripture, he brought the deliberation to a conclusion. Rather than ignoring the concerns of those clinging to the teaching of Moses, James affirmed that Moses was "read in the synagogues every Sabbath" (15:21).

- **They discerned and followed the leading of the Holy Spirit.**
  God worked in each of their lives, and they listened to the leading of the Holy Spirit: "For it seemed good to the Holy Spirit and to us" (Acts 15:28). A thorny issue, a vigorous debate, a powerful report of what God was doing, a key passage of Scripture, the mind of the Holy Spirit was discovered, and a devastating division was averted. Wise leaders. Wise leadership. A great example for the church today.

COMMON GROUND FOR HEALTHY MEETINGS

Many best practices for a board meeting apply in a God Meeting as well. It makes good sense to prepare an agenda for the meeting and keep minutes. Common courtesies are essential: be on time, listen, don't interrupt. Don't get your exercise jumping to conclusions, running others down, clawing your way to the top, side-stepping responsibility, throwing your weight around, or making mountains out of molehills. It is helpful to have a written Ministry Position Description (MPD) of the qualifications and expectations for all team members. I recommend reading the MPD aloud and agreeing to it yearly, and every time a new leader joins the group. This helps keep everyone on track.

It is also helpful to have a Board Policy Manual (BPM) of established policies and past decisions. Trying to recall a decision made three years ago leads to selective memory and possible conflict. "I thought we decided to …" "No, I remember it quite differently." Effective leadership teams purposefully stay out of meddling and micro-managing. Instead of tightly controlling everything, they practice releasing many issues to the staff and ministry leaders, giving them the freedom to be creative and do their work. "Boards that attempt to address anything and everything become immersed in minutiae."[5]

Wise leaders are forward-looking and focused on big-picture priorities. They guard against chasing multiple bunny trails. Church leaders would do well to note the Russian proverb: "If you chase two rabbits, you will not catch either one."

Dan Busby and John Pearson have written an excellent book entitled *Lessons from the Church Boardroom*. This easy-to-read, practical book has short chapters offering insights for exceptional governance. One of their recommendations is creating a Prime Responsibility Chart indicating the assigned roles for the pastor, board, and staff. This helps prevent confusion and potential conflict regarding personnel, financial, and ministry decisions.

Before presenting a problematic issue to the group, I recommend thorough research and development of a solution-based plan of action. According to Busby and Pearson, wise leaders don't throw red meat on the table—a gnarly issue brought up without a plan of action.[6] This will inevitably lead to frustration and futility.

In addition, give careful thought to the meeting location. Too many meetings are held in rooms that are cold and sterile, have cramped uncomfortable seating, or are dulled by poor lighting. After a particularly rough meeting, Pastor Larry Osborne suggested the board gather at his home for the next meeting. The move changed everything. "By changing the environment, I had inadvertently changed behavioral expectations. Right away, I noticed that we were noticeably more cordial when dealing with dicey issues. When reviewing the budget, we weren't quite so picky. When someone talked, no one rudely leafed through reports, even if they wanted to. … When someone talks to you in the living room, you're supposed to listen. And when you disagree—no matter how much you disagree—when you're sitting on my couch, you're not allowed to be a butthead about it."[7] Where you meet changes group dynamics, so choose wisely.

Why Have a Meeting?

Even more critical than good practices in a meeting is a strong sense of purpose. I am convinced that much of the frustration in board meetings relates to a lack of meaningful purpose. Some meetings are painfully boring. In a church where I served, a sweet-hearted deacon would fall asleep when the meeting was dull. And then he'd start snoring. As he was enjoying himself, we'd look around the room and see the smiles—his snoring had a way of breaking the boredom, but this isn't the kind of meeting any church wants.

The solution for board meetings is not just improving procedures—it's sharpening the purpose. Sometimes board meetings are "the well-intentioned in full pursuit of the irrelevant."[8] Ask the members of the board in your organization, "Why do you go to board meetings? What is the purpose of the meeting?" You may be surprised by some of the responses.

"Someone has to keep an eye on the pastor and staff."

"By-laws require it."

"We monitor the money."

"Complaints need to be aired."

"I don't know—something to do on Tuesday evenings."

I firmly believe there is one reason, one transcending purpose, for leaders to gather: *Leaders meet to meet with God.* It's that simple. I can't think of anything more important than meeting with God. Leaders stand on holy ground, lift up holy hands, listen to the Word of God, and discern God's marching orders. Leaders purify their lives before God, surrender to God's authority, discover where God is working and what he wants done ... and then, they do it. Yes, there are other reasons to meet, but none is more important than meeting with God.

If your board meetings have become "bored meetings," it's time for an infusion of purpose. Make your next gathering a God Meeting. You may have an experience with God that will thrill your soul and live in your memory for years to come.

Reflection and Discussion

Quick Recall

- What was the origin of board meetings? _____
  _____

- What is the timeless lesson from Numbers 16 mentioned in this chapter? Don't go to a God Meeting with a _____ or a _____
  _____.

- Which exercise tempts you most often?
  ___ Jumping to conclusions
  ___ Running others down
  ___ Clawing your way to the top
  ___ Side-stepping responsibility
  ___ Throwing your weight around
  ___ Making mountains out of molehills
  ___ Other

Thinking It Through

1. If you could have participated in one of the five God Meetings mentioned in this chapter, which would you choose and why?

2. What is the difference between "lording it over" and "leading"?

GOD MEETINGS | 73

3. Like Moses, most pastors experience burnout at some point in their ministry (nearly three out of four). What, in your opinion, contributes most to a leader experiencing burnout?

   ___ Long working hours

   ___ Disgruntled people

   ___ Little or no time away

   ___ No sabbath or day off

   ___ Lack of others sharing the load

   ___ Frustrating circumstances

   ___ Feeling inadequate for the task

   ___ Little or no time for intimacy with Jesus

   ___ Other factors

4. Discuss this statement: "Effective leadership teams purposefully stay out of meddling and micromanaging. Instead of tightly controlling everything, they practice releasing many issues to the staff and ministry leaders, giving them the freedom to be creative and do their work."

Then Moses, Aaron, Nadab, Abihu, and the seventy elders of Israel climbed up the mountain again. There they saw the God of Israel. Under his feet there seemed to be a surface of brilliant blue lapis lazuli, as clear as the sky itself. And though these nobles of Israel gazed upon God, he did not destroy them. In fact, they ate a covenant meal, eating and drinking in his presence! (Exod. 24:9-11)

—5—

BOARD MEETINGS OR GOD MEETINGS?

What's the Difference? Why Is the Outcome So Different?

If the disciples had a board meeting, it might have gone something like this.

MEETING OF THE BOARD

By Richard K. Wallarab

Pete: This meeting has been called at the request of Matt, John, Tom, and Little Jim. Bart, will you please open with prayer?

Bart: Almighty God, we ask your blessing on all we do and say and earnestly pray that you will see our side as your side. Amen.

Pete: Jesus, we have been following you around for some time, and we are getting concerned about the attendance figures. Tom, how many were on the hill yesterday?

Tom: Thirty-seven.
Pete: It's getting to be ridiculous. You're going to have to pep things up. We expect things to happen.
John: I'd like to suggest you pull off more miracles. That walking on water bit was the most exciting thing I have ever seen, but only a few of us saw it. If a thousand or so had a chance to witness it, we would have more than we could handle on the hill.
Little Jim: I agree. The healing miracles are terrific, but only a limited number really get to see what has happened. Let's have more water to wine, more fish and chips (it never hurts to fill their stomachs), still more storms, give more signs. This is what the people need.
Pete: Right. And another thing, publicity is essential, and you tell half the people you cure to keep it quiet. Let the word get around.
Matt: I'm for miracles, but I want to hear a few stories I can understand. This "those who have ears to hear, let them hear" business just clouds the issue. You have to make it clear, or most of us aren't going to be able to take anything home.
Big Jim: I'd like to offer an order of service. First a story, then a big miracle followed by an offering, then maybe a saying or something, followed by a small miracle to bring them back next time. Oh yes, and a prayer if you like.
Tom: We have to do something.
Little Jim: That's for sure. Attendance has been awful.
Judas: I'd like to say if we are going to continue to meet in this upper room, we ought to do something about the carpet.[1]

Sometimes we need to laugh rather than cry. On the other hand, it's heartbreaking to see this kind of ridiculous nitpicking and wrangling actually infect churches. How do we avoid these pitfalls?

Getting Past the Trivia Trap

Trivia is the enemy of the eternal as it sucks up our most valuable possession—time. The reality is too many governing boards are tied up in the trivial rather than the eternal. Consultant John Carver states, "In my experience, most of what the majority of boards do either does not need to be done or is a waste of time when done by the board. Conversely, most of what boards need to do for strategic leadership is not done."[2] Management expert Peter Drucker said, "There is one thing that all boards have in common, regardless of their legal position. They do not function. The decline of the board is a universal phenomenon of this century."[3] So cancel board meetings? Yes. Replace them with God Meetings.

As I interact with church leaders, I'm discovering a yearning for meetings that move beyond the mundane, meetings that accomplish more than trivia. Do leaders need to debate for 45 minutes whether to buy pens or pencils for the pews? A Dallas Seminary professor described his experience as sitting in an elders' meeting until the early hours debating a trivial choice of color.[4] I picture the Devil and his minions conniving, "Let's get them arguing about 20 lb. vs. 80 lb. paper for the worship folder. They'll never get to planning evangelism." Think this is far-fetched? My experience says otherwise.

One of my pastor friends found a bargain on toilet paper, and he wanted to save the church some money, so he bought a couple of cases for the church. The board found out and went ballistic. "Who authorized you to purchase toilet paper? That's our responsibility. We make those kinds of decisions." It festered for several months and became known as the "issue of the tissue."

Things need changing. Before we micromanage ourselves into oblivion, we need to find a better way of doing kingdom work. It's time for a radical overhaul of how leaders work together and make decisions, and God Meetings can make a difference. If your leadership team is already incorporating these concepts, I commend you.

WHAT MAKES FOR A GOD MEETING?

While there are similarities, there are also significant differences between traditional board meetings and the new way of meeting with God I recommend. The issue is not so much procedural as it is attitudinal, relational, and spiritual. Several characteristics distinguish one type of meeting from the other:

1. **God Meetings are led by God through a servant-leader.**

In a God Meeting, a designated chair directs the group in looking to the Holy Spirit to preside and guide the meeting. You can sense when the chair of a meeting is "lording it over" the process rather than leading with a heart surrendered to the will of God.

2. **God Meetings are directed by God's Word and God's will.**

In a board meeting, personal opinions and preferences tend to dominate the decision-making process. As a last resort, someone may ask, "What does the Bible say about this?" In a God Meeting, Scripture is regularly consulted though there isn't necessarily a verse regarding every subject to be discussed. The leaders continuously remind themselves, "'My thoughts are nothing like your thoughts,' says the LORD. 'And my ways are far beyond anything you could imagine. For just as the heavens are higher than the earth, so my ways are higher than your ways and my thoughts higher than your thoughts'" (Isa. 55:8-9). Rather than saying, "Well, my personal opinion is ..." (which we're all prone to do), you'll hear, "I've been asking God for clear leading. Here is what I'm sensing from the Lord."

3. **God Meetings aim for a spirit of oneness and harmony.**

Discord, bitter jealousy, selfish ambition, abusive language, rage, deceit, or slander may seep into board meetings. The atmosphere turns sour with contention and animosity. Backs stiffen, knuckles turn white, tension freezes the air. Not so with God Meetings. There may be a vigorous debate over issues in a God Meeting—nothing wrong with that—but the debate is respectful rather than personal. Instead of put-downs, there will be build-ups—uplifting, encouraging words. After the discussion, individuals park their personal preferences and ask the key question, What is the mind of God on this? The goal for a God Meeting is this: "Now may the God who gives perseverance and encouragement grant you to be of the same mind with one another according to Christ Jesus, so that with one accord you may with one voice glorify the God and Father of our Lord Jesus Christ" (Rom. 15:5-6 NASB). Underline the ones here: one another, one accord, one voice. Oneness and being of the same mind bring glory to God.

4. **In a God Meeting, God directs the final decision through a Spirit-led consensus.**

There are several factors to consider in this crucial topic. Let's take them one at a time.

What about voting in the Bible? In reviewing Scripture, this instance came to mind: the decision of whether to enter the Promised Land or not. The twelve spies who checked out the land agreed on the facts—it's a honey of a land, fruitful to the max, but giants are lumbering around. When they voted, two were staunchly in favor of marching forward to conquer the land, while ten voted for the grasshopper amendment—we looked like grasshoppers in their sight and couldn't possibly conquer the land (Num. 13:25-33). Both groups reasoned from the same set of facts. It all depends on what you combine with the facts—fear or faith.

FACTS + FEAR = DEFEAT
FACTS + FAITH = VICTORY

As you probably already know, voting didn't work out too well for the Israelites—they spent thirty-eight years wandering in the wilderness. How different could it have been if the ten spies had listened to God rather than their fears?

The vote is the final verdict in a board meeting, even if it's six opposed and five in favor. Those who were voted down may leave feeling disgruntled and proceed to voice their opposition among the congregation. This has the potential to ignite smoldering embers of resentment toward leadership, or it may plant the seeds for a split. The spirituality of the board may be questioned, particularly if the decision had to do with a significant spiritual endeavor. *Split votes? Think of splinters—slivers of wood that get under the skin and get infected.*

What about discussion before a decision? I make a distinction between unity before a decision and unity after the decision. Prior to making a decision, there should be a free expression of all perspectives. I told team members,

"You may have input that seems far out, so you're hesitant to share it. You have my 100 percent backing to express any idea no matter how ridiculous, because it may be just the perspective we need to hear." After the decision, unity is essential.

Is it wise to proceed if the decision is not unanimous? Scripture mentions frequently being of the "same mind" (Rom. 12:16; 15:5; 1 Cor. 1:10; Phil. 2:2) or "one mind" (Acts 1:14; 2:46; 15:25; Phil. 1:27) along with similar words such as "one accord" (Acts 4:24; 5:12; Rom. 15:6), "one spirit" (Phil. 1:27), and "united in spirit, intent on one purpose" (Phil. 2:2 NASB). Paul tells the Corinthians, "Now I exhort you, brethren, by the name of our Lord Jesus Christ, that you all agree and that there be no divisions among you, but that you be made complete in the same mind and in the same judgment" (1 Cor. 1:10 NASB).

There are four key phrases: *you all agree, no divisions among you, same mind, same judgment.* It is difficult to reconcile a split vote on a major decision with the Scriptures above. To become of one mind is a work of the Holy Spirit, a miracle, because it is contrary to our natural state of mind. Sometimes I can't even agree with myself. Is the Holy Spirit directing a meeting when a decision is ramrodded through and wins by one vote? Is the Spirit of God divided? Split decisions may lead to a divided team and a divided church. If the proposal that wins by a divided vote doesn't work out well, those who voted against it will be prone to say, "I didn't vote for it."

However, if it's a minor issue and no one objects to moving forward, I recommend proceeding. For example, I remember a discussion regarding camp scholarships. Some wanted to provide the full amount for students in need. Others felt paying half was sufficient. The opinions were divided, but no one had strong feelings one way or the other. While the majority favored providing the full amount, the minority viewed it differently but agreed to move forward with the majority. It was a minor difference of opinion, and there was no division in the group's unity.

However, if it's a major issue regarding the direction of the ministry and opinions are sharply divided, I believe it is best to slow the process, pray, and seek God's direction. With surrendered hearts, wait for the confirming consensus of the Holy Spirit. There have been times when our team chose to wait and pray because something wasn't clear. After a month of prayer, the Lord brought an entirely different set of factors into view. Had we pushed it through, a major mistake would have been made.

What happens after a decision? Following a decision in a God Meeting, the team chooses to be one. I told members of our leadership team, "After we make a decision, we roll together. We do not criticize one another. We don't talk against the decision." I cringe when I hear a sports figure criticizing the coach's decision or the play of a team member in an interview. That tears a team apart. Board members who backbite a decision cause a similar rift. Oneness following a decision honors one another and God.

What is the ultimate form of decision-making? Throughout history, there have been many forms of government: communism, socialism, oligarchy, monarchy, fascism, and democracy, to name a few. In my opinion, democracy is an excellent form of government, but it's flawed. A theocracy is the ultimate—the supreme form of government. It rises above all the others because Jesus is in charge. One of the salient features of the coming kingdom is that Jesus will be King. If we're doing kingdom work now, shouldn't Jesus be in charge? Absolutely.

5. **In a God Meeting, there is the freedom to be authentic and vulnerable.**

Despite board members' best intentions, putting on a pretense of strength and invincibility tempts many. Pastors and leaders may go to great lengths to hide their limitations, believing weakness is for wimps. When we look at it from God's perspective, weakness is for winners. "A great weakness is a pretense of strength; a great strength is a humble acknowledgment of weakness."[5] According to the Bible, weakness is a good thing. Paul asked God to take away his weakness, but God responded, "My power works best in weakness" (2 Cor. 12:9). In other words, *God uses weak people mightily.* Why? When we try to impress others with our gifts and knowledge, we seek our own glory and not much happens spiritually. But God is glorified by displaying his power in weakness and lives are changed. Like Paul, I have learned that "when I am weak, then I am strong" (2 Cor. 12:10).

Pastors may acknowledge the biblical truth that God uses authentic and vulnerable leaders, but many still try to bury their burdens. One-third of pastors are currently at high or medium risk of burnout,[6] and 71 percent report experiencing burnout at some point in their ministry.[7] Few confide this in a trusted friend or mentor. Almost half of pastors have faced depression at some time during their ministry,[8] and 35 percent of pastors are regularly battling depression or fear of inadequacy.[9] Effective leaders are not immune. Depression had a significant impact on Moses, King David, Jeremiah, and Paul, to name a few. Charles Spurgeon, who battled depression, said this.

> We have the treasure of the gospel in earthen vessels, and if there be a flaw in the vessel here and there, let none wonder. Our work, when earnestly undertaken,

lays us open to attacks in the direction of depression. Who can bear the weight of souls without sometimes sinking to the dust? ... To see the hopeful turn aside, the godly grow cold, professors abusing their privileges, and sinners waxing more bold in sin—are not these sights enough to crush us to the earth?[10]

Pastors may be exhausted, hurting, or experiencing depression, but they think it is too risky to share. I know. I was one of those pastors. For twenty-five years, I experienced twice a year depression that lasted three or four weeks. When I finally opened up and shared my struggle, my fellow leaders were understanding and supportive. I shared it with the congregation, and the doors opened wide for an entirely new dimension of ministry. My vulnerability encouraged others to come to me with their struggles. Thanks be to God, my last episode of depression was over twenty years ago. By opening up, I identified the factors contributing to my depression—buried woundedness and bitterness—plus healthy practices that include eating right, exercise, journaling, and talking to trusted confidants.

Remember, concern over appearing weak isn't limited to pastors. Volunteer leaders are often reluctant to mention a struggle they're having at work, a crisis at home, or personal discouragement. In a God Meeting, however, every team member is equal—we're all weak and often under attack. When we acknowledge this and share our pain, the gathering takes on authenticity. We deepen relationally by praying and caring for one another.

6. **In a God Meeting, God makes things happen.**

When we put on a pretense of being strong, we are relying on the flesh. We may expect money to make things happen or manipulation to get things done. Ministry is never about money, manipulation, or numbers. Numbers in the early church were neither ignored nor promoted. Early in the ministry of Jesus, the crowds numbered in the thousands. As Jesus focused on the cost of following him, the numbers went down. In John 6, the crowd showed up hoping for another fish sandwich. They were not amused when Jesus said, "I am the bread of life. Whoever comes to me will never be hungry again. Whoever believes in me will never be thirsty" (v. 35). People really coughed and sputtered when Jesus said, "Anyone who eats my flesh and drinks my blood remains in me, and I in him" (v. 56). That did it. I imagine them saying, "We're outta here. Let's go to that chicken and wings spot down the road."

John records the pivotal moment: "At this point many of his disciples turned away and deserted him" (v. 66). Trends of attendance and giving, while important, should not be the final determination of whether God is at work. When Jesus evaluates the churches in Revelation 2 and 3, there is no indication of how many were attending or the size of their budgets. God always checks the internal temperature in making an appraisal—cold, hot, or lukewarm (Rev. 3:15–16). There's more on this topic in chapter 13, "Storm No. 3: Unrealistic Pressure to Succeed."

Some say, "Money makes things happen." Not so. *God* makes things happen—with or without money. The Bible gives us a great example of this in 1 Thessalonians.

> So you can see we were not preaching with any deceit or impure motives or trickery.
>
> For we speak as messengers approved by God to be entrusted with the Good News. Our purpose is to please God, not people. He alone examines the motives of our hearts. Never once did we try to win you with flattery, as you well know. And God is our witness that we were not pretending to be your friends just to get your money!

As for human praise, we have never sought it from you or anyone else. (1 Thess. 2:3-6)

As the apostle Paul did, we need to abandon fleshly techniques. We do this in God Meetings, where *God* makes things happen.

7. **A God Meeting is focused on building lives.**

Most board meetings in the business model focus on building the organization. In the church, the organization is secondary to building lives. Paul was passionate about people: "After all, what gives us hope and joy, and what will be our proud reward and crown as we stand before our Lord Jesus when he returns? It is you! Yes, you are our pride and joy" (1 Thess. 2:19-20). These verses provide us with a great model for establishing healthy leadership priorities.

8. **The goal of a God Meeting is to please God.**

With critics and enemies hounding him, Paul made it clear, "Our purpose is to please God, not people" (1 Thess. 2:4). It's easy to get caught in the people-pleasing trap. Most churches have one or more squeaky wheels—sometimes well-intentioned, though perpetually discontent, people. What's the solution for a squeak that drives you batty?

Adjustments may or may not work. I have a rocking dining room chair that squeaks. I have taken it apart, oiled it, adjusted it, removed and reinstalled the spring—numerous times—and it still squeaks. So, we avoid sitting in that chair, and we're looking for a new dining room set. In the church, one squeaking wheel puts everyone on edge. One negative, contentious person drains the joy and gums up the inner workings. Forward momentum grinds to a halt. Important plans get tabled.

I recall a whiny wheel with a considerable following and a long history in the church. For several years, I tried numerous ways of connecting with him and correcting things to please him. Efforts to change things or make him happy were futile. He'd pick at stuff as if he were deboning a chicken. If I took the lead on something, he opposed it. Ultimately, he wanted to be in control and did everything possible to undermine my leadership. If I could do it over, I would take another leader with me, meet with him in private, and explain how things would be different: "I've listened to you for a considerable length of time, and I've attempted to correct many of the things you've brought up. When I change something, you're discontent about something else. You repeatedly undermine my leadership. This has been confusing for me because what I hear from you and what I hear from God are not the same thing. I choose to follow the voice of God, and I won't be listening to your complaints any longer. I will also let others in leadership know about my choice, and if you continue sowing seeds of discord among the congregation, the next step will be to disassociate from you, according to Titus 3:10." This meeting may have introduced new problems, but it would have ended my efforts to satisfy one cantankerous member.

We've all seen that a squeaky wheel can distract the entire group from perceiving what God wants and where he is directing. Marshall Shelley, a former senior editor of *Christianity Today*, writes about those he calls dragons in the church—well-meaning Christians who leave ulcers, strained relationships, and hard feelings in their wake. Shelley says, "If pastors become preoccupied with the dragons, afraid to challenge them or at least too concerned about 'fighting only the battles that need to be fought,' they often lose their spontaneity and creativity. ... If the first casualties in dragon warfare are vision and initiative, the next victim is outreach. When a pastor is forced to worry more about putting out brush fires than igniting the church's flame, the dragons have won, and the ministry has lost."[11] God Meetings keep a board's focus on pleasing God above all else.

9. **God Meetings have a dress code.**

Peter reminds leaders, "All of you, dress yourselves in humility as you relate to one another, for 'God opposes the proud but gives grace to the humble'" (1 Pet. 5:5). Pride is the lurking enemy for every spiritual leader, and the leader who fails to prune their pride will meet their downfall. Godly leaders dress in humility so don't show up sporting an attire of pride and arrogance.

10. **A God Meeting is forward-looking.**

The most effective teams spend most of their time looking toward the future. In *Lessons from the Church Boardroom*, Dan Busby and John Pearson recommend investing 80 percent of the time working on the future and 20 percent on the past.[12] I heartily agree. Staying stuck in the past is a problem. I'll explore this principle further in the next chapter, but here are initial symptoms to watch for:

- When fresh thinking raises eyebrows—not enthusiasm
- When status and *status quo* are synonymous (someone said, *status quo* is Latin for "the mess we are in")
- When programs are maintained because "we've always done it that way"
- When church members spend most of their time talking about the good ol' days
- When rigidity sets in like rigor mortis

Solomon wisely observed, "Do not say, 'Why is it that the former days were better than these?' For it is not from wisdom that you ask about this" (Eccl. 7:10 NASB). Looking forward and grasping opportunities is the primary work of leadership.

Putting It Into Perspective

As you can see, while there are similarities, there are also significant differences between traditional board meetings and this new way of functioning—meeting with God. On the next page is a side-by-side comparison of the characteristics that distinguish one type of meeting from the other.

Are you tired of contentious, bullheaded board meetings? Cancel them. With the Sovereign Ruler of the Universe at the helm in God Meetings, servant-leaders are empowered to do phenomenal kingdom work.

Board Meeting	God Meeting
1. Led by a human leader	1. Led by God through a servant-leader
2. Dominated by personal opinions and preferences	2. Directed by God's Word and God's will
3. Spirit of contention and conflict	3. Spirit of oneness and harmony
4. Majority rules	4. God rules through a Spirit-led consensus
5. Pretense of strength and invincibility	5. Freedom to be authentic and vulnerable
6. Money makes things happen	6. God makes things happen (with or without money)
7. Building organizations	7. Building lives
8. Focused on pleasing people	8. Focused on pleasing God
9. Dress code: attitude of self-dependence and pride	9. Dress code: clothed in humility and God-dependence
10. Bemoaning or reliving the past	10. Forward looking

GOD MEETINGS | 91

REFLECTION AND DISCUSSION

Quick Recall

- Trivia is the _____ _____.
- Split votes? Think of _____ _____.
- Facts + Fear = _____.
  Facts + Faith = _____.
- As a general principle, Dan Busby and John Pearson in *Lessons from the Church Boardroom* recommend investing _____ percent of the time working on the future and _____ percent on the past.

Thinking It Through

1. Consultant John Carver states, "In my experience, most of what the majority of boards do either does not need to be done or is a waste of time when done by the board. Conversely, most of what boards need to do for strategic leadership is not done." Discuss the ramifications of this and possible solutions.

2. What does the trivia trap look like for your team? What kind of issues do you get stuck on? What steps can you take to remedy this?

3. Paul said, "Our purpose is to please God, not people." How does this phrase shape your work and attitude as a leader?

4. Do you have squeaky wheels in your organization? What's your game plan to deal with squeaky wheels? What can you learn from their concerns? What do you perceive are the needs in their life, and how could you come alongside them?

So you can see we were not preaching with any deceit or impure motives or trickery.

For we speak as messengers approved by God to be entrusted with the Good News. Our purpose is to please God, not people. Never once did we try to win you with flattery, as you well know. And God is our witness that we were not pretending to be your friends just to get your money! (1 Thess. 2:3-5)

—6—
A MEETING WITH GOD!

A Powerful Purpose to Meet and a Pattern to Follow

How many of us have rushed into a leadership meeting with adrenaline still pumping after a crazy, stress-filled day? We fight traffic, inhale a burger and fries, skid into the parking lot, dart inside, grab a seat, and look over the agenda (primarily to assess the length of the meeting).

The chairman opens, "Let's get started. I'm going to get us out of here by 9:30 p.m. All in favor?"

Wholehearted approval resounds. "All right, Bill, lead us off in prayer."

Bill shoots up a prayer about the length of a hefty sneeze, and like the Kentucky Derby, the horses are off and running.

Five agenda items are quickly checked off when the chairman announces, "Next agenda item: how often should we have the church carpets cleaned?"

The meeting hits a snag.

Sam and Bill feel the carpets need a professional cleaning every six months. "It's important how the facility looks to visitors. Have you counted all the coffee stains?" they contend.

Phil and Jeff see it differently. "It seems like a lot of money. Once a year should be sufficient."

Then quiet Joe surprises everyone with an opinion. "Let's have people in the congregation clean the carpets with a rented machine. We'll save a lot of money."

The conversation drifts further.

Agitated, Ralph grouses, "The solution is no coffee in the carpeted area."

The discussion wrangles on. Eyes are rolling over this trivial issue. This one is a yawner. Some are holding their phones below the table to check their messages.

After fifty-five minutes with no resolution in sight, the chairman lifts his wrist in the air and points at his watch, "We're never going to get out of here by 9:30 if we don't get moving."

Carpet cleaning tabled.

This is a board meeting—not a God Meeting.

Most of us enter meetings with our own set of expectations. Typically, we're concerned that our perspective is heard and respected, our proposals approved. Humans instinctively default to a "What's in it for me?" mindset. This outlook isn't inherently bad, but it is often short-sighted and can be dangerous. Unless we surrender our will, we will not discover the will of God. As much as we may hate to admit it, we can get in the way of Christ's eternal purposes. At that moment, Peter was concerned more about his own natural human desires and feelings than the plan of God.

It still happens today. Too many leadership meetings are "seeing things merely from a human point of view, not from

God's." Satan weasels his way into a leadership meeting through self-serving interests. To thwart his schemes, we must consciously place our plans at the foot of the cross and yield them to Jesus. Otherwise, fleshly impulses will get in the way.

Let's examine how this could be different.

The Almighty Awaits

Your invitation to a leadership meeting is a personal invite to meet with God. The Almighty wants to meet with you. It's as simple as that—and as astounding.

The thought of meeting with God rattles my cage, and it should. I'm awestruck. I'm humbled. I identify with Isaiah, who said, "Woe is me, for I am ruined! Because I am a man of unclean lips, and I live among a people of unclean lips; for my eyes have seen the King, the LORD of hosts" (Isa. 6:5 NASB). Isaiah said, "Woe is me"—not "Wow is me!" Humility gripped him with a deep awareness of his sinfulness.

The prophet identifies three ways to prepare for a meeting with God.

- **Set your focus on Jesus.**

"My eyes have seen the Lord," Isaiah exclaims. That changes everything. We, too, come seeking an audience with the Lord God Almighty, the King of Kings. Shift the focus from the concerns of the day and focus on "Jesus, who both began and finished this race we're in" (Heb. 12:2 MSG). When entering a God meeting, breathe a silent prayer: *I'm here to worship, adore, and glorify you, Lord Jesus. I am awed and honored to be in your presence.*

- **Ask God to purify your lips.**

Isaiah had an unforgettable experience of God purifying his lips. "Then one of the seraphim flew to me with a burning coal he had taken from the altar with a pair of tongs. He touched my lips with it and said, 'See, this coal has touched your lips. Now your guilt is removed, and your sins are forgiven'" (Isa. 6:6-7). If the lips are unclean, the heart is polluted as well. Jesus said, "The words you speak come from the heart—that's what defiles you" (Matt. 15:18). Like Isaiah, we need our lips and hearts cleansed. It's so easy to pop off with hurtful words. We're prone to say things we later regret, so we need spiritual mouthwash. Our tendency is to be judgmental and critical of others. We are wired to self-justify and become defensive. As you prepare for meeting with God, pray, "May the words of my mouth and the meditation of my heart be pleasing to you, O LORD, my rock and my redeemer" (Ps. 19:14).

- **Surrender your will to serve.**

Isaiah prayed, "Here I am. Send me" (Isa. 6:8), and so should we. Come into God's presence wearing the garment of servanthood. Whatever you want, Lord, start with me. I'm available. Wash everyone's feet—no problem. Make or clean up the coffee—consider it done. Make the phone calls needed? Yes. Come with a listening and willing heart, ready to serve.

A BIBLICAL PATTERN FOR A GOD MEETING

In chapter 4, we examined the God Meeting in Jerusalem to resolve a highly explosive issue. A closer look at Acts 15 reveals a natural flow of the meeting that helps establish a pattern for God Meetings today.

1. **The leaders gathered with joy to seek God and his will.**

A group of delegates along with Paul and Barnabas traveled to Jerusalem, and "they stopped along the way in Phoenicia and Samaria to visit the believers. They told them—much to everyone's joy—that the Gentiles, too, were being converted" (Acts 15:3). They could have been fretting and stewing about the upcoming meeting. Instead, there was great joy on their journey to seek God's direction for the churches. Don't abandon joy even when facing a difficult or agonizing decision.

2. **The leaders reported the wonderful things God was doing.**

"When they arrived in Jerusalem, Barnabas and Paul were welcomed by the whole church, including the apostles and elders. They reported everything God had done through them. ... Everyone listened quietly as Barnabas and Paul told about the miraculous signs and wonders God had done through them among the Gentiles" (15:4, 12). Hearing the awesome work of God was crucial before tackling the thorny issue at hand.

3. **The leaders discussed the issue to discover the will of God.**

There was vigorous debate. Peter stood and explained how Gentiles had received the Holy Spirit, cleansing their hearts by faith. James followed this with the Old Testament prophecy about the Gentiles. In this meeting, which could have been disastrous, everyone sought God's will by reading the Scripture and listening to each other. God brought about a Spirit-led consensus: "... *it seemed good to us*, having become of one mind" and "... *it seemed good to the Holy Spirit and to us* to lay upon you no greater burden than these essentials" (15:25, 28 NASB emphasis mine).

4. **The leaders set in motion a plan to do what God had directed.**

A letter was drafted, and Paul, Barnabas, Judas (called Barsabbas), and Silas were assigned to deliver it to the churches (15:22-34). There was great joy throughout the churches as the encouraging report was read (v. 31).

Schism averted. Mission accomplished.

PLANNING GOD MEETINGS

Based on this pattern, we can discern a general flow for a God Meeting that is not restrictive and allows room for creativity. Here are the four essential components.

Part One: Surrender Before God

The first part is certainly the most important because it prepares our hearts to do the Father's business. Following are several ways to prepare your heart, either with the entire group or in groups of two or three. Select what works best for your situation and change it from time to time to keep it fresh. The first twenty to thirty minutes of a God Meeting are the most crucial part.

Be still. Take time to slow down and breathe deeply. There must be a conscious shift from the stress of the day to stillness before God to hear the quiet voice of the Spirit. As the Psalmist said, "Cease striving and know that I am God" (Ps. 46:10 NASB). Be still, release the stress, be quiet, focus on God. Don't make this too short or too long. These are moments to read Scripture, pray, and yield your life to God. Like David told his son Solomon, "Now set your heart and your soul to seek the LORD your God" (1 Chron. 22:19 NASB).

During this time of surrender, the team will find great benefit in silence. "Silence frees us from the need to control others. One reason we can hardly bear to remain silent is that it makes us feel so helpless. We are so accustomed to relying upon words to manage and control others. A frantic stream of words flows from us in an attempt to straighten others out. We want so desperately for them to agree with us, to see things our way. We evaluate people, judge people, condemn people. We devour people with our words. Silence is one of the deepest disciplines of the Spirit because it puts a stopper on that."[1]

Confess sin. We know sin blocks our relationship with God, but how many meetings open with a brief opportunity to confess sin? Far too few! We can't meet with God and expect his guidance while harboring unconfessed sin. If you had a spat with your spouse or yelled at your kids on the way out the door, it would be appropriate to step out of the meeting, call your wife or kids, apologize to them, and then return to the meeting, ready to yield before God.

Stand or kneel. This isn't required, but it is a good practice to stand or kneel in the presence of King Jesus for reading Scripture, confession, and prayer. While I was the program director and pastor at Mt. Gilead Bible Conference Center in Northern California, the board's monthly meeting didn't start until 8 p.m. due to the camp schedule. Rather than rushing into the meeting, this group always spent thirty to forty-five minutes on their knees in prayer. Some had a two-hour drive to get home, and they still took the time to pray. While I don't recommend the late start time for meetings, these godly men sensed the presence of God in the discussions, and the harvest of souls in the camp ministry confirmed the power of prayer.

Establish spiritual cohorts or prayer partnerships. As an alternative to open the meeting, consider small groups. I suggest pairing two or three leaders for the term of service. The intent is to know each other personally—work, family, and life challenges—and pray for each other during the month. At the start of the meeting, cohorts or prayer partners report in and pray for each other for about twenty minutes. If someone has faced a big disappointment or a personal hurt during the day, this provides the opportunity to share it and receive prayer. Following this, the entire group stands as a brief passage of Scripture is read, followed by a prayer of confession and surrender.

At this point, we get nervous. We assume if we spend twenty to thirty minutes in spiritual readiness, the meeting will go till midnight. Let me offer a principle and a challenge: Seek first the kingdom of God, and he'll take the kinks out of your meeting. I've witnessed it over and over—when leaders seek God, it's amazing how smoothly and quickly the rest of the meeting flows. You'll also be less inclined to spend time on trivial matters.

If there's just too much to cover in one meeting, I highly recommend this alternative. Schedule a separate "shepherds' meeting." Facing the dilemma of a too-long agenda crowding out the spiritual, Pastor Larry Osborne started this practice.

> I hit upon an idea and suggested something I never thought I'd support: *why not schedule an extra monthly meeting to deal exclusively with these important but neglected priorities?*
>
> I called it a "shepherds' meeting," intending to highlight the spiritual and leadership dimension that came with shepherding the flock that God had given us.
>
> I had no clue if it would work or if anyone would agree to come to another meeting. But I asked anyway, positioning these extra meetings as exclusively set aside for three things:
>
> 1. Team building
> 2. Training
> 3. Prayer
>
> The board agreed to give it a shot for six months. ...

It wasn't long until our shepherds' meeting became a permanent fixture. Today, I can't imagine trying to build a healthy and unified lay leadership team without it. It has become the key vehicle for building trust, finding common ground, and deepening relationships.[2]

In this second meeting, the leadership team functions as a small group. So rather than just decision-making, the group becomes a setting for disciple-making. This is what Jesus said matters—making disciples (Matt. 28:19-20). We have to be the people of God before we can do the work of God.

Spiritual surrender and discipleship are not just for church leadership teams. My close friend, Pastor Lou Damiani, spent nine years serving on the leadership board for a Christian school. The group chose to meet twice a month. One of the meetings was on Saturday morning when they spent about two hours in the Word and prayer. Lou said they became like a "body life board"—thriving in their relationships with each other and deepening in their walk with God. The other meeting was on a Monday evening. They opened the meeting with time in the Word, followed by prayer in groups of two or three. The following two hours of healthy discussion and decision-making helped to grow their unity and relational trust while minimizing power struggles. Was this a small school with very few things to discuss? Hardly. The school had 1500 to 2000 students and a staff of 150 to 175 across five campuses.

Include focused prayers. This is another resource for the team. In the book *Lessons from the Church Board Room*,[3] there are thirty-nine prayers grouped in seven sections: 1) thank you, 2) report honestly, 3) see clearly, 4) listen objectively, 5) speak cautiously, 6) plan wisely, and 7) remain unified. Each prayer provides insight into the challenges every leadership team faces, so include one or two of these prayers when appropriate as the team surrenders before God.

Part Two: Report What God is Doing

Most meetings include reports from the pastors, staff, and leaders of various ministries. A great way to start a report is to ask, "What are you celebrating? What are you thankful for?" so leaders can share an answer to prayer or an area of victory, either personal or ministry-related. Our human tendency is to think negatively and focus on problems, but Scripture reminds us, "Always be joyful. Never stop praying. Be thankful in all circumstances for this is God's will for you who belong to Christ Jesus" (1 Thess. 5:16-18). This reverses negative thinking, which tends to spiral downward, and sets the tone for a healthy meeting.

Reports are an opportunity to discover and encourage what God is doing. As you listen to someone share what God is doing in their ministry, look for the unique ways God is at work, then identify ways to partner with God in that work. In *Experiencing God,* Henry Blackaby and Claude King recommend that leaders look for where God is at work and adjust to joining him in that work.[4] While a report is shared, you may sense a tired or discouraged teammate. This is an excellent opportunity to pause and pray. As a group, gather around, laying hands on them as you pray. They will never forget the experience.

I've often seen volunteers or staff members attempting to give an enthusiastic report of what God is doing in their ministry. Across the table, I see glum looks and scowls—it looks more like a congressional investigation. Warm smiles and nods of affirmation go a long way toward affirming and encouraging ministry rather than imparting deep pain. "Death and life are in the power of the tongue, and those who love it will eat its fruit" (Prov. 18:21 NASB). Listen for what God is doing, join him in it, and encourage, encourage, encourage your teammates.

I vividly recall a time when this didn't happen for me. Following our honeymoon, Joanne and I jumped into our first ministry. We worked ourselves to the bone doing youth work and running day camps in a Presbyterian church. I felt it had been a good three months of ministry, with many decisions for Christ. At the end of the summer, I was called before the session to give a report. I was nervous but enthusiastic. About halfway through my report, an elder interrupted and launched into a scolding. He was upset I hadn't spent more time with his rebellious son. He had expected me to fix his son, who had no intention of getting fixed. During this dressing-down, he blasted me and the entirety of our work that summer. I exited the meeting and stood alone in the courtyard as burning tears trickled down my face. The experience etched deep wounds in my heart—wounds that healed slowly and left a painful memory. I pray your teammates never experience something similar as they report what God is doing.

Part Three: Discover the Will of God

At this point in a God Meeting, the group begins asking God for specific guidance regarding a variety of agenda items. It is best to establish the agenda in advance, so someone who wants to add something to the agenda should contact the chairman a day or two before the meeting. However, allow flexibility for an urgent item as needed.

As I mentioned in the last chapter, the most effective teams focus their agenda and spend most of their time looking toward the future. Dan Busby and John Pearson recommend the 80/20 rule: invest 80 percent of the time on the future and 20 percent on the past. They call this avoiding the rearview window syndrome.[5] You need to have rear window visibility in your car mirror to see what's behind, but driving a car looking primarily out the back window would be disastrous. Follow the 80/20 rule to "get your ministry past the traditional focus on lagging indicators, such as church attendance and weekly collection (indicators that essentially tell you about your past performance), and on to leading indicators, such as innovative programs in the pipeline, member satisfaction, and available staff and volunteer talent (indicators that tell you where you're headed in the future)."[6]

Agenda items and future thinking may include concerns from the congregation, but these should be presented only with names attached. Congregational complaints are often introduced with a statement like, "I've been talking with some people, and they are concerned about ..." I encourage leaders to immediately ask, "Do *they* have names?" It is impossible to deal with the concern objectively if the source is not identified. When Paul addressed the concerns brought to his attention at Corinth, he identified the source (1 Cor. 1:11). Financial giving can be anonymous but not criticism.

In every God Meeting, as teammates pray and discern together, God wants to impart wisdom (insight beyond human perspective) and courage (rising above human limitations). A prayer over every agenda item can quickly become rote; however, stopping to pray over major decisions is essential. The chairman should clarify that any member of the group can give a time-out signal, like a referee, to stop and pray at any point.

Part Four: Do the Work of God

How many times have you seen a great idea falter because no one followed through? As each God Meeting comes to a close, look back over the discussion and make a concrete plan. Phone calls? Personal appointments? Written communication? Write down the action steps, make assignments, and identify completion dates. Be specific and hold each other accountable. The meeting minutes should indicate the assignments and due dates and be reviewed at the next meeting to determine next steps.

For further help, see the agenda worksheet in Appendix 1.

Laugh and Have Fun in a God Meeting

While focusing on meeting with God and surrendering our lives, don't forget to smile and laugh. Board meetings often become very intense, serious, and solemn, but where did we get the idea that fun isn't spiritual? Laughter is a God-given lubricant in human relationships, a salve removing friction and stress. It assists us with living in the present rather than agonizing over the past or worrying about the future. Laughter helps us accept our imperfections and frees us from being negative and trying to control everyone and everything. While in prison, Paul wrote, "Always be full of joy in the Lord. I say it again—rejoice!" (Phil. 4:4) or, to put it another way, "Celebrate God all day, every day. I mean, *revel* in him!" (Phil. 4:4 MSG). To maintain a healthy balance, lighten up, relax, laugh, and enjoy the journey.

Announcing a God Meeting

Churches frequently make announcements like, "On Sunday, we have our worship services. Tuesday evening is the business meeting of the elders." In other words, Sunday's agenda is spiritual, while Tuesday's sounds primarily secular. We'd never say it aloud, but when we enter into "business meeting" mode, it's almost as if we're saying, "God, we'll take over now and sort things out the way the world does." Such an idea is foreign to biblical teaching, which makes no distinction between the spiritual and the secular. Instead, we should announce, "On Sunday, we gather to worship God, and on Tuesday evening, the elders will be seeking God and his leading for the church." In the list of what's happening for the week, you can include this: 6:30 p.m. Tuesday: Elders' God Meeting. The church will appreciate that you're meeting to seek God. And after you do, give the church a summary of action items. This simple practice goes a long way in keeping everyone on the same page.

THE FIREPLACE FOR REVIVAL

In these dark days, churches need a fresh awakening. What stands in the way of revival? One of the major obstacles is the behavior of leaders in traditional board meetings. In too many cases, the Holy Spirit has little say as the elected leaders assume power and authority, muscling their way through to reach their own goals. In one church where I worked, two leaders on the board had a long-standing feud. They openly campaigned against and boycotted each other's ministry. Their public anger and displays of ungodly temper stymied the church. Getting these two leaders to meet and resolve their issues was about as easy as extracting a shark's tooth. Sadly, similar scenes play out in many churches.

Board members do some horrific things. Infighting, outbursts of anger, bitterness, cutting remarks, petty jealousies, selfish ambition, backbiting, and dissension all block revival. Like pawns on a chessboard, people are often discarded with little concern for their well-being. The result is long-term damage and wounding to the individual and their family. Such calloused treatment of people grieves the Holy Spirit (Eph. 4:30-32).

Pastor Chuck Smith wrote, "Do you know why the early church was so successful? It enjoyed God's favor because the Holy Spirit directed all of its activities. The early church allowed the Holy Spirit to direct where it should go and what it should do. He was in charge. The Spirit ordained and established the leadership of the church."[7] We may have charts, graphs, statistical analysis, data mining, budget forecasting, regression analysis, spreadsheets, sentiment analysis or opinion mining, demographic studies, SWOT analysis, PEST analysis, MOST analysis, heptalysis, but where's the Holy Spirit? I'm not opposed to any of these tools, but "the tragic mistake of the modern church is its declaration of independence from the Holy Spirit. We have declared we no longer need the Spirit to direct our activities."[8] My concern is that we've substituted techniques and tools for the power of the Holy Spirit released in humble and surrendered lives.

God Meetings are the fireplace to ignite the flames for revival. When leaders humble themselves before God, confess sinful behavior, and allow the Holy Spirit to direct their meetings, sparks burst into flame. Soon others gather around the hearth, and the warmth invades the entire church.

Jesus, speaking of the last days, said, "Sin will be rampant everywhere, and the love of many will grow cold" (Mt 24:12).

It's cold and getting colder.

Let's light the fireplace.

REFLECTION AND DISCUSSION

Quick Recall

- Isaiah didn't say, "_____ is me!" He said, "_____ is me."
- There are three steps to be prepared for a God meeting.
  Set the focus _____.
  Ask God to _____.
  Surrender _____.
- What are the four suggested parts for a God Meeting?
  S_____ before God.
  R_____ what God is doing.
  D_____ the will of God.
  D_____ the work of God.

Thinking It Through

1. What helps you most get in tune with God at the beginning of a meeting—praying together, silence, reading Scripture, worship in song, kneeling, or standing?

2. Discuss the rearview window syndrome and how it impacts ministry.

3. What is the best way to discover what the Holy Spirit is communicating to each person?

4. How do you discern if there is a consensus to move forward?

Now set your heart and your soul to seek the LORD your God. (1 Chron. 22:19 NASB)

Trust in the LORD with all your heart;
do not depend on your own understanding.
Seek his will in all you do,
and he will show you which path to take.
(Prov. 3:5-6)

—7—

HOTHEADS AND BULLIES NEED NOT APPLY

CHOOSING LEADERS GOD'S WAY

Board bullies plague far too many churches. Whether the lead pastor or a volunteer, bullies assume the position entitles them to carte blanche grab the horns of power and rule the church. Disguised as servants of God, they become ruthless dictators, eliminating those who oppose them and maneuvering to get their way. They are status seekers.

A small church in the Midwest was in serious need of leadership. Enter Dan (names have been changed in this story) and his family, new in town. The church discovered he was a take-charge guy, seemingly just what they needed. They were impressed when Dan mentioned his experience as the lead pastor of two churches. However, he conveniently failed to mention his first pastorate lasted eighteen months and his second less than a year. In both churches, Dan was asked to leave because of his oppressive style of leadership and his intense anger when his views met resistance. He was stubborn, manipulative, argumentative, and domineering—but no one in town knew this ... yet.

In short order, Dan was elected to the leadership team and quickly became the chairman. Initially, it seemed to work well as the more passive team members willingly followed Dan's lead. He helped recruit and select the church's first full-time pastor, Pastor Jerry. Their relationship started well since Jerry went with the flow of Dan's agenda.

A servant-hearted shepherd, Pastor Jerry led the church in building a new worship center along with adjoining classrooms to start a Christian school. Meanwhile, tension was brewing. Never one to *assist* someone in succeeding, Dan would *insist* things be done his way. He formed a power base that opposed and undermined the leadership of Pastor Jerry. After five years of power struggle, Pastor Jerry finally resigned—wounded, betrayed, and bewildered.

The church greatly loved and respected Pastor Jerry. Though these were trusting folk, they were also discerning. They knew what had actually taken place (no matter how much spiritual-sounding lipstick Dan put on the pig of his ugly power grab), yet they felt powerless to do anything about it. Dan had successfully undermined and run off their beloved pastor. He was the status-driven, unofficial "church boss," a role he relished.

Pastor Chuck was selected as the next pastor. He quickly surmised that coming under Dan's dominance was his ticket to survival. Chuck became the consummate peace-keeping pastor, cowering in fear and placating Dan's pushiness. By continually caving and catering to Dan's directives, he further emboldened the church bully. When the invitation came to pastor a larger church in a major city, Pastor Chuck eagerly accepted—relieved to exit the dictatorship of Dan.

Pastor Zach was chosen as the next pastor. It became abundantly clear from the first week there would be no "honeymoon period"—he had walked into a firestorm. Dan launched public and private attacks on Pastor Zach—his teaching, family, leadership, and motives. Having seen this pattern before, the leadership team, along with Pastor Zach, began the peacemaking work that had been neglected for years. They confronted Dan's bullying behavior with "truth in love" sessions. He was defensive, accusatory, and demeaning. The situation came to a head when the entire staff resigned one week before the start of school. For the first time, not one leader supported Dan. With one voice, the group finally stood up to the bully. He soon resigned his position and left the church in shame and disgrace that he'd brought on himself.

Whether it's the lead pastor, a volunteer leader, or a long-time member, bullies wreak havoc. This church could have prevented years of heartache and pain by checking Dan's track record and qualifications before selecting him for leadership. Unfortunately, thousands of churches have experienced a similar story because the cavernous need for leadership often leads to a careless selection process. A biblical plan to choose godly leaders can prevent the selection of status seekers who use and manipulate people and create division.

Better Than Casting Lots

Wouldn't it be nice if we could cast lots or flip a coin to choose the right person for leadership? In replacing Judas Iscariot, the disciples searched for the right candidate, someone who had witnessed the life and resurrection of Jesus. Two candidates were qualified, and it seems the apostles had a hard time deciding between the two. "So they nominated two men: Joseph called Barsabbas (also known as Justus) and Matthias. Then they all prayed, 'O Lord, you know every heart. Show us which of these men you have chosen as an apostle to replace Judas in this ministry, for he has deserted us and gone where he belongs.' Then they cast lots, and Matthias was selected to become an apostle with the other eleven" (Acts 1:23-26).

Prior to Pentecost and the Holy Spirit indwelling believers, many decisions were made by casting lots, a practice that appears over seventy times in the Bible. Today, flipping a coin or rolling dice would be similar to casting lots. Proverbs says God controls every throw of the lot and uses it to accomplish his purpose: "The lot is cast into the lap, but its every decision is from the LORD" (Prov. 16:33 NASB). However, I don't recommend giving your nominating committee a set of dice to make those dicey leadership decisions. You don't want to rely on the luck of the draw, flipping coins, or drawing straws to choose spiritual leaders. Why not? Because you have the Holy Spirit to direct you to the right person. After the Holy Spirit came in Acts, there is no record of casting lots to select leaders.

LEADERS SELECTED BY THE HOLY SPIRIT

In Paul's farewell meeting with the elders in Ephesus, he reminds them to "feed and shepherd God's flock—his church, purchased with his own blood—over which the Holy Spirit has appointed you as elders" (Acts 20:28). Did you notice who appointed them? The Holy Spirit. This confused me. Did the Holy Spirit send a list by "divine mail" with the names of those chosen to be the leaders? I realized God oversees the selection process through the Holy Spirit. The following three principles invite the Holy Spirit's direction in the selection process.

Principle One: Candidates are selected by spiritually mature leaders who seek God with fasting and prayer.

We don't often hear of a church selecting leaders with fasting and prayer, but there is a purpose behind this practice. As we refrain from food for one or more meals or abstain from luxury foods (Dan. 10:2-3), we become more God-conscious and alert to the leading of the Spirit, less focused on externals and more attune to spiritual qualifications. How can we discern leaders "appointed by the Holy Spirit" without seeking God in fasting and prayer?

Prayer and fasting became the norm for the New Testament churches. "Paul and Barnabas also appointed elders in every church. With prayer and fasting, they turned the elders over to the care of the Lord, in whom they had put their trust" (Acts 14:23). The word *appointed* (Grk. *cheirotoneō*, also used in 2 Cor. 8:19) means 1) to stretch out the hand, 2) to appoint by show of hands, or 3) to appoint or elect without regard to the method.[1] The process could have been stretching out the hand (pointing to individuals and saying, "I select you, and you, and you.") or a show of hands ("All in favor, raise your hand."). One of my professors, Dr. Robert Saucy, favored the view that the names were presented to the congregation, who indicated their approval with a show of hands.[2]

The biblical account makes no mention of nominations from the floor. "I would like my brother-in-law Marcus to be an elder. He's made a lot of money selling sardines." I was in an annual meeting when an individual stood and asked that his name be added as a candidate. The chairman wisely refused his request. After the meeting, I watched this individual, now with a beet-red face, shouting at the chairman. His anger confirmed why he was not nominated.

I have heard church announcements like this, "We need three more elders to serve. Let us know if you want to be an elder." What? Unbelievable. Almost as disastrous is the announcement, "We're getting ready to select leaders for next year. If you would like to serve on the nominating committee, let Bill know after the service." These two practices open the door for disqualified people to assume positions of leadership. And once you get a cantankerous, self-centered person in leadership, it's very difficult to remove them. A couple of times, I had to approach an individual and ask them to change their behavior or step down. It's not fun, and it rarely goes well. Guard the door rather than getting the wrong person.

Give careful thought in selecting the nominating team as well. Spiritual maturity and sensitivity are essential. Let candidates know the seriousness of the task, and ask them if they are willing to fast and pray in preparation. Sometimes the pastor is shut out from the selection process, which is a tragic mistake. I would not serve in a church that locks the pastor out of the selection process for leaders. How can a pastor build a team without a say in who is selected? As a senior pastor, I always met with the nominating group. Before considering names, we reviewed the biblical qualifications of leaders.

Following this, I explained the policy we would follow. "As we consider candidates, all of our conversations are to be kept strictly confidential. This is not a setting for character assassination. As we come to a name, you may hear me say, 'Let's move on to the next person.' Why? It means I have a strong hesitation regarding that individual, possibly because of confidential information from counseling or personal interaction. It would be wrong for me to share this. If you have compelling hesitation regarding someone, you also have permission to say, 'Let's pass on this person.' I ask that we reject a nomination only as led by the Spirit, never because of personal dislike."

Principle Two: Candidates are selected according to biblical responsibilities.

To choose the right leader, match the candidate with the role they will fill. There are two levels of leadership for the local church: elders and deacons. "To all the saints in Christ Jesus who are in Philippi, including the overseers [elders] and deacons" (Phil. 1:1 NASB brackets mine). The roles of the elder (a term synonymous with pastor or overseer) and deacon are different. *The work of the elder or pastor is very specific: shepherd the flock and oversee the flock* (1 Pet. 5:1-2). Feed and lead. Sometimes, it is feed and weed. Thorny issues are part of the pastoral ministry. *The work of the deacon is very general.* Because of this, the role can be defined according to the needs of the individual church. In our world of complex organizational structures, the biblical pattern of elders and deacons is surprisingly simple for the smallest church and flexible for the expanding ministry of the larger church. To help your selection process, let's sharpen the focus on the differences between these two roles.

Elder, Overseer, or Pastor

Don't be confused by these three interchangeable terms used for the spiritual leaders of New Testament churches (Acts 20:17, 28; Titus 1:5-7; 1 Pet. 5:1-2). The word *elder* (Grk. *presbuteros,* root of the name presbyterian) indicates spiritual maturity and wisdom. The Jews were familiar with this term, which originated with the appointment of the seventy elders by Moses. A second term, *bishop* or *overseer* (Grk. word *episkopon,* root of the name episcopal), is a compound word *epi* meaning "before or over" and *skopeo* meaning "to look over or watch." This was a common word in the Greek and Roman world, used to designate overseers of public work projects who were sent to the various cities to organize and govern them. The third term, *pastor* (Grk. word *poimen*), is a word from the rural community, meaning a shepherd who faithfully tends, feeds, guards, and cares for the flock. In the crisscross of cultures—Greeks, Romans, and Jews—the use of three different words to describe the same person makes sense. When you combine the three words, you have a spiritually mature person (elder) who watches over (overseer) and shepherds the flock (pastor).[3] In the New Testament, the elders who worked hard, particularly at teaching and preaching, were to receive "double honor," a Greek word referring to appreciation expressed by an honorarium or compensation (1 Tim. 5:17). Elders may be vocational or volunteer, but here's the crucial point: *biblically, a pastor is an elder, an elder is a pastor.*

Sometimes I ask elders, "How's it going caring for the needs of people?"

Some look perplexed. "As elders, we meet monthly to make decisions. The pastors care for the people."

I counter, "Elders are pastors, and the heart and soul of being an elder is caring for people. Being an elder extends beyond meeting once a month. The work of an elder is to 'shepherd the church of God' (Acts 20:28 NASB) and 'shepherd the flock of God among you' (1 Pet. 5:2 NASB). You're a partner with your pastors in caring for the people of God."

In 1 Peter 5, "The verb 'shepherd' (Greek, *poimaino*) is in the emphatic position and the imperative mood, indicating that shepherding the flock is the essential work of the elder according to Peter."[4] The role of the elder-shepherd is four-fold: 1) *knowing* the sheep by name (i.e., caring for them personally), 2) *feeding* the sheep, 3) *leading* the sheep, and 4) *protecting* them from danger.[5]

On a beach around a charcoal fire, the first commissioning service for an elder-shepherd took place. Peter had denied Jesus three times before the crucifixion, then repented. After the resurrection, Jesus asked Peter three times to affirm his love.

> After breakfast Jesus asked Simon Peter, "Simon son of John, do you love me more than these?"
>
> "Yes, Lord," Peter replied, "you know I love you."
>
> "Then feed my lambs," Jesus told him.
>
> Jesus repeated the question: "Simon son of John, do you love me?"
>
> "Yes, Lord," Peter said, "you know I love you."
>
> "Then take care of my sheep," Jesus said.
>
> A third time he asked him, "Simon son of John, do you love me?"
>
> Peter was hurt that Jesus asked the question a third time. He said, "Lord, you know everything. You know that I love you."
>
> Jesus said, "Then feed my sheep." (John 21:15-17)

The question remains the same for elders in every local church today: Do you love Jesus? If so, feed and care for his sheep. Leaders may wonder what that means. William Barclay provides a vivid—and challenging—description of a shepherd:

> His life [the shepherd] was very hard. No flock ever grazed without a shepherd, and he was never off duty. There being little grass, the sheep were bound to wander, and since there were no protecting walls, the sheep had constantly to be watched. On either side of the narrow plateau, the ground dipped sharply down to the craggy deserts, and the sheep were always liable

to stray away and get lost. The shepherd's task was not only constant but dangerous, for, in addition, he had to guard the flock against wild animals, especially against wolves, and there were always thieves and robbers ready to steal the sheep. Sir George Adam Smith, who traveled in Palestine, writes: "On some high moor, across which at night the hyaenas howl, when you meet him, sleepless, far-sighted, weather-beaten, leaning on his staff, and looking out over his scattered sheep, every one of them on his heart, you understand why the shepherd of Judaea sprang to the front in his people's history; why they gave his name to their king and made him the symbol of providence; why Christ took him as the type of self-sacrifice." Constant vigilance, fearless courage, and patient love for his flock were the necessary characteristics of the shepherd.[6]

The Bible further emphasizes that biblical elders were assigned to care for a specific group of people in the church. Peter urges, "Don't lord it over the people assigned to your care, but lead them by your own good example" (1 Pet. 5:3). The word *assigned* is *kleron* in Greek, meaning an "assignment by portion or share." According to New Testament scholars Arndt and Gingrich, this refers to the "various parts of the congregation which have been assigned as 'portions' to the individual ... shepherds."[7] A pastor of a congregation with two hundred or more people can run themselves ragged trying to tend to every personal need. This is one of the reasons many churches stop growing when attendance reaches a hundred fifty or two hundred. God's plan is for a group of elders to care for people together. Elder assignments can be made based on geographical location, age groupings, or small groups. Whatever the approach, elders share the work of shepherding.

When leaders see themselves more as rulers than shepherds, major problems are brewing. I've seen it too often. A dictatorial mindset settles in. "We're in charge around here. We supervise the pastor, staff, and other ministries." Elders who don't regularly care for the hurts and struggles of the people tend to rule with a harsh severity. Understanding, forgiving, and healing are replaced by judgmental rigidity. In a stinging rebuke against the spiritual shepherds of Israel, Ezekiel warned, "You have not taken care of the weak. You have not tended the sick or bound up the injured. You have not gone looking for those who have wandered away and are lost. Instead, you have ruled them with harshness and cruelty" (Ezek. 34:4). May it never be so with us! I've seen some disastrous decisions inflict deep wounds when leaders acted as calloused rulers rather than tender shepherds. Yes, there are tough calls to make, and not every decision will be popular. But when elders are faithful shepherds laying their lives down to care for the flock, the tough calls, with few exceptions, will be respected rather than resisted.

I hear the term "ruling elder" tossed about frequently these days. Implied, at least in some cases, is an authoritarian and domineering style of leadership, sort of a license to throw weight around and wield power. I've even seen it twisted to justify abusive behavior. The words "ruling elder" come from 1 Timothy 5:17, "The elders who rule well ..." (NASB), but the Greek word translated *rule* here is *proistemi,* meaning "to stand before," which pastors do as they lead the congregation. The sense is to guide, direct, or lead in a way that encourages a voluntary following. It does not imply authoritarian or dictatorial leadership. Yes, Scripture says, "Obey your spiritual leaders, and do what they say. Their work is to watch over your souls, and they are accountable to God. Give them reason to do this with joy and not with sorrow. That would certainly not be for your benefit" (Heb. 13:17). The people are to obey, and the elders are ultimately accountable to God, but balance this with the injunction we highlighted earlier: "Don't lord it over the people assigned to your care" (1 Pet. 5:3).

Growing up in rural South Dakota, I learned that cattle are driven from behind. Sheep, on the other hand, follow a gentle shepherd who leads from the front. Notice how the Good Shepherd works with us, his sheep, in Psalm 23:2-3, "He *lets me rest* in green meadows; he *leads me* beside peaceful streams. ... He *guides me* along right paths" (emphasis mine). When leaders are frustrated with a lack of results, they may be tempted to start a sheep drive and, in the process, beat the sheep into submission. A good shepherd never drives or beats the sheep.

It ultimately boils down to this: when choosing leaders, avoid status seekers hungry to rule and always look for a shepherd's heart.

Deacon and Deaconess

The terms *deacon* and *deaconess* come from the Greek word *diakonos*, meaning "to wait at tables" or "one who serves." The root of the word traces back to *diako* "to run on errands." While their function is not tightly defined in the New Testament, we see deacons serving the early church in a number of practical ways. The idea of a deacon behaving as an authority-wielding ruler is entirely foreign to biblical teaching. The general sense of the word serving, *diakonos* included giving food and drink, extending shelter, providing clothes, and visiting the sick and prisoners (Matt. 25:34-44), serving meals (Matt. 8:15; Luke 10:40), assisting and counseling people in their time of need (Rom. 16:1-2, 1 Cor. 16:15), supervising the common meals and distribution of food (Acts 6:1), and administration of offerings and their distribution (2 Cor. 8:18-21). Deacons "served as assistants of the church leaders. Certainly, that was clearly the role of deacons by the second century. Deacons continued to fill an important role in the ministry of the early church, serving the needs of the poor, assisting in baptism and the Lord's Supper, and performing other practical ministerial tasks."[8] In 104 A.D., deaconess duties were to "take care of the sick and poor, to minister to martyrs and confessors in prison, to instruct catechumens, to assist at the baptism of women, and to exercise a general supervision over female church members."[9]

Were deaconesses a separate office from the deacons, or were they the wives of the deacons? This is not a point to be dogmatic about, but I believe deaconesses were a separate office for these reasons. "First, the use of likewise (cf. 1 Tim. 2:9; 3:8; Titus 2:3, 6) argues strongly for seeing a third and distinct group here in addition to elders and deacons. Second, there is no possessive pronoun or definite article connecting these women with male deacons. Third, Paul gave no qualifications for elders' wives. Why would he do so for deacons' wives? Fourth, Paul did not use the word 'deaconesses' because there was no such word in the Greek language; the masculine form of *diakonos* was used of both men and women (cf. Rom. 16:1)."[10]

Paul thought very highly of Phoebe, whose name meant "bright and radiant." "I commend to you our sister Phoebe, who is a deacon in the church in Cenchrea. Welcome her in the Lord as one who is worthy of honor among God's people. Help her in whatever she needs, for she has been helpful to many, and especially to me" (Rom. 16:1-2). While some think the word deacon simply means she was serving in the church, I believe that, in this context, *diakonos* indicates Phoebe was a female deacon or deaconess. In the churches

I have served, I have had the privilege of working with some wonderful Phoebe-like women. I applaud them. May the number of "bright and radiant" women who serve the Lord as Phoebe multiply greatly! We need them.

Principle Three: Candidates are selected according to biblical qualifications.

If you check the qualifications for a chief executive in the business world, you will discover they differ greatly from the requirements for a servant-leader in the church. Candidates should not be selected simply because they're sharp in business, donate a lot of money to the church, or their family helped found the church. This doesn't eliminate them, but be certain they meet the biblical qualifications. Don't choose candidates because they represent a disgruntled group. Scripture provides a clear list of qualifications for elders in 1 Timothy 3:1-7 and Titus 1:5-9 and deacons and deaconesses in 1 Timothy 3:8-13. In Acts, when the disciples chose the seven who would lead the food distribution, the apostles selected candidates who were "respected and full of the Spirit and wisdom" (Acts 6:3). How do you know if someone is "full of the Spirit and wisdom"? Use Galatians 5:22-23 to evaluate the characteristics of a spirit-filled person and James 3:13-18 to identify a person filled with God's wisdom.

In bringing these various Scriptures and qualifications together, here are five questions for the nominating team to ask regarding each candidate.

1. Are they respected?

"A life above reproach"—no grounds to be accused—heads the list of qualifications in both 1 Timothy and Titus. A "blameless life" is core to their fitness to serve in leadership, and they must have a good reputation (Grk. *maturia*, meaning "a good witness") with those outside the church. Look for those who are self-controlled (i.e., sober-minded or clear-headed)—this disqualifies heavy drinkers or substance abusers. Are they sensible and wise, just and fair—without partiality toward others? Do they have a good grip on their personal life? Do they maintain a clear conscience before God and others? Leaders must not be in love with money or dishonest in handling it. Consider whether a large donation would sway them to make an unwise decision.

2. Are they a team player?

Look for people who fit relationally with others. Are they likable? Are they good listeners? Do they work well with others? Are they approachable? Qualified elders enjoy having guests in their home, a natural setting to care for people. Pass on selecting contentious, quarrelsome people. Hotheads do damage. Watch out for those with a sharp tongue who attack others with cutting remarks. Are they double-tongued, talking out of both sides of their mouth, saying one thing to one person and something different to someone else? If someone demonstrates selfish ambition—obsessed with controlling and running things—they're not a good fit as a servant-leader. Pass on conspiracy-driven candidates who promote fringe issues and partisan politics. Isaiah cautioned, "Don't call everything a conspiracy, like they do, and don't live in dread of what frightens them" (Isa. 8:12). Look for those who are gentle, patient, and kind—not pushy. The wise person, according to God, is first pure, peace-loving, gentle at all times, willing to yield to others, full of mercy and good deeds, showing no favoritism, sincere, and peacemakers (James 3:17-18).

3. Are they growing in spiritual maturity?

Scripture specifies leaders are not to be new believers, lest they get a big head and get tripped up by the devil.

Instead, look for those committed to the Word of God. Elders must be able to explain Scripture and refute any who contradict the gospel message. Ask questions like: Do they display the fruit of the Spirit? Do they have a joyful, positive attitude, or are they negative? Are they peaceful or turbulent? Are they open to correction? Where do they stand on offering grace or playing hardline legalism? Without question, they must be devoted to the Lord.

4. Are they good managers of their home?

Evidence of a well-managed life and home precedes the responsibility of caring for the family of God. Are they faithful and devoted to their spouse? There are different views regarding the phrase "husband of one wife," a requirement Paul sets forth. Some believe this eliminates a previously married candidate. Others believe it refers to marital faithfulness. The phrase "husband of one wife" means literally "'a one-woman man,' i.e., a husband who is consistently, both inwardly and outwardly, devoted and faithful to his wife (cf. 1Ti 3:2). An otherwise qualified single man is not necessarily disqualified. This is not speaking of divorce, but of internal and external purity in the sexual area."[11] The candidate's children are to believe and behave. This doesn't mean their children will never do anything wrong, get in trouble, or do some of the things kids do. The issue is whether they obey when told to do or stop doing something ("under control," 1 Tim. 3:4). The word for children (Grk. *teknon* from *tickto* "to give birth" and "keep warm"—"little children" in 1 John 2:12) is a "nursery term for a small child" (*Kittel's Theological Dictionary of the NT*). While sometimes used for children of various ages, the word does not refer to grown adult children.

Many outstanding men and women of God have agonized over a wayward son or daughter. It seems if Satan can't take a Christian leader down, he goes after their children.

In his commentary on Titus 1:6, Chuck Swindoll noted, "Let's face it; many of the very best families have a child who goes astray, at least for a time. The patriarch of an otherwise believing household is not disqualified for having a prodigal child."

5. Are they faithful and dependable?

Do they follow through on assignments? Are they teachable? Deacons must be tested before being chosen, and all candidates should have a proven track record of faithfulness—one of the fruits of the Spirit.

Appendix 2 is a quick reference tool called Biblical Qualifications for Leadership.

Dangers and Cautions

Qualifications—watered down or too rigid?

One misstep is to view a candidate's qualifications hopefully rather than actually. In other words, don't select someone hoping they will stop being contentious or develop a sudden deep interest in spiritual things. This doesn't work. Qualifications are preconditions. Another mistake sets the standard so high no one measures up. God's leaders haven't arrived spiritually—they're not perfect. Look for people who have a heart for God and a desire to learn with sufficient evidence of growth in the qualifications.

Vacancies and urgency?

Avoid the pitfall of urgent pressure to fill every vacancy immediately. Let's say there are three vacancies but only two qualified candidates. The tendency is to fill that third position with a questionable candidate hoping it will work out. It rarely does. It's far better to leave the position vacant than place the wrong person in leadership.

Multiple governance boards with equal authority?

Some churches attempt a division of authority by having one board deal with the temporal and financial while another group is responsible for the spiritual care. This inevitably leads to strife and confusion. I firmly believe in one leadership team overseeing the work. There may be subgroups managing finances or the facilities, but they report directly to the leadership team.

Leadership team—how large is too large?

Building relationships and maintaining clear communication become more difficult as a team gets larger. Patrick Lencioni, an insightful organizational expert, writes:

> So many teams I've encountered struggle simply because they're too large. This is a big problem and a common one. A leadership team should be made up of somewhere between three and twelve people, though anything over eight or nine is usually problematic. There is nothing dogmatic about this size limit. It is just a practical reality. Having too many people on a team can cause a variety of logistical challenges, but the primary problem has to do with communication. When it comes to discussions and decision-making, there are two critical ways that members of effective teams must communicate: advocacy and inquiry. A professor at Harvard, Chris Argyris, introduced this idea. Advocacy is the kind of communication that most people are accustomed to, and it is all about stating your case or making your point. ... Inquiry is rarer and more important than advocacy. It happens when people ask questions to seek clarity about another person's statement.
>
> What does this have to do with the size of a team? Plenty! When more than eight or nine people are on a team, members tend to advocate a heck of a lot more than they inquire. This makes sense because they aren't

confident that they're going to get the opportunity to speak again soon, so they use their scarce floor time to announce their position or make a point. When a team is small, members are more likely to use much of their time asking questions and seeking clarity, confident that they'll be able to regain the floor and share their ideas or opinions when necessary.[12]

Lencioni's words resonate with my fifty years of experience. In a group of twenty or twenty-five, the outspoken members will dominate the discussion while the quieter ones may not speak up. The speed of getting things done will resemble something like a turtle with a bad case of arthritis. In my opinion, the leadership team should be twelve or fewer for maximum effectiveness, even in a large church or organization.

Terms of service?

The silence of Scripture regarding terms of service allows for flexibility of approaches and caution against dogmatism. In some churches, volunteer elders serve without interruption and potentially for life. In other churches, elders serve a specified number of years, often with a year or more off between terms. The selection of deacons and deaconesses usually follows a rotation pattern.

"Three-quarters of church boards have term limits, usually ranging from one to five years. But 'the impact of term limits is limited' because 45 percent of churches 'don't limit the number of terms a governing board member may serve,' according to a survey of five hundred churches by the Evangelical Council for Financial Accountability (ECFA). 'While 18 percent of churches require at least a year off between terms, 67 percent of churches allow back-to-back terms without time off, and 12 percent allow three terms without a mandatory break.'"[13]

I have read arguments for and against lifetime appointments for elders. Either approach is workable, but I often see problems develop with elders who perpetually remain on the governance team. If an elder becomes difficult to work with or loses the respect and confidence of the people, it's nearly impossible to remove them. It's the belligerent ones who hold on to their position no matter what others say. As they age, they may become set in their ways and a roadblock for the church moving forward. I'm all in favor of elderly elders, as long as they stay flexible and teachable. When there is a pastoral transition, an elder appointed for life can be a thorn in the side of the new pastor, particularly if the pastor feels led to move in a new direction.

However, if an elder rotates on and off the governance team, I see no problem with a lifetime assignment as a shepherd caring for people. Since elders are first and foremost shepherds, knowing and caring for the needs of people, the number of elder-shepherds will need to expand as the church grows. Pastor Phil Taylor encountered this in his work with the Mosaic Church in Orlando, Florida. When the church was small, their direction team had ten elders. As the church grew, they trained and added elder-shepherds until they had twenty-five. Pastor Phil realized twenty-five people sitting around a room making decisions was a recipe for disaster. To correct this, they established the direction team of elders would not exceed eleven. The other elders were active as shepherds caring for the people.[14] A large church easily could have twenty-five or thirty elder-shepherds serving on an ongoing basis. At the same time, a much smaller number would comprise the governance team, who would be nominated and selected by the congregation for a specified term.

The rotation system has advantages and disadvantages. With rotation, there is the opportunity to bring in new leaders and fresh thinking. If someone is shirking their duties or gumming up the works with a grumpy attitude, there is a built-in opportunity for them to exit. Disadvantages? Continual turnover can make developing a cohesive team more difficult. You may lose a highly valued team member forced to rotate off at a crucial moment when their leadership is needed most. My recommendation is that the governing team be selected for a specified term—one, two, or three years—with no limit on the number of consecutive terms. This allows highly effective leaders to continue serving, and it provides a "painless way to remove painful people."[15] The Scripture leaves terms of service undefined, so select the approach that works best for your situation.

SELECTION OF A LEAD PASTOR

The selection of a new senior or lead pastor is one of the crucial moments in the church. God gives to the local church pastor-teachers "for the equipping of the saints for the work of service, to the building up of the body of Christ" (Eph. 4:12 NASB). The search process discovers God's choice to lead the fellowship forward. Building on the selection process for leaders already discussed in this chapter, choose the selection team based on their spiritual maturity and wisdom. You want people who are willing to seek God in fasting and prayer. If they want to serve because they represent a disgruntled segment of the congregation, politely turn them down. You don't want issue-driven people on the team. Proceedings need to be confidential, but keep the congregation informed of progress. The search process usually takes a minimum of six months and may extend to one or two years.

Seek to know the candidate as a real person. Remember, you're selecting a pastor—not a savior. I sometimes share the following profile of the perfect pastor to lighten things up and get the search team past absurd idealism.

PERFECT PASTOR

After hundreds of years of research, a model pastor to suit everyone has been found.

- He preaches exactly 20 minutes, then sits down. He condemns sin but never hurts anyone's feelings.
- He works from 8 a.m. to 10 p.m. in every type of work from preaching to custodial service.
- He makes $60 a week, wears good clothes, buys good books regularly, has a nice family, drives a good car, and gives $30 a week to the church. He also stands ready to contribute to every good work that comes along.
- He is 26 years old and has been preaching for 30 years.
- He is tall and short, thin and heavyset, handsome.
- He has one brown eye and one blue, hair part in the middle, left side dark and straight, the right brown and wavy.
- He has a burning desire to work with teenagers and spends all his time with older folks.
- He smiles all the time with a straight face because he has a sense of humor that keeps him seriously dedicated to his work.
- He makes 15 calls a day on church members, spends all his time evangelizing the unchurched, and is never out of the office.
- He had a nervous breakdown at age 37 and now lives in a rest home for the elderly.[16]

If the search process involves hiring someone outside the congregation, employ additional measures to know them well. A résumé and the real person are not the same thing. Check references. Ask the person giving the reference to provide additional names to contact and then go three or four deep in checking references. For married candidates, I strongly recommend using the Prepare and Enrich marriage assessment to understand the strengths in their marriage and identify areas where growth may be needed. Additionally, interview the spouse and get to know any children. Find out the spouse's attitude toward ministry, as it will significantly impact the candidate's ministry.

Ask probing questions to get below the surface. In his classic book, *Dangerous Calling*, Paul David Tripp recommends getting to know candidates by asking questions like: What are their hopes, dreams, and fears? What are their deep desires that fuel and shape the way they do ministry? How do they work with a team of leaders? What are the things that have the potential to derail them? What are their temptations, weaknesses, and failures? What drives them deeper in their walk with God? Are they dogmatic or pushy? Are they teachable? What do they do to take care of their physical and emotional health?[17]

Most interviews check for a pastor's doctrinal beliefs, which is important, but very little attention is directed to their ability to work with others. This is surprising because most of the biblical qualifications deal with relational issues. It's difficult to identify an oppressive, dictatorial leader in an interview. Because they usually display confidence and a clear road map of the future to impress search teams, digging deep to discover how they work with others is crucial. Ask, "How would you respond if half the leadership team was opposed to your proposal?" Contact members of the board from their previous ministry to see how they responded when their viewpoint was challenged. Doing so may spare you and the church heartache.

Finally, don't focus on externals. As the Lord told Samuel, "Don't judge by his appearance or height, for I have rejected him. The LORD doesn't see things the way you see them. People judge by outward appearance, but the LORD looks at the heart" (1 Sam. 16:7). Above all, seek to discern the heart of the person. Tenderness toward God and suitability for the task will be key components for an excellent leader.

THE HUMAN FACTOR

In looking back over fifty-plus years of selecting people, I've chosen some leaders who exceeded all my expectations, and I've made some poor choices as well. My weakness is that I view people optimistically, seeing potential rather than problems. As a result, I've overlooked some red flags and occasionally rushed the process.

While allowing the Holy Spirit to direct the process, we must understand the reality of human fallibility. The best leaders make some poor choices along the way. Even with a thorough search process, you still have limited knowledge of the candidate. Pray, ask questions, take your time, listen to the input of others, stay open-minded, pray some more, and move forward, allowing the Holy Spirit to appoint the right person. When spiritually mature people seek God with fasting and prayer and choose according to biblical qualifications, they select the right person with few exceptions.

It's better than casting lots!

REFLECTION AND DISCUSSION

Quick Recall

- Why do we no longer cast lots to select leaders? ___
  _____
- The work of the elder or pastor is very specific: _____ the flock and _____ the flock (1 Pet. 5:2). The work of the deacon is very general.
- Biblically, a pastor is an _____, an elder is a _____.

Thinking It Through

1. What are the ramifications of choosing leaders simply because they're sharp in business, donate a lot of money to the church, represent a disgruntled group, or their family helped found the church?

2. "When leaders see themselves more as rulers than shepherds, major problems are brewing." Do you agree or disagree with this statement? Why?

3. How are leaders selected in your church? In what ways is this working well? What do you suggest to improve the process?

So guard yourselves and God's people. Feed and shepherd God's flock—his church, purchased with his own blood—over which the Holy Spirit has appointed you as elders. (Acts 20:28)

—8—

PURSUING DREAMS TOGETHER

LEADERS LISTENING TO GOD AND EACH OTHER

The level of distrust in this California church was thick and rampant. Few trusted anyone but their closest friends. The staff was suspicious of the board, the seniors were wary of the young adults, board members distrusted each other, the worship team was at odds with the worship committee, and the remaining teenagers had all but written off the church. Everywhere I turned, I faced hidden agendas and power blocks preventing any group from taking control. Even the factions had factions. The hurt and fear that accompanied this distrust were heartbreaking and destructive—like a bark beetle infestation in a healthy tree.

During a transition between lead pastors, I was asked to step in as the interim senior pastor, which I have done for several churches. When I attended my first board meeting, I joined a dozen others at the conference table. The board meeting was held in a large classroom with about forty additional chairs, like a gallery. Before the meeting started, a crowd began to fill all the seats in the gallery. Thinking there must be a special presentation or topic scheduled for this many people to turn out, I gently jabbed the guy next to me.

"What are all these people here for?"

"They come every month to keep an eye on the board," he replied.

My jaw dropped. "What? Every month? How do you discuss a confidential matter?"

"Oh, we have to go into executive session."

This felt more like a city council meeting. While I was trying to wrap my mind around this level of distrust, the meeting commenced with an explosive issue. Bam! The sparks began to fly. I silently wondered, *What have I gotten myself into?*

Previously, this had been one of the great churches in the city and the region. Gone were the glory days when the numbers swelled into the thousands, and they built a magnificent facility to accommodate the crowds. The music and preaching ministry of the church was renowned, and it was considered the flagship church in the conference. When I interviewed, I listened to the church's history, how it started, how it grew, and what it had been through since those glorious days. There were moral failures, church splits, and many sad stories. At one point, I offered my observation. "If you made a checklist of every possible problem a church could experience, I think you've covered them all." There were numerous attempts to turn things around, and the church had careened from one style or emphasis to another. The squabbles were legendary. At one point, someone hung a noose over the balcony to indicate their disapproval of leadership. All I could do was shake my head in disbelief.

About six months into the work, I went before the Lord with a broken heart. Despite all the distrust, I found good people who longed for a thriving church. And they were committed—otherwise, they would have left years earlier. These were wounded sheep. I had grown to love these people, and I felt their ache. After a painful weekend, I drove home, reflecting on recent developments. The board had taken a mean-spirited stance toward a ministry leader in retaliation for his action twenty years earlier. Several members disagreed with the board's action, resigned, and left the church. My tears flowed as I prayed, "Lord, this is your body. They are crucifying you again. When will the bleeding stop?"

My heart was grieved and broken, but I didn't have a clue what to do. With all my schooling and years of experience, I honestly was stumped. Some of the trusted leaders acknowledged they felt much the same. The situation seemed beyond repair.

During several weeks of agonizing prayer, I sensed the Lord directing me to invite the people to what I called "Saturday Mornings at the Summit." The burden on my heart was to bring people together to seek God, surrender themselves and the church totally to him, and listen to God and each other. I asked participants to purchase two books: *Intimacy with the Almighty* by Charles Swindoll and *Well-Intentioned Dragons* by Marshall Shelley. To my surprise, thirty-five to forty people came to the summit once a month. In the back of my mind rang the words of my college Bible professor, "To a church that was in danger of dividing, Paul mentions Jesus Christ ten times in the first ten verses of 1 Corinthians. The answer for a divided church is Jesus." I didn't provide new formulas to try, a new program to roll out, or profound teaching. I focused on Jesus and called the group to surrender, repentance, and prayer.

Marshall Shelley's book consists of several case studies of church conflicts led by well-intentioned members who become dragon-like, manipulating others and creating conflict. As our group went through the material, people would pull me aside and say, "Pastor, this is just like our church." I smiled and said, "Keep reading." I began referring to "dragon breath"—harmful, hurtful things we say that damage one another. I suggested we gently remind each other if we lapse into destructive communication, "My friend, you're probably not aware of it, but I'm getting a whiff of dragon breath." Little by little, a change of heart and attitude began to occur.

Ultimately, a miracle took place. There was no astounding, cataclysmic breakthrough, but the walls slowly crumbled. The seniors called me one evening to come to a meeting. Different than meetings in the past, they weren't upset about anything. "Pastor," they asked, "what do we need to change, and how do we respond differently to pass this ministry on to the next generation?" A new spirit began to impact the church. Saturday Mornings at the Summit were an important start but just the beginning. After I served for two years, the church called a new senior pastor—a warm-hearted, godly leader with decades of experience. He provided strong, caring leadership, a catalyst to continued healing and renewal. At his invitation, I directed six leadership training and prayer retreats for about thirty-five people over the next two years. As we listened to God, flames of love sparked and fanned within our hearts—love for one another and our community. It gives me great joy to report the church continues to move forward with a thriving ministry today.

Churches need leaders who listen to God and each other. After all, it was listening to God that resolved the fears and friction of the early church leaders (Acts 1:13-14). Listening leaders are required not only for the church in crisis but also for healthy churches. Together, leaders ask this critical question.

What's on the Heart of God?

Some say it's the role of the senior or lead pastor to seek God and establish the vision for the church. What do people hope from this scenario? Perhaps the pastor will go away to a mountain cabin for a week or two and return with a face glowing from meeting God. Tucked in his briefcase are tablets etched with a grand vision from God for the future of the ministry. The pastor shares it with the leadership and congregation, and everyone says in unison, "Amen. So be it." Sorry to burst anyone's bubble, but church life doesn't work that way. More often than not, the pastor faces pushback or flat-out opposition, partly because others had no part in developing the vision. So even if God gives the pastor a missional mountain top vision, it's best to engage the entire leadership team in developing and sharpening the vision.

Leaders Listening to God

I propose you gather the leaders for a Listening to God retreat for discernment and direction at least once a year. This could be a weekend together or a couple of Saturday mornings. Intentionally include a larger group than your core leadership team—pastors and elders, deacons and deaconesses, staff and ministry leaders. This connects the governing leadership with those in the trenches doing the work. Be purposeful about who to include or exclude— look for those who have a positive vision for the church. If someone has a reputation for stirring up trouble, it is best to pass on inviting them. This is not a gripe session or an opportunity to railroad a pet cause. In one form or another, I have been doing this for the past twenty years, and I keep discovering the joy of discerning the will of God with a group.

My close friend, Frank Winans, served as my associate pastor for fourteen years. Together, we made discerning the will of God a top priority for the leadership team. Frank is a man of God, and we had a great partnership. When I retired, he stepped in as senior pastor and took leadership cohesiveness to a new level. Each September, he gathers the leadership team, staff, and ministry leaders. He reminds them, "You were chosen because of your spiritual maturity, desire to serve God, and willingness to surrender personal ambitions and agenda before God. Our purpose in meeting is to discover the mind of God for our lives and our church." And then he leads them in seeking God.

Heart preparation to hear from God must precede the entire process. Experienced business leaders, executives, and strategic planners may resist this part of the process, thinking it's unnecessary. It all depends if you want God to lead the ministry or not. We need Jesus to calm the internal chaos of living in a frenetic, high-stress world. How do we hear the voice of God when bombarded incessantly by noise clamoring for our attention? Healthy leaders lean into the whispers of their Lord.

Elijah—in a lonely cave, running for his life, depressed and discouraged—heard a still small voice, "the sound of a gentle whisper" (1 Kings 19:12). God was speaking. In the quiet of the night, Samuel prayed, "Speak, LORD, your servant is listening" (1 Sam. 3:10). In solitude, spiritual leaders hear God speak—not audibly (though God certainly could choose to do that). Rather, through Scripture and the prompting of the Holy Spirit, they gain a growing sense of clarity, conviction, and urgency. They discover the secret sound of silence.

If you want to lead others in listening to God, begin with heart-searching and confession of sin. Don't rush this time. Prepare a handout with several verses such as these:

> Listen! The LORD's arm is not too weak to save you,
> nor is his ear too deaf to hear you call.
> It's your sins that have cut you off from God.
> Because of your sins, he has turned away
> and will not listen anymore. (Isa. 59:1-2)

> People who conceal their sins will not prosper,
> but if they confess and turn from them, they will receive mercy. (Prov. 28:13)

> Search me, O God, and know my heart;
> test me and know my anxious thoughts.
> Point out anything in me that offends you,
> and lead me along the path of everlasting life. (Ps. 139:23-24)

> Have mercy on me, O God,
> because of your unfailing love.
> Because of your great compassion,
> blot out the stain of my sins.
> Wash me clean from my guilt.
> Purify me from my sin. (Ps. 51:1-2)

> If we claim we have no sin, we are only fooling ourselves and not living in the truth. But if we confess our sins to him, he is faithful and just to forgive us our sins and to cleanse us from all wickedness. If we claim we have not sinned, we are calling God a liar and showing that his word has no place in our hearts. (1 John 1:8-10)

Pray as you read through the Scriptures. Allow time for each person to examine their heart, confess sin, and let go of every questionable practice. Pray for a fresh filling of the Holy Spirit. As Frederick Buechner noted, "To confess your sins to God is not to tell him anything he doesn't already know. Until you confess them, however, they are the abyss between you. When you confess them, they become the bridge."[1]

Enter into God's presence with songs of worship and praise as well. As you continue in prayer, either in the large group or in groups of two or three, cry out to your Lord. "O Great and sovereign God. You own us. You own this church. We surrender before you. Give us eyes to see where you're working and hearts to cooperate with what you're doing. Keep us from getting in the way. We yield our motivations and ambitions to you. Burden our hearts with the things that weigh heavy on your heart. What do you want to do through your people this year and in the years ahead? By your Spirit, stir in us a passionate desire for your will. Give us a picture of something bigger than ourselves, beyond the limitations of our minds and our human resources."

Ruth Haley Barton, writing in *Pursuing God's Will Together*, recommends three types of prayer.[2] The first is a "prayer of quiet trust." "In God, whose word I praise, in God I have put my trust; I shall not be afraid. What can mere man do to me?" (Ps. 56:4 NASB). The second is the "prayer of indifference." At first, this wording may seem strange, but this is simply a prayer of abandonment—letting go of your own agenda. In praying this way, we become indifferent to anything but the will of God. The third is the "prayer for wisdom." "If you need wisdom, ask our generous God, and he will give it to you. He will not rebuke you for asking" (James 1:5). Ask God for wisdom. As leaders in the body of Christ, we all need it.

Along the way, take a break and allow your team to find a quiet place to listen to God on their own. The solitude and silence will enable each person to hear the voice of God. Pray, wait, and listen. Reflect on where God is at work and write down thoughts—even random ones—about what God is saying regarding the future. Let these thoughts percolate, and then gather to share what you're hearing from God.

Spirit-filled Desires are the Fuel

David wrote in the Psalms, "May he [God] grant your heart's desires and make all your plans succeed. May we shout for joy when we hear of your victory and raise a victory banner in the name of our God. May the LORD answer all your prayers" (Ps. 20:4–5). Anticipation oozes from these verses—shouting for joy, raising a victory banner. Psalm 37:4 says, "Take delight in the LORD, and he will give you your heart's desires." The desires of the heart precede the plans that succeed. Spirit-filled desires—not self-centered or greedy desires—are the fuel that ignites the fire for goals that flourish. As you're waiting before the Lord, cultivate kingdom-driven desire, the source for discovering God's will. Check out these verses.

> He grants the desires of those who fear him;
> he hears their cries for help and rescues them.
> (Ps. 145:19)

> The desire of the righteous will be granted. (Prov. 10:24 NASB)

> The desire of the righteous is only good. (Prov. 11:23 NASB)

> Desire realized is sweet to the soul. (Prov. 13:19 NASB)

> Hope deferred makes the heart sick,
> But desire fulfilled is a tree of life. (Prov. 13:12 NASB)

The tree of life represents a fruitful life. Delight yourself in the Lord and let your desires dance. For a moment, set aside all limitations—cost, time, and resources. Later, you'll have the opportunity to bring cost, time, and resources into consideration. What picture do you see for an exciting and fruitful future? What yearning desire rises from the depth of your soul? If it is for God and his kingdom, pursue it.

Daring to Dream as a Team

It's no accident that God placed you and your church in your community for this precise moment in history. There's a purpose God wants to accomplish that is unique and different from the church down the street. I don't believe God wants every church to be a mega church. He has a specific plan for your church, whether you're fifty people in a small community or five thousand in a bustling city. I don't believe it's necessarily a numerical goal. Numerical growth is a by-product of something that may be good, but not always. Growth should always be driven by two questions: "Where is God at work, and how can we join him in what he is doing?"[3] and "What is on the heart of God for us to accomplish?"

Think of the church community (those in the church) and your neighborhood community (those outside the church). What are the hurts of people? Jesus said to his disciples, "The harvest is great, but the workers are few. So pray to the Lord who is in charge of the harvest; ask him to send more workers into his fields" (Matt. 9:37-38). Preceding this prayer, Jesus was moved as he looked at the crowds. Jesus had a spiritual radar to perceive the deep-seated needs of people, and his heart was moved with compassion for them. "When he saw the crowds, he had compassion on them because they were confused and helpless, like sheep without a shepherd" (Matt. 9:36). The word *confused* (Grk. *eskulmenoi*, from *skullo* "to cut, flay, skin, or lacerate") means wounded, mangled, bewildered, or beat. This describes the wounded person who has been mistreated or abused. The second word, *helpless* (Grk. word *errimménos*), means cast down or knocked down, tossed aside, depressed, laid low, and unable to get back up.

Who in your sphere of influence has been wounded, mangled, beat, cast down, and tossed aside? How many are depressed, laid low, and feeling no one understands? Ask God to give you "Jesus eyes"—a spiritual radar to sense the deepest hurts in people. Look for needs like loneliness, depression, unemployment, divorce, addictive behaviors, or teens in rebellion.

Paul told Timothy,

> You should know this, Timothy, that in the last days there will be very difficult times. For people will love only themselves and their money. They will be boastful and proud, scoffing at God, disobedient to their parents, and ungrateful. They will consider nothing sacred. They will be unloving and unforgiving; they will slander others and have no self-control. They will be cruel and hate what is good. They will betray their friends, be reckless, be puffed up with pride, and love pleasure rather than God. (2 Tim. 3:1-4)

Does this sound like what's going on in your community?

Let God ignite fresh dreams in your hearts. There may be teenagers who walk past the church every afternoon who are without a purpose in life, and God grips your heart to reach them. You may sense the call to initiate a new work or become a church that cares for persecuted believers worldwide. You may consider distributing food to the needy in your neighborhood. As people receive a bag of groceries, ask how you can pray for them. Look for the lonely, the depressed, the disillusioned.

Where have you seen passionate individuals already ministering? We know a couple who started a "Laundry Love" ministry at laundromats in their community—offering quarters to help people in need pay for washing and drying their clothes. Most are delighted with the offer and open to talking as they wait. Many face loneliness, disappointment, or broken relationships and are receptive to being prayed for as they wait. Several have come to Christ. Their ministry has grown, and now it is supported by their church.

What are the needs within your church family? Spiritual growth, discipleship, counseling? Do the people of the church feel needed, included, and valued? Are volunteers recognized and appreciated? Are new people invited to a small group? Are the widows lonely and isolated? Do the seniors feel discarded? Does the nursery need to be expanded?

Be creative, dare to dream big, let the vision develop slowly, and see which dreams you feel confirmed by God to pursue. They may become part of the DNA of your church for decades to come.

Defining Goals and Preparing Budgets

As your Listening to God retreat continues, begin the process of articulating the dream as a goal (or more than one goal). In most cases, there will be dozens of ideas that will surface, but you can only choose a few. Use a method of prioritizing the most important ones. A "goal" and an "objective" are not the same, despite the terms being used interchangeably. A goal is a dream-driven, desirable result with a long-term impact, while an objective is a measurable action toward a goal. For example, you may have a goal to communicate to each person in the church their worth, importance, and giftedness and to value them in a way that reflects the enormous love God has for them. A goal like this may have ten or fifteen subpoints or objectives, like writing letters or making phone calls, in order to reach the goal. Also, you may have any number of organizational objectives independent of a larger goal, things like adding restroom signs or buying tables for the youth room. These are *not* goals. A goal grows out of a strong desire. A goal is a godly desire with a deadline. A personal goal is something you *really* want to do. The same is true for a group goal.

Many years ago, a $100,000 research project asked the question, "Why are some goals achieved while others fizzle?" At the heart of the research, they discovered strong desires always drive successful goals. Some people and organizations set goals hoping to kindle the motivation to achieve them. These goals fail. Don't establish a goal because you think it is something you *ought* to do. Establish a goal because it is something you passionately *desire* to do. Allow it to become an obsession—something you think of during the daytime and dream of at night. Let your collective desires catch on fire, and don't let anyone stomp out the flame.

Following this, clarify and sharpen the goals and objectives and begin preparing the budget. A smaller task force can be assigned to do further research and develop each goal. The next chapter will help you prevent a budget blow-up while preparing a visionary biblical budget.

After a discernment retreat, how do you communicate goals, objectives, and budgets to the congregation? Some churches have annual meetings to cover these items. In other churches, these matters are decided by the leadership with no requirement for a congregational meeting. In either situation, it's essential to connect with the church body. If leaders make top-down decisions without listening to the people, eventually, there will be a breakdown and a rift. In the western world, we tend to think of organizational charts and lines of authority, but the church is an organism—a living, breathing body—not just an organization. A healthy body is connected, sending and receiving messages, and highly dependent on the healthy function of each part. An itching toe tells you one thing, a pain in the shoulder something different, and blurry vision sends an alarm. A wise person listens to the signals from their body. Similarly, wise leaders are sensitive to signals from the church body.

Risk Assessment

Listening to the Holy Spirit together unites a team like nothing else. Why, then, do leaders resist bringing others into the goal-setting process? From my own experience, I resisted this for a long time because I didn't want others messing with my plans. I didn't trust the Holy Spirit to communicate his will with a larger group. I plowed ahead with my own goals and wondered why others couldn't get on board and stop resisting. As a result, I forfeited the power of the Spirit working through a team that is passionate and committed to the goals.

However, I acknowledge there are risks involved. For example, when bringing a group together for setting goals, you may have those interested in airing their grievances or beating a contrary drum. Provide an alternate time for them to express their concerns and clarify that contention is not the purpose of a Listening to God retreat. Instead, you gather to seek God's will—not your will; to repent of sin—not resist leadership; to surrender before God—not fight for your cause; to look to the future with faith—not lament the failures of the past.

GOING DEEP

A Listening to God retreat is an opportunity to grow deeper in spiritual intimacy. The Psalmist said, "You thrill me, LORD, with all you have done for me! I sing for joy because of what you have done. O Lord, what great works you do! And how deep are your thoughts" (Ps. 92:4-5). Human perception and understanding are shallow, but God's thoughts are deep. "'My thoughts are nothing like your thoughts,' says the Lord. 'And my ways are far beyond anything you could imagine'" (Isa. 55:8). Leaders in a big hurry will never discover and discern the depth of the mind of God.

"Be still, and know that I am God!" (Ps. 46:10) is the invitation to listen, to experience the stillness that calms the storm. "Be still" means to let go, to take your hands off, to relax, to cease striving. Delightfully paraphrased, "Step out of the traffic! Take a long, loving look at me, your High God, above politics, above everything" (Ps. 46:10 MSG). Leaders who gather and listen to God will find creativity, communication, compassion, and renewed commitment.

Spiritual renewal always brings relational renewal. You'll smile when you see two people who get on each other's nerves praying together. Don't be surprised when relational rifts and ripples of discontent vanish during a Listening to God retreat. It happens.

It happened. One hundred and twenty feisty, frightened, confused, self-serving leaders prayed in an upper room. They became of "one mind."

And they turned their world upside down ... or right side up!

Reflection and Discussion

Quick Recall

- If God gives the pastor a missional mountain top vision, it's best to engage _____ _____.
- What are the three types of prayers recommended by Ruth Haley Barton for leaders seeking God's will?
Prayer of _____
Prayer of _____
Prayer for _____

Thinking It Through

1. When and where do you go for silence and solitude?

2. When have you had "dragon breath" or observed others with it? What kind of spiritual mouth wash do you recommend for "dragon breath"?

3. If your Listening to God retreats produce thirty-five or forty good ideas for ministry, how do you decide which ones to pursue? How do you prioritize ministry desires and goals?

Take delight in the LORD, and he will give you your heart's desires. (Ps. 37:4)

The desire of the righteous will be granted. (Prov. 10:24 NASB)

The desire of the righteous is only good. (Prov. 11:23 NASB)

Desire realized is sweet to the soul. (Prov. 13:19 NASB)

—9—
PREVENTING A BUDGET BLOW-UP

AVOIDING THE PITFALLS OF A PLAY-IT-SAFE OR PRESUMPTUOUS BUDGET

As I sat in the congregational meeting, I felt nervous about the presentation of the proposed annual budget. It reflected some modest visionary goals the leadership had developed for the new year. Nothing grandiose, but challenging nonetheless. I watched the church chairman squirm as one of the long-time members launched into a full-scale assault on the budget. "Last year, even though we ended the year in the black, we didn't meet the budget. What makes you think we'll meet a larger budget this year? I think we should be cutting things back—a decrease in the budget from last year. We should be spending less, not more."

Like a heavy fog, a spirit of gloom settled over the audience. I felt like countering this dismal outlook but kept quiet. The budget was tabled for a future meeting, and I felt defeated and deflated. The leaders were unified regarding the priorities, but I knew if we tried to push it through that night, it would have gone down in defeat. I didn't sleep well that night. Around 2 a.m., I was mulling over this play-it-safe budget mindset. The attitude was "keep the doors open and the lights on," but not much more. I asked God, "Does a play-it-safe budget please you? Didn't you make it clear that without faith, it is impossible to please you?" I turned the light on and began writing. A couple of hours later, I had identified and outlined three types of budgets. When I taught what God showed me to the congregation a week later, the budget—without revision—was unanimously approved.

This story ended happily, but storms swirl around the budget process at many churches. As a pastor, I often felt trapped between those who urged me to be more visionary and the naysayers who shot down anything I proposed. Budgeting heightened this tension. Some of the nicest people turn into spitfires talking about money. I admit there have been times when I thought I could live the rest of my life in peace and contentment if I never had to be in another heated, budget-wrangling session.

The Listening to God retreat, described in the previous chapter, enables the leadership team to discover what is on the heart of God. Spending goals should organically develop from that time of listening. This chapter will examine how churches can follow a balanced, sensible approach to developing a visionary budget.

THREE TYPES OF BUDGETS

Money and ministry have built-in tension. God's resources are unlimited, but the resources for ministry are limited while the needs of people seem endless. I believe God set it up this way. Indeed, this money-ministry friction is a *good* thing—God intended—though sometimes it doesn't feel that way. God could easily dump a ton of money into every God-honoring ministry, but what would it be like if we had unlimited funds? I imagine we'd spend a lot of money foolishly. And we wouldn't have to get on our knees to ask God to provide. We'd be "faith infants," knowing little of mountain-moving faith. We'd tend to use money as a solve-all for any problem, trusting money rather than God.

Is budgeting biblical? If you check your Bible, you won't find the word *budget*. The first church I served didn't believe in having a budget ... at all. They spent only the money that came in. Sounds simple, right? Wrong! Every expenditure had to be approved at the monthly congregational meeting, attended by a handful of the elderly. The congregation of about five hundred was poorly represented at the monthly meeting. If the high school group needed $100 to sponsor a pizza-night outreach, the elderly at the monthly business meeting didn't understand why they should pay for pizza. If a room needed fresh paint, it required unanimous approval to buy a couple of gallons of paint. Someone would inevitably object, "I looked at the room, and it looks fine to me." And more often than not, there would be an argument about buying cheap paint or premium paint or wallpaper. It turned into monthly wrangling about trivia—depressing and demoralizing. The church finally decided it needed a budget.

A budget is simply an estimate of income and expenditures. The biblical equivalent to the word *budget* is the word *plan*. As Proverbs says, "We can make our plans, but the LORD determines our steps" (16:9), or we could say, "We make our budgets, but the Lord determines the future—including unforeseen opportunities, needs, emergencies, shortfalls as well as surpluses of income."

That means our plans need to be flexible—leaving room for the Lord to direct and determine the outcome. In the process, "Commit your actions to the Lord, and your plans will succeed" (Prov. 16:3). Remember, "Plans go wrong for lack of advice; many advisers bring success" (Prov. 15:22).

I've been in hundreds of budget planning sessions. Though it's subtle, something shifts in our thinking as we put our Bibles away and get out our calculators, computers, reports, projections, and spreadsheets. For the most part, we pivot to a business mindset. The finance chair usually directs the discussion. We haven't disinvited Jesus from the meeting, but he usually isn't acknowledged as being in control.

This is a moment to stop before you start. A budget meeting is *still* a God Meeting. God wants to direct your budget planning. That doesn't mean discarding good business tools for planning, but remembering instead to "trust God from the bottom of your heart; don't try to figure out everything on your own. Listen for God's voice in everything you do, everywhere you go; he's the one who will keep you on track" (Prov. 3:5-6 MSG). Begin the meeting, acknowledging the lordship of Christ and asking for his direction regarding every decision. If and when you hit a serious snag, stop and spend time in prayer, seeking his direction.

Planning is biblical, and a budget is a plan. Budgets are, at best, an educated guestimate of the future. Why, then, do we carve them in granite? Unforeseen needs will arise, so I recommend having a simple, straightforward policy to change the budget as needed during the year. And just because something is a line item in the budget, don't spend the money if funds aren't available.

The budget meeting with the congregation should be primarily a discussion of the future. Meetings become negative or boring when weighed down with a line-by-line discussion of last year's expenditures. "How come we spent $73.19 on animal crackers for the toddlers? Saltine crackers would be less expensive." Meanwhile, the person in charge of the nursery hears this question came up in the meeting. With feelings of hurt, they wonder, *Why are they questioning the snacks for the kids? They must not value the ministry I'm doing.*

Friends, there is a simple way to overcome this ... and related issues too. When you distribute copies of the financial report and proposed budget, include the name and phone number of the person overseeing that area of the budget. Announce to the congregation, "We have included the name and phone number of the person who oversees each section of the budget. If you have questions about expenditures or the proposed budget, contact them personally before the meeting. They'll be glad to provide whatever information you need." Make it clear that there will be no line-by-line discussion of the budget in the congregational meeting, but the leadership will be available to answer questions afterward. Individual salaries should not be discussed in a public forum since this invites a painful evaluation of the worth of the person. If a church member wants salary specifics, they should make an appointment with the board chairman. How I wish I had these guidelines when I jotted down the following three budgets during a sleepless night.

1. The Play-It-Safe Budget

This budget appeals to our comfort zone. There is little or no vision in it, and it's based on maintaining the status quo. This budget promotes a "mattress mindset." Success for the play-it-safe budget is cash in the bank. This budget avoids risk and focuses on spending as little as possible. Fearful thinking is coddled and caressed. To paraphrase a familiar quote, "Fear is Satan's darkroom for developing negative thinking."[1] Fears readily emerge as bullies in budget meetings.

Whenever I see an organization with a play-it-safe budget, it's usually ironclad—violators who overspend their budget are marched off the proverbial gangplank. Some volunteer board members feel their term of service was a success if there was no scandal, the attendance stayed steady, the budget was met, and plenty of money sits in the bank. This may be tragic in the sight of God. I recall a church with over a million dollars in the reserve fund. This was not a building fund—they had no plans to expand facilities. They were a congregation of about a hundred fifty people striving to maintain what was. Mediocre was their mindset, and money in the bank was their security blanket. Meanwhile, young families were leaving the church because the leaders refused to select a student ministry pastor. A few years later, the church closed its doors.

This church had an attitude like the unfaithful servant Jesus described in Matthew 25:14-15. "Again, the Kingdom of Heaven can be illustrated by the story of a man going on a long trip. He called together his servants and entrusted his money to them while he was gone. He gave five bags of silver to one, two bags of silver to another, and one bag of silver to the last—dividing it in proportion to their abilities. He then left on his trip." This is called the parable of the talents, so we usually think in terms of natural ability. However, the word talent in this passage refers to a large sum of money.

The servants entrusted with the five bags (five talents) of money and two bags (two talents) handled their investments wisely and doubled it. The person receiving one bag of money (one talent) was afraid and buried it. *The Message* paraphrase captures the drama of the master's confrontation with the unwise servant: "The master was furious. 'That's a terrible way to live! It's criminal to live cautiously like that! If you knew I was after the best, why did you do less than the least? The least you could have done would have been to invest the sum with the bankers, where at least I would have gotten a little interest. Take the thousand [one talent] and give it to the one who risked the most. And get rid of this 'play-it-safe' who won't go out on a limb'" (Matt. 25:26-28 MSG, bracketed word mine). This parable illustrates the heartbreak of wasted opportunity.

Jesus makes it clear. No-risk leadership is a catastrophe. Leaders who fail to invest and take risks in planning for the future will lose what they have. Churches and ministries never standstill. Though it may seem they stay about the same, organizations either move forward or gradually decline and go downhill. Don't allow no-risk leadership to derail your church's future.

In the last century, Montgomery Ward was a highly successful chain of department stores. Today, they are long gone. What happened? If you traveled back to the 1950s and the plush office of Sewell Avery, chairman of Montgomery Ward and Co., you'd find a highly prosperous company that pioneered the mail-order catalog and the money-back guarantee. Sewell Avery was credited with leading the company out of the Great Depression. He also amassed a huge sum of working capital. In fact, they had so much cash, Montgomery Ward had a dubious Wall Street nickname: "the bank with the department-store front." How could such a successful company collapse and finally declare bankruptcy? Sewell Avery decided to take no risk. It was a boneheaded business strategy that he refused to give up. From 1941 to 1957, Sewell Avery refused to open a single new store. "When urban and suburban America boomed, Ward's was stuck with its dowdy 'green awning' stores in small towns nationwide."[2] Montgomery Ward piled up cash—and foolishly sat on it.

Churches do well to heed the warning bell sounded by stories like this. In the final analysis, a play-it-safe budget defaults to walking by sight and not by faith (2 Cor. 5:7). Don't be misled—"It is impossible to please God without faith" (Heb. 11:6). No-risk, play-it-safe leadership is tragic and unacceptable to God, and play-it-safe churches are on the road to closure.

2. The Presumptuous Budget

The polar opposite of the play-it-safe budget is the presumptuous budget. This budget is risky and grandiose. There are at least three dynamics specific to this form of budgeting.

Perpetual Emergency. Some ministries charge ahead with bold plans and insufficient money to accomplish them. About halfway through, they send out the plea. "Help! We're in crisis. If we don't receive $25,000 by the end of the month, the electricity will be shut off. We'll miss our payment on the mortgage and incur late charges, and we'll start laying off employees." Employees are treated almost like hostages, "Bail us out, or they're gone." This is their planned fundraising strategy. I'm sensitive to crises in Christian organizations, and I often try to help. But when it's a persistent pattern, people catch on. They know which organization is always out of cash due to poor planning, and they begin to roll their eyes rather than cough up the emergency money. Financial experts agree a well-run organization should have three to six months of operating expenses in reserve. Proverbs says, "There is precious treasure and oil in the dwelling of the wise, but a foolish man swallows it up" (21:20 NASB). The perpetual emergency is presumptuous planning.

Extravagant Spending. The prosperity gospel movement is rooted in presumptuous promises—false claims that God will give the follower abundant wealth and health. Many prosperity gospel leaders enjoy huge salaries and bonuses, several multi-million-dollar homes, private jets, and luxurious cars while promising their followers much of the same if they give more. "In popular culture, the movement was best known for Jim and Tammy Faye Bakker, the de facto king and queen of 1980s televangelism. Their media empire toppled when Jim was convicted of financial fraud, and the scandal cemented in most people's minds the idea that the prosperity gospel was fundamentally about gold faucets, thick mink coats, and matching his-and-her Mercedes—and very little else."[3] While in prison, Jim Bakker read the entire Bible for the first time. In 1996, he wrote *I Was Wrong*, stating, in part, that he misused Bible passages out of context to support his prosperity theology.

Presumptuous behavior isn't strictly a modern problem. David asked God to keep him back from committing presumptuous sins—grievous, high-handed, haughty, though unintentional, infractions (Ps. 19:13). The biblical word *presumptuous* is an adjective meaning "proud or arrogant, haughty rather than humble." Presumptuous behavior goes beyond sensible reason into risky foolishness. It's like this conversation between the business owner and his friend. The businessman announced, "You know I hired this 'professional worrier,' so I don't have to worry anymore." The friend was impressed with the businessman's savvy, "Wow, that sounds great. How much do you pay him?" The businessman replied, "I pay him $500,000 a year." A bit puzzled, the friend asked, "How are you going to afford that?" The businessman quickly replied, "That's his worry." And that's presumptuous thinking.

James counsels prideful planners with strong words: "Look here, you who say, 'Today or tomorrow we are going to a certain town and will stay there a year. We will do business there and make a profit.' How do you know what your life will be like tomorrow? Your life is like the morning fog—it's here a little while, then it's gone. What you ought to say is, 'If the Lord wants us to, we will live and do this or that.' Otherwise, you are boasting about your own plans, and all such boasting is evil" (James 4:13-16).

Presumptuous budgeting and spending involve some form of boldly charging forward with or without funds, spending money before it comes in or using money from restricted funds, using guilt to coerce people to give more, or assuming God is obligated to bail an organization out because it's doing the work of God. When people are pressured to give more, the organization becomes money-driven rather than ministry-driven. When plans fail to materialize, those who didn't give are often blamed for their lack of commitment; ultimately, God may even be blamed for human foolishness. What a travesty. I'm familiar with a church that followed the lead of a prosperity gospel preacher and initially raised a lot of money. The next year, the preacher continued the emphasis with "give to get" teaching and guilt-driven pressure in every message. People eventually smelled the greed and stopped giving. Greed-driven plans will always backfire, and this preacher was later convicted of securities fraud.

Excessive Borrowing. As Jesus zeroed in on the cost of discipleship, he employed a pointed illustration. "Don't begin until you count the cost. For who would begin construction of a building without first calculating the cost to see if there is enough money to finish it? Otherwise, you might complete only the foundation before running out of money, and then everyone would laugh at you. They would say, 'There's the person who started that building and couldn't afford to finish it!'" (Luke 14:28-30). To give an updated example of this parable, I wrote this all-too-familiar scenario.

The neighborhood church dreamed of building a three thousand-seat worship center on the eight acres they owned in an unincorporated area. The two hundred fifty people who attended the Sunday services were enthusiastic about the possibilities. The phrase "If you build it, they will come" caught on like wildfire. County approval of their plans and a million dollars in cash donations were all the affirmation they needed, so they broke ground. But they were shocked and disappointed when the bank turned down their request for a ten-million-dollar loan. Other attempts at financing proved futile. Finally, they obtained a loan for five million, but things went sour. They couldn't make the payments on the loan and began laying off staff. People started to leave the church. Two years later, they had a concrete slab and nothing more. The people were disillusioned, and the local skeptics of Christianity made fun of the project.

This church didn't decline due to a lack of vision. Its downfall was presumptuous planning. As a general rule, debt payment should not exceed 33 percent of annual income for most churches and up to 40 percent for fast-growing churches. In addition, the maximum debt owed should not exceed 2.5 times the church's annual income for the previous year.[4] Henry Morris wrote, "Many ambitious Christian leaders have brought embarrassment (or worse) upon themselves and their followers by undertaking ambitious building programs or other projects without adequate financing. A good principle is not to go into debt (Romans 13:8) without positive assurance that all obligations can be paid on time."[5] Proverbs says, "The rich rules over the poor, and the borrower becomes the lender's slave" (22:7 NASB). I've led the way in several capital expansion campaigns and three building programs, so I'm not opposed to building programs and sensible debt to accomplish kingdom goals.

Prudence keeps churches in step with the Holy Spirit. Presumptuous planning gets ahead of God and calls it faith. It's not faith—it's foolishness. There is a better way.

3. The Prayer and Faith Budget

Rather than a play-it-safe budget or a presumptuous budget, churches need a prayer and faith budget. It's based on *discovering what God wants to do through his body, the church*. It's established based on God's will, not on financial resources. The prayer and faith budget is forward-looking but not foolish. It allows God to do the extraordinary without being reckless. It trusts God to do over and above what seems humanly possible while granting God permission to change, disrupt, or redirect the plan. Believing God and prayer form the basis of this budget.

Tough times are no barrier if God is in the planning. In Macedonia, there were believers in great affliction and living in "deep poverty" (2 Cor. 8:2). The word for deep in Greek is *bathos,* from which we get the English word *bathysphere*, a deep-sea submersible vessel used to explore the bottom of the ocean floor. They were so deep-down poor the poor people called them poor. Were they gloomy? Hardly—they were overflowing with joy. Paul was astounded. "For I can testify that they gave not only what they could afford, but far more. And they did it of their own free will. They begged us again and again for the privilege of sharing in the gift for the believers in Jerusalem. They even did more than we had hoped, for their first action was to give themselves to the Lord and to us, just as God wanted them to do" (2 Cor. 8:3-5). Notice the leaders were not begging them to give. The people were begging for the opportunity to give. What a switch!

A prayer and faith budget is based on cheerful giving from the heart—never high pressure or guilt. "You must each decide in your heart how much to give. And don't give reluctantly or in response to pressure. 'For God loves a person who gives cheerfully'" (2 Cor. 9:7). At the start of a year, I used to give one message on the goals and vision of the church and another message on God's principles for giving. Some pastors are reluctant to teach on giving, but it is an essential biblical topic that helps believers mature in their faith. I've included a resource for speaking on the topic in Appendix 3, A Cheerful Giver.

What are the practical steps in putting together a prayer and faith budget?

First, determine all that God wants to do. Make a complete list of every possibility and then prioritize it. Don't eliminate something solely because it seems impossible or too costly. Allow the Holy Spirit to clarify the most important priorities of all the possibilities.

Next, develop the who and the why. Leaders often present a budget explaining what they plan to do, how they will do it, and when it will be done, but they wonder why the presentation falls flat. The essential ingredients are missing: who will be impacted by this goal, and why is it important to advance the kingdom of God? No budget item is ready to be presented until it has a clear who and why statement—even paving the parking lot. "We believe paving the parking lot is essential to move forward in our work for the kingdom of God. If an unbeliever hits that pothole at the front of our parking lot on their first visit to the church, they'll probably curse God, the church, and the person who invited them—and we'll miss our opportunity to introduce them to Jesus."

Third, develop the budget in two or more parts. The first part is the operational budget, based on the input of various ministries regarding objectives and needs. The other is the challenge budget—faith challenges dependent on God providing. You can introduce the challenge budget this way, "As God provides $100,000 over and above in the next twelve months, these are the things we anticipate moving forward on." The oft-quoted phrase "Where God guides, God provides" reflects rock-solid truth. Isaiah 58:11, in essence, says the Lord will guide and abundantly provide. The challenge budget may include a fund for additional staff, but I urge you not to list current salaries as challenge items.

Even within prayer and faith budgets, friction may exist. One continuous point of tension in the churches I served was what percentage of the budget to direct to world missions. Advocates made passionate speeches about increasing missionary giving from 10 percent to 15 percent to 20 percent of the budget while slashing expenditures for the local church ministry. Others disagreed. After several years of friction, we hit on an idea that resolved the conflict. We established a separate budget for missions. Individual believers could direct 10 percent, 20 percent, or 100 percent of their giving to world missions if they felt led to do so. We discovered our giving to world missions increased every year. Amazingly, so did the giving to the operation and faith challenge budgets. Prayer and faith budgets minimize friction and allow God to provide over and above.

Rising to a Challenge

My life-long friend, Pastor Bob Thune, took on the challenge of an eleven-million-dollar debt when he stepped in as senior pastor of a large church. He sized it up as a debt load—appropriately named since it put enormous pressure on the ministry. The interest alone was just shy of a million dollars yearly. Bob set the challenge before the congregation. "Imagine the possibilities when we are no longer making payments on this loan. Think of how many missionaries we could support with interest alone." To put a face on the monster, Bob named the eleven-million-dollar debt "Goliath" and adopted the motto, "Let's slay Goliath." He had a lot of fun with the theme of slaying the giant, and in three years and nine months, the church toppled Goliath. Wow! What a celebration. It brought renewed freedom to the ministry.

Henry Blackaby led a small church with an income of $74,000. They had several exciting sessions to consider what God wanted them to do as a church. These discussions established an operational and challenge budget totaling $164,000 for the coming year. That's an enormous stretch of faith for a small church. The people embraced the challenge, and at the end of the year, God had brought in $172,000. Blackaby said budget forecasting—envisioning what God was going to do—became one of the most exciting times in the church's life.[6]

I've been in budget meetings with so much pessimism and defeatism, you'd think God had filed for bankruptcy, and everyone's heavenly mansion was up for sale. Do you think budget projecting could change a gloomy gathering to a celebration of what God is going to do? I do, and here's why.

A Journey of Faith

When I became senior pastor of Woodbridge Community Church, we had about a hundred forty to a hundred fifty people meeting in a crackerbox building. As the ministry developed, we eventually held four worship services on a Sunday, though not all were full, and one was the Filipino congregation birthed from our church. Initially, we had eight badly deteriorated parking spaces left over from a small bank that had been on the property. This left a negative impression, so we removed them, leaving us with no on-site parking. Our people parked at the school district or the medical center on either side of our property. If a visitor found the church and discovered where to park, we knew God sent them—they wouldn't find it any other way.

Daring to Dream

God began to stir our hearts with a strong desire to reach a rapidly growing community with on-site parking, a larger worship center, and education facilities. We dreamed ... and we drew up plans. The process seemed endless and sometimes futile. The amount of money required loomed over us. But God gave us a burden, a clear directive to move forward. Dreams are rarely a straight, smooth path. Instead, they zigzag and include delays, disappointments, and even dead-ends. Little did we know that it would take more than ten years to realize our dreams.

Deciding to Take Steps of Faith

Rick Warren stated, "A dream is worthless until you decide to do something about it."[7] Each year, we chose challenge goals, the first being to pay off the mortgage. In two years, we knocked this out and celebrated with a "Put the Mortgage on the BBQ" service. One of our charter members put it on a barbeque at the close of a worship service, accompanied by thunderous applause and thick smoke. I'm still amazed the smoke alarm didn't go off, and the sprinkler system didn't baptize the congregation. It was a great Sunday. Over the next two years, we built and dedicated a new educational wing for $500,000, and in the years following that, we constructed the courtyard with a gazebo and baptistry for $60,000 and a sports square for youth ministry for $24,000. We were taking challenging but manageable steps forward.

During this time, a developer approached us to build storage units behind the church in an abandoned dry ditch. He had one problem: he needed access to the storage units from the main street. After years of negotiating, we granted his customers the right to drive through our property (only a few cars weekly), and he gave the church $920,000. He also paid for and put in all the parking we needed and agreed to maintain it into the future. Also included in the deal was the right of access for a Jewish Chabad behind the church. The total package value came to about $2 million, the amount we had prayed for.

Difficulties, Delays, and Dead Ends

Did everything roll along smoothly? Hardly. I had some hard lessons to learn and made some mistakes. When I exerted some high-handed leadership on a personnel issue—contrary to what I recommend in this book—it backfired. A worship service was disrupted, and a faction developed that opposed just about everything we attempted. The congregation had approved the master plan, but a factious few dubbed it the "disaster plan" and eventually persuaded the congregation to vote it down. The morning after, the staff gathered in my office, and we wept in our pain and disappointment. It felt like the death of a dream—from our perspective. Instead, God changed the picture and brought an unforeseeable advantage we would never have discovered without the defeat. The revised master plan was approved unanimously less than two months later. Getting the new plan approved by the city was another hurdle, as we waited for a city council member to rotate off and trudged through numerous reviews and appeals. Final approval took six years.

In the midst of all this, I had quadruple bypass heart surgery, though thankfully with no heart attack and no heart damage. Of the three major arteries to my heart, two were 100 percent closed, and the third was 92 percent blocked. I was a walking, bike-riding miracle. It was astounding that I didn't drop dead on some bike trail. Doctors were amazed, explaining my bike riding had created natural bypasses around the blockage. As I recovered, my wife, a nurse, urged me to read the ninety-six-page book by Dr. Ever E. Mann entitled, *Everything Men Knew About Taking Care of Themselves Before Women Came Along*. It didn't take long to read—all ninety-six pages are blank. While I was out for two months on medical leave, I sought the Lord regarding his plan for the church. I could name a dozen reasons why it wasn't a good time to build, but the Lord impressed on my heart that he was leading the way. It was time!

When I returned, I shared the confirming direction I sensed from the Lord. The people were ready. We drew up plans for a new 735-seat worship center and offices, family life center, sports court, and parking (paid for by the developer). I began the preliminary work for a "Building for Life" campaign in the fall to raise the needed funds. Even though the church was debt free, the issue of raising enough money still seemed impossible.

One morning, the leadership team chairman, Don Nordstrom, and finance chairman, Tom Ells, called me at home and asked to come over. These are two wonderful, godly men, champions in the cause, but when leadership chairs want to make a house call on a Wednesday morning, there's usually a big problem brewing at the sheep ranch.

Don started with a joke. I thought, *Maybe he is softening things before the bad news.*

"Uncle Charlie inherited a million dollars," Don began. "But he had a bad heart. The family didn't know how to break the news to him, afraid he might have a heart attack and die. Finally, they decided to ask the pastor to break the news. 'He's very diplomatic. He'll know how to break the news to Charlie, so he doesn't drop dead from the shock.' The pastor visited Charlie in his home. Trying to think of a way to approach the topic, he started with a question, 'Charlie, what would you do if you inherited a million dollars?' Without hesitation, Charlie calmly replied, 'Why, I'd give it all to the church!' The pastor had a heart attack."

We all laughed uproariously. Then the chairman said, "We don't want you to have a heart attack, but we have just received a gift of $2.5 million to build the new worship center and family life center." My heart fluttered a little, but I didn't have a heart attack. I was floored and thrilled beyond words. Tears of thanksgiving welled up in my eyes. "Yes, God, you've led us every step of this journey."

It was still a stretch, and the entire project from start to finish, including the value of the donated parking, was over $6 million. More than ten years of dreams, discouragements, defeats, dead ends, and delays preceded the dedication. It was a great team effort and a wonderful experience of prayer and faith planning.

> My joy overflowed with glory to God.
> Where God guides, God provides!

Reflection and Discussion

Quick Recall

- _____ and _____ have a built-in tension.
- What word in the Bible is the equivalent to the word *budget*? _____
- What is the difference between an operational budget and a challenge budget?
- _____
  _____

Thinking It Through

1. Discuss the characteristics and cautions of the three types of budgets: play-it-safe, presumptuous, and prayer and faith.

2. What are your thoughts about including the name and phone number of the person overseeing each area of the budget so people can contact them directly with questions?

We can make our plans, but the Lord determines our steps. (Prov. 16:9)

Commit your actions to the Lord, and your plans will succeed. (Prov. 16:3)

Plans go wrong for lack of advice; many advisers bring success. (Prov. 15:22)

—10—

GOD MEETING WITH THE PEOPLE

ENGAGING THE CONGREGATION TO CATCH THE VISION AND TRANSFORMING BUSINESS MEETINGS INTO SACRED ASSEMBLIES

It was a dark day, a day of national disaster. Like an invading army, locust swarmed into the land, so thick they darkened the sky, devouring every piece of vegetation. Crops were ruined. The economy teetered on the verge of collapse. The countryside became a moonscape, a dust bowl of dirt. It was a time to weep and mourn. Like a bride dressed in black, mourning the death of her fiancé, grief swept into every home. In this time of national calamity, the prophet Joel called for a sacred or solemn assembly—a congregational God Meeting.

> Consecrate a fast,
> Proclaim a solemn assembly;
> Gather the elders
> And all the inhabitants of the land

> To the house of the LORD your God,
> And cry out to the LORD. (Joel 1:14 NASB)
>
> Blow a trumpet in Zion,
> Consecrate a fast, proclaim a solemn assembly,
> Gather the people, sanctify the congregation,
> Assemble the elders,
> Gather the children and the nursing infants.
> Let the bridegroom come out of his room
> And the bride out of her bridal chamber.
> Let the priests, the LORD's ministers,
> Weep between the porch and the altar,
> And let them say, "Spare Your people, O LORD,
> And do not make Your inheritance a reproach,
> A byword among the nations.
> Why should they among the peoples say,
> 'Where is their God?'" (Joel 2:15-17 NASB)

Like Joel, we live in dark days. We're members of a decaying culture. Spiritual locusts have invaded the land. They have stripped biblical morals, gnawed at family values, crept into our courts, and swarmed into our schools. It's time to mourn and weep. Proverbs says, "Where there is no vision, the people are unrestrained" (29:18 NASB). The word *vision* means revelation—the proclamation of God's Word. The *New Living Translation* puts it this way, "When people do not accept divine guidance, they run wild" (Prov. 29:18). Gone wild! What a description of our world today. Believing hearts cry out for revival in our land.

> Upright citizens are good for a city and make it prosper, but the talk of the wicked tears it apart. (Prov. 11:11)
>
> Godliness makes a nation great, but sin is a disgrace to any people. (Prov. 14:34)
>
> When the godly succeed, everyone is glad. When the wicked take charge, people go into hiding. (Prov. 28:12)

> When the godly are in authority, the people rejoice. But when the wicked are in power, they groan. (Prov. 29:2)

Desperate times call for decisive leadership. It's time for leaders to invite the people to meet with God in a sacred assembly.

WHAT IS A SACRED ASSEMBLY?

Biblically, sacred assemblies—annual or in response to a crisis—were an occasion for God's people to worship, confess sin, pray for one another, remember God's faithfulness, seek his will for the future, and call on God's intervention. In simple terms, they were God Meetings. "The prescribed sacred assemblies (or holy convocations) for Israel included the Sabbath (Lev. 23:3) and seven other days of sacred assembly: the first (Passover) and seventh days of the Feast of Unleavened Bread (Lev. 23:4-8), the Feast of Weeks (Pentecost, Lev. 23:15-21), the Feast of Trumpets (Lev. 23:23-25), the Day of Atonement (Lev. 23:26-32), and the first and eighth days of the Feast of Tabernacles (Lev. 23:33- 36)."[1] Lest we think it was all somber, these were called festivals—times for worship and celebration, fasting as well as feasting. Psalms 113–118, the "Great Hallel" or "Great Praise," were sung at Passover, Feast of Weeks, and Feast of Tabernacles. The Passover Jesus celebrated with the disciples became the observance of the Lord's Table, a sacred assembly.

In the Old Testament, a sacred assembly was often called in response to a looming disaster; at other times, it was called after everything fell apart. Claude King traces the examples through Israel's history:

> These times for renewing a right relationship with God were called sacred assemblies (or solemn assemblies,

holy convocations). In the Old Testament we see two approaches to the use of sacred assemblies. One comes before the disaster and the other comes after the disaster.

Before. When King Jehoshaphat saw a vast army coming against the nation, he called for a fast and a time to seek help from the Lord (2 Chron. 20:1-30). God responded and saved the people. When Jonah preached a message of coming destruction, a wicked and pagan city and king repented, and God withheld the disaster (Jonah 3). When King Josiah heard God's Word read, he tore his robes in anguish, realizing how much his nation had offended God by violating His commands. When Josiah humbled himself before the Lord and then guided the people to repent, God spared that generation from destruction (2 Chron. 34:14-35:19).

After. In 586/7 BC, God used a wicked king of Babylon to execute judgment on Jerusalem and Judah, and Nebuchadnezzar carried God's people into exile in Babylon for 70 years. After experiencing such great judgment, Ezra and Nehemiah guided the people to stand before God in repentance so God would heal and restore the land (Neh. 8-10)—and God did![2]

And God did ... what a remarkable phrase. The Bible clearly indicates that God responds when his people gather, pray, and confess sin. Let's look at the reasons your church will benefit from a sacred assembly.

WHY CALL FOR A SACRED ASSEMBLY?

As leaders, you establish vision and goals based on listening to God and each other. But how does this vision capture the hearts of the people? How do they become engaged with the direction of the ministry? Too often, an us-versus-them gap develops between leadership and the people. A sacred assembly is a unique opportunity to build a visionary bridge with the people.

A carefully planned sacred assembly provides the setting to accomplish three things: 1) cry out to God as a body of believers for the crisis in your church, community, nation, or the world, 2) convey the vision and listen to and engage the congregation in the mission of the church, and 3) prepare God's people to do the business of the church.

Later in this chapter, I discuss planning a sacred assembly, but let's first discuss why it's essential that churches find a new way to do God's business.

The "Black Eye" of Church Business Meetings

I've met some wonderful, down-home folk on my ministry journey. They're not the ones who receive accolades and applause, but I love them. They're real. Unpretentious. Uniquely different and priceless.

Meet Flo. I crack a smile at the mention of her name. Well into her 80s, with frizzy hair and missing a couple of teeth, Flo wandered into church one Sunday from the nearby rest home. She found the people friendly and decided to show up every Sunday, arriving five to ten minutes late. Oblivious to making a grand entrance, Flo marched down the center aisle, waved at me, and so everyone could hear, loudly announced, "Good morning, Pastor Dave," before sitting down in the second row. Everyone smiled. Everyone loved Flo. If she had a question, she might ask it in the middle of the message. She loved to hear about Jesus, and it wasn't long till she opened her heart and invited him into her life. Immediately, she wanted to be baptized. My wife assisted her in getting ready. She was okay with wearing the white robe but refused to take off her girdle. When I brought her into the baptistry, I asked the usual questions,

"Do you believe Jesus Christ is God's Son and the Savior of the world?"

"Yup," she replied.

"Have you invited Jesus Christ into your life?"

"Yup."

That was good enough for me, and I baptized her, girdle and all. She came out of the water, thrusting her arms up in celebration and grinning from ear to ear.

One Sunday, we had a business meeting following the worship service, and Flo decided to stay. You've probably been in church business meetings when the mood becomes tense and somber. A funeral dirge is upbeat compared to some church business meetings. This church had a history of explosions at business meetings, so folks came with residual fear, not knowing what might hit the fan. Flo sat and listened to the proceedings for about thirty minutes. Finally, she stood up and spoke her mind, "You're not talking about Jesus. I'm going home." And she marched out.

Flo's comment struck a note of truth, and everyone sensed it, but we didn't know what to do about it. We didn't talk about Jesus in business meetings other than opening with a prayer. Minutes, motions, mundane reports, contentious issues, "I want it this way" speeches, disagreements, uncomfortable, pointed questions, and Robert's Rules held more sway than Jesus. In that church, I don't ever recall praying before an important congregational decision or a vote. Maybe Jesus felt like Flo. "They're not talking about me. I'll exit." We know that Jesus knocked at the door of the lukewarm Laodicean church, which basked in its wealth but didn't know it was naked. "Look!" He exclaimed, "I stand at the door and knock. If you hear my voice and open the door, I will come in ..." (Rev. 3:20). I wonder how often Jesus knocks and waits at the door in church business meetings.

Meetings for Business

Most states require nonprofit organizations to have at least one meeting of the membership annually. Generally, this meeting aims to select new officers, review financials, adopt a new budget, and confirm goals for the upcoming year. Churches with no formal membership usually designate the board as the church members, so a board meeting is a membership meeting. There are constitutional requirements for membership meetings in most churches, and I'm not suggesting working around these. I advise following what the written documents require or revising them. I also recommend thinking biblically about every meeting.

The Bible does not mention a "business meeting" of the church as we generally think of it. The closest to it would be the selection of leaders (Acts 6:1-5), carrying out church discipline (1 Cor. 5:4-5, 13), sending out missionaries (Acts 13:1-3), and receiving the letter from the Jerusalem Council (Acts 15:30). I was led to Christ through Yorba Linda Friends Church (a church in the Quaker tradition) and later served as pastor for seven years. One thing that stuck with me was their firm conviction that a meeting to conduct the church's affairs was a worship service. They emphasized no distinction between sacred and secular, between business and spiritual. The meetings included silent and group prayer, Scripture reading, and worship.

Would that all churches operated with these priorities in place, but the opposite usually occurs. Thom Rainer, an insightful pastor and church consultant, shares his observations about business meetings in many churches.

- There are still many churches today where the business meeting is primarily a gathering of critics and malcontents. The happy church member tends to avoid the meetings for obvious reasons.

- There is a clear trend toward less frequent business meetings. Quarterly meetings are becoming common, and many churches have moved to annual meetings only.

- Though I have not actually done a precise statistical study, I am confident in saying that there is a high correlation between the size of the church and the way a congregation does business meetings. Larger churches tend to have less frequent meetings. And smaller churches are more likely to require votes on more issues than larger churches.
- Most pastors and staffs dislike, even dread, church business meetings.
- The most common item covered in church business meetings is the finances of the church. For those congregations with annual meetings only, the church budget is the primary item brought as business.
- Relatively few churches discuss ministry in these meetings.[3]

Regardless of what form of governance a church embraces, business meetings too often follow the dismal pattern Rainer describes. There are several types of church government, and it is not my goal to change your church polity. There is a time and a place for that. But, in the final analysis, I believe in one ultimate type of church government: *Jesus is the head of the church* (Col. 1:18). When Jesus is Lord, first in everything, things work out on his timetable. If you believe in the authority of the Scripture, you're probably quick to say amen, but how do we make this a practical reality in the decision-making of the church?

To start, we should acknowledge that church business meetings are not inherently bad. They're not the eleventh plague leftover from the Exodus, though I know some would argue otherwise. I applaud churches that have God-honoring business meetings where the Spirit of God superintends the process, and the work of God advances. However, I have deep concerns about business meetings that waste kingdom time or provide a platform for cantankerous conduct and ungodly behavior.

Mind-Numbing, Monotonous Meetings

Through the years, I don't know how many people have told me they don't attend congregational meetings because they are boring and a waste of time. I don't disagree with them. There have been times when I outlined my sermon in a congregational meeting, made my to-do list, and when I was done, counted my teeth with my tongue and checked for lint in my navel. While a couple of people are bickering about a piddly issue, others are rolling their eyes, checking their phones, or wondering how they can slip out without being noticed.

In one church, the business meeting started at 7 p.m. and went until midnight. The issue still hadn't been decided, so they agreed to continue the dispute the following evening. Finally, after six hours of contentious debate, they reached a decision. What was the issue? Whether to have standard or chrome wheels on the people mover. Another church met for hours debating what type of lawnmower blades to purchase. Seriously? Another congregation had a two-hour meeting discussing donuts. Now we're talking about an important issue![4]

Churches that spend valuable time on issues like this tend to stay small or decline. But take heart, not all church business meetings are mundane. Some are heated and nasty.

Contentious and Divisive Meetings

In the fruit of the flesh identified in Galatians 5:19-21, Paul calls out sexual sin, idolatry, wild parties, drunkenness, and witchcraft—behaviors believers wouldn't think of condoning. But in the same list, he includes practices allowed in too many congregational business meetings: "hatred and fighting, jealousy and anger, constant effort to get the best for yourself, complaints and criticisms, the feeling that everyone else is wrong except those in your own little group" (Gal. 5:20 TLB). Be truthful. Have you seen behavior like this in a church meeting? I have, and I've heard people rationalize it too. "Well, we've got to let people have their say," or "He's really a nice guy, but his temper gets out of control in business meetings." Why do we allow this to go on?

The book of James confronts the problem head-on. "What is the source of quarrels and conflicts among you? Is not the source your pleasures that wage war in your members?" (James 4:1 NASB). Quarrels (Grk. *polemos*) is a general word for fights, elsewhere in the New Testament translated as war. From this word, we get the word *polemics*, a strong verbal or written attack on someone. James also uses the word *conflicts* (Grk. *mache*), a narrower term for fighting, such as a personal vendetta. *Wage war* (Grk. *strateuomenon* from *strategos*, to lead) is a military term meaning to lead an attack. Our word *strategy* comes from this Greek word. The word *pleasures* (Grk. *hedonon*), the source of our word hedonism, is self-gratification.

I've seen James 4:1 played out in living color—divisive strategizing, war-like quarrels, and heated conflicts—during church business meetings. It may appear those involved want the best for the church, but James says the source is the internal conflict in the soul. Driven by hedonistic, self-seeking pleasure, people strategize to get their own way regarding any issue. "I want what I want, and I want it now. And if I don't get it now, I'll fight for it." Even their prayers are self-centered—praying amiss (James 4:3). They know nothing of abandoning self-centeredness and praying, like Jesus, "I want your will to be done, not mine" (Matt. 26:39).

James describes an out-in-the-open campaign of conflict. And this still goes on today. My longtime friend, Pastor Roy Roberts, wrote,

When a conflict like this arises, all the factions of the church come out of the woodwork. It is a "show-down" at the congregational business meeting corral. I know of a case where the color of carpet was up for grabs. One faction in the group wanted blue, and the other schism wanted red. At Sunday's business meeting, it was to be settled by vote. During the week, the town's phone lines were humming as each group called their supporters to instigate a voting-block rally at the impending meeting. People showed up at church who had not been there for years! Well, the "reds" won, and the "blues" promptly stood to their feet and left en masse. The church was split over the color of the carpet. They were divided over a personal preference. Whether or not it was a Bible issue never entered anyone's mind! The church was incredibly weakened, and Satan scored a point. The local church was the real loser.[5]

It's one thing to have a disagreement or a difference of opinion. That's normal. Disagreement, in my book, starts with a small "d"—a healthy part of any vibrant organization. Divisiveness is a big "D" word—unhealthy and destructive! Big "D" sometimes occurs because little "d" is squelched.

There are many types of church business meetings—monthly, quarterly, or annual meetings, information meetings, church dinner/business meetings, issue-centered meetings, emergency meetings, and sometimes unofficial meetings. All of them can become contentious and divisive. The issues to be decided by the congregation vary widely from selecting leaders, approving budgets, evaluating staff, receiving or removing members, approving expenditures that exceed the budget, approving contracts, loans, or building programs. Some churches do not have congregational meetings since the governing leadership makes all the decisions. Whatever their nature, business meetings have given the church a black eye far too long.

We could have a long debate about what issues should or shouldn't be decided by the congregation, but this is not my purpose. There is a better solution: *make every meeting of the church to discuss and make decisions a God Meeting.*

CALLING FOR A SACRED ASSEMBLY

Why not transform business meetings into a meaningful highlight of church life? Rather than calling it a business meeting or an annual meeting, I suggest renaming it a sacred assembly or a congregational God Meeting. The name emphasizes a consecrated and holy gathering with God. The church leadership invites everyone to arrive prepared to meet with God, ready to behave like a guest in God's living room, the throne room of heaven.

It's not a town hall meeting—to rally people to your cause, to ramrod your proposal, to create a voting block, to complain and whine. It's a time to listen to the sovereign ruler of the church, the Lord Jesus Christ. We go to a God Meeting not to scheme but to surrender, not to fight but to follow Jesus.

Some may think it a stretch to call a business meeting a sacred assembly, but I ask, "Why not?" Church business meetings are notorious for disgraceful behavior, and something needs changing. Is God glorified when there is a big blow-up at a business meeting? If an unbeliever visits an ugly church meeting, would they walk away from Christianity? Major disputes sometimes hit the local or national news, and Jesus is disgraced.

If sacred assembly is too radical, consider referring to it as "The Father's Business Meeting"—a meeting with your Heavenly Father. Jesus said he was intent on doing the Father's business (Luke 2:49)—we should be too. Gathering to do the Father's business forms the foundation for a sacred assembly. Let's look at some additional, practical steps to guide your process.

How to Plan a Sacred Assembly

Though there are many possible formats for various types of meetings, I have based the following on the annual business meeting model used by many churches for the sake of simplicity.

1. **Establish a significant and clear purpose for the assembly.**

A wisely constructed sacred assembly can accomplish the constitutional requirements for a business meeting while accomplishing so much more. Use it as an opportunity to bring spiritual renewal and stir revival. When planned with an engaging purpose, you'll likely discover hunger among the members to draw close to God and interact with their leaders. Scheduling a business meeting without a meaningful spiritual cause creates a purposeless vacuum that invites contentious issues. Establishing a compelling reason to meet—praying with urgency for a spiritual crisis—overcomes the drift to the negative.

There are three questions to ask in establishing the purpose of a congregational God Meeting: What is the spiritual crisis in the church, community, nation, or the world? What is the vision to communicate to the church to engage them in dialogue, prayer, and action? Finally, what are the procedural matters to discuss or transact?

2. **Call for a sacred assembly—a meeting with God.**

Announce the date and extend an invitation to God's people to gather and seek the Lord. Invite God's people to pray and fast regarding a single, compelling issue. It could be the crumbling morals of the nation or persecuted believers in various parts of the world. If there is an economic downturn, pray for families and those looking for work. Pray also for the ministry of the church, the leaders, and goals for the new year. When the early church selected leaders and sent out missionaries, they did so with prayer and fasting (Acts 13:1-3; 14:23). Why should we do anything differently? When believers embrace a burden to reach the lost and a greater sense of purpose, they'll be less prone to debate lesser matters. Get past trivia by setting a focus of spiritual urgency.

Next, help your people get ready to meet with God. Before gathering the Israelites at Mt. Sinai, God told Moses, "Go down and prepare the people for my arrival. Consecrate them today and tomorrow" (Exod. 19:10). Provide a guide for prayer and fasting; distribute the names of candidates for leadership and the financials. Those who love to stir up trouble, criticize, and create division are unlikely to attend a sacred assembly ... if they do, perhaps they'll be led to repentance.

3. **Open the meeting by setting the focus on God.**

The pastor or chairman should welcome everyone, set the tone for the gathering, and outline the general flow of the meeting. I suggest opening with Scripture that describes a meeting with God. For example, God told the people of Israel, "I will meet with you and speak with you. I will meet the people of Israel there, in the place made holy by my glorious presence" (Exod. 29:42-43). In like manner, the pastor can say, "I invite the people of our church to meet God in this place, made holy by his glorious presence. This is a sacred assembly of God's people. Lord, we worship you and adore you." When a meeting is initiated with, "Holy, holy, holy is the Lord God, the Almighty—the one who always was, who is, and who is still to come" (Rev. 4:8), or "Praise the LORD! For the Lord our God, the Almighty, reigns. Let us be glad and rejoice, and let us give honor to him" (Rev. 19:6-7), a sense of awe and wonder descends and transforms the meeting. Why not start with repentance instead of reading the minutes (save this for later)? Or open the session kneeling before King Jesus. The first order of business in a sacred assembly is getting right with God.

4. **Sing and share what God is doing.**

A sacred assembly is a meeting for worship, prayer, and celebration—trade hand-wringing for hand-clapping. Replace the furrowed brows with smiles of anticipation. Focus on God's sovereignty and promises. Open with songs about faith and victory with all the leaders seated in front, facing the audience. If the meeting follows the Listening to God leadership retreat, ask several to share what God did during the discernment process. Following this, the pastor shares God's leading for the goals and vision, then explains what will be discussed or decided. "Surrendered before God, we will discuss where God is leading and how to wisely use the resources he has provided." In addition, leaders can present the challenge budget and explain, "This is what we're putting on God's to-do list. By faith, we're trusting him to do this in his time and according to his purpose."

5. **Break into small groups.**

Connect the leadership with the people by spreading them among the groups. The small group dynamic prevents a disgruntled person from grabbing a microphone and spewing their negativity in the larger group, allows a quiet person to speak up, and unites leadership with the people on a personal level.

Provide a passage of Scripture about examining the heart to pray-read together. Here's one.

> So humble yourselves before God. Resist the devil, and he will flee from you. Come close to God, and God

will come close to you. Wash your hands, you sinners; purify your hearts, for your loyalty is divided between God and the world. Let there be tears for what you have done. Let there be sorrow and deep grief. Let there be sadness instead of laughter, and gloom instead of joy. Humble yourselves before the Lord, and he will lift you up in honor. (James 4:7-10)

After praying through the passage together, allow time for private prayer and listening to God. Follow this with prayer for the identified crucial need, the church goals, and the selection of leaders.

6. **Listen to God and one another.**

Continuing in the small group, the leader can ask, "What is God saying to you for our church to be or do?" Notice the wording of the question. This is not a gripe session. This is what you're hearing from God. The leader needs a pen and notepad to take notes. Allow each person to share without passing judgment or debating what they said. Clarify their comment if needed and include their name. This is the body of Christ connecting—sending and receiving messages with Jesus at the center.

Listening is part of the fine art of effective leadership— and it may be the most neglected. When leaders neglect listening to the people, their concerns build up like steam in a pressure cooker. One day the lid will blow off. A sacred assembly provides the opportunity for leaders to listen to the people in an appropriate setting.

7. **Transact the issues to be discussed and decided.**

Reassemble as a large group. Read the minutes from a previous meeting. Proceed with whatever actions are required. It may be approving the candidates for leadership, goals, and budget for the year that follows. Some churches have a history of a verbal report from every ministry. Assess whether this is a beneficial or poor use of time. When the building and grounds chairman gives a fifteen-minute report detailing changing eight sprinkler heads, oiling the door hinges, resetting the light timers, and cleaning the chairs in the youth room, even though this is important, it is not a good use of people's time. It's far better to include some information in a written report.

There are two options at this juncture. One option is to take action on the goals, budget, and nominees for leadership before concluding the meeting. The other option is a separate meeting, perhaps one week later. Make it clear that this second meeting is not for discussion. Open the meeting by explaining what is to be decided, spend time in prayer, and proceed to vote. This rarely takes longer than fifteen or twenty minutes.

In presenting a proposal for a vote, refrain from common business parlance: "How many of you are in favor of this? How many are opposed?" This makes it a matter of personal opinion and preference—which is not the main point. What matters is whether God is leading to proceed. Henry Blackaby suggests a more appropriate question: "With all the information and all the praying that we have been doing, how many of you sense that God is directing us to proceed in this direction?"[6] You're not conducting an opinion poll. You're asking them to give voice to the leading of the Spirit of God. And that makes all the difference.

8. **Be available for questions and comments following the meeting.**

Conclude the meeting with all the leaders returning to the front. Sing a song of victory before dismissing. Announce that anyone with further questions is welcome to talk with the leadership following the meeting. The point is not to squelch negativity or concerns but to give them proper expression in an appropriate context. You're building bridges between the people and the leadership.

9. **Review input from the congregation.**

Compile all the input from the congregation, including the name of the person who shared each idea. You may hear some fresh thinking that will contribute to the direction of the church. Often, you'll discover the congregation and leadership are hearing much the same things from God. How confirming! Remember, people will more readily embrace the goals and contribute time and money to the cause if leadership takes the time to listen and include them in the process.

10. **Arrange the timing, flow, and format that works best for your congregation.**

You may find it helpful to create a general pattern for the process. For the sake of illustration, let's assume a January to December fiscal year.

- **August or September:** Schedule a Listening to God leader retreat.
- **October:** Prepare goals, budget, and nominations for elected office, introduce the vision and goals to the congregation, and distribute copies of the goals, budgets, reports, and names of candidates.
- **November:** Call for a sacred assembly of fasting and prayer. Proceed with whatever action is required. Celebrate the weekend before Thanksgiving with a festive, all-church dinner.

Of course, there are many variations of this. Be creative and keep it fresh. A sacred assembly is not a solve-all.

Anticipate spiritual attacks because you're allowing Jesus Christ to assume his rightful position as the Lord of the church. Once, I had a couple upset because there was no free-for-all gripe session. They were stoked when everyone got stirred up and spewed what was upsetting them. Vexing and venting were like a gladiator event. I smiled and replied, "We want to hear from people in the right setting, but most of all, we desire to meet with and hear what Jesus wants for his church." People will still have issues, but setting boundaries for expressing concerns is a big step toward addressing them appropriately.

ANTICIPATING A MEETING WITH GOD

A sacred assembly can be a highlight in church life. Blow the trumpet and gather the people. Sing songs of faith, victory, and surrender. Listen to the Word of God, and focus on God's sovereignty and promises. Talk about the future with faith—rather than focusing on fears and futility. Confess sin and worship the Lord. Talk about ministry—not just money. You may want to put up biblical banners to set the focus.

> The LORD of Heaven's Armies is here among us. (Ps. 46:11)
>
> Don't be afraid, for I am with you.
> Don't be discouraged, for I am your God. (Isa. 41:10)
>
> Nothing will be impossible with God. (Luke 1:37 NASB)
>
> May he grant your heart's desires and make all your plans succeed.
> May we shout for joy when we hear of your victory and raise a victory banner in the name of our God.
> May the LORD answer all your prayers. (Ps. 20:4-5)

Celebrate like the Israelites on the seventh day and seventh trip around Jericho. Watch the walls of defeatism and despair crumble and fall. And if an unbeliever happens to observe your sacred assembly—singing, praying, listening, rejoicing, and doing the business of God in a harmonious, God-honoring way—they may exclaim, "God is truly here among you."

GOD MEETINGS | 197

REFLECTION AND DISCUSSION

Quick Recall

- There are several types of church government, but in the final analysis, there is one ultimate type of church government: Jesus is _____ _____ (Col. 1:18).
- If it's too radical to call your God Meeting a sacred assembly, consider referring to it as _____—a meeting with your Heavenly Father.
- D_____ is a small "d"—a healthy part of any vibrant organization. D_____ is a big "D"—unhealthy, destructive!

Thinking It Through

1. What has been the history of congregational meetings in your experience in the church?

2. What causes break your heart—in the church, community, nation, and world? Which of these would be important to focus on in a sacred assembly?

3. What would you like meetings with the congregation to be like in the future?

> Consecrate a fast,
> Proclaim a solemn assembly;
> Gather the elders
> And all the inhabitants of the land
> To the house of the LORD your God,
> And cry out to the LORD.
> (Joel 1:14 NASB)

SECTION TWO

PREVENTING PROBLEMS

SAFEGUARDING THE MINISTRY FROM SHIPWRECK

> Fight the good fight, keeping faith and a good conscience, which some have rejected and suffered shipwreck in regard to their faith. (1 Tim. 1:18-19 NASB)

The dramatic movie *The Perfect Storm* tells the true story of courageous fishermen who lost their lives at sea on Halloween in 1991. On their last fishing expedition of a disappointing season, they met up with three raging weather systems that collided to produce fifty-foot swells and waves ten stories high—the fiercest storm in modern history.

Perfect Storms are ravaging the church and Christian ministries. When moral or ethical failure topples a spiritual leader and the ministry crumbles, an intersection of storms usually contributes to the tragedy. "Perfect storms in the leader's life happen when dark, powerful forces converge within the soul of the leader,"[1] wrote Stephen W. Smith.

Three storms—unrealistic expectations, an unrealistic schedule, and an unrealistic pressure to succeed—join forces, creating a perfect storm in a leader's soul. Stopping the shipwreck of leaders and ministries is urgent. Discover the solutions to prevent the three storms and gain a playbook for God's team.

> **Each chapter has a featured video by a Christian leader. See pages 399-400 to access the code for free access to the video series.**

—11—

STORM NO. 1: UNREALISTIC EXPECTATIONS

PREVENTING MISUNDERSTANDING AND DISCOURAGEMENT

Joanne and I grieved as a young, multi-gifted pastoral couple told us, "If this is ministry, we want out." They had warm personalities, a heart for ministry, and both had solid Bible and seminary training. As the associate pastor for a church of about five hundred (and the only ministry staff other than the senior pastor), he was responsible for the nursery, the children's program, the junior high, senior high, college ministries, and young families—everyone from birth to age thirty. He was expected to organize and run VBS and teach four times a week. Part of their vacation included an exhausting week as counselors at the youth camp. The trustees expected his wife to recruit workers and oversee the nursery even though the church did not employ her. His anger and frustration boiled over, "The trustees call me in for a review twice a month and ask why I can't get more done? They often follow with another question. 'Why do you think you need to study five to ten hours a week to teach four times?'" These were hard-nosed businessmen, and the senior pastor was a former executive who decided to apply his business savvy to running a church. The two pastors rarely talked, and they never had staff meetings. The underlying philosophy of the church was to spend very little of their substantial cash reserves on staff.

After several meetings, I honestly expected this young couple to resign and leave the ministry. Finally, I replied, "At this point, you don't have much to lose. Getting fired would be a promotion and a blessing. Why don't you meet with the pastor and trustees and tell them the pressure you feel? Just lay it out there." With fears of being fired, he met with the trustees and senior pastor. He explained he couldn't meet the demands of the position, and if they wanted to replace him, that would be acceptable.

God turned the situation around dramatically. When we met with the couple a few weeks later, I couldn't believe we were meeting with the same people. Their body language had an air of confidence, and they were bubbling over with enthusiasm. "Everything has changed. We love the ministry again." For the first time, he felt heard and validated, and his wife was excited about their future. He and the senior pastor started supporting each other with frequent meetings. The trustees didn't want to lose this dynamic couple, so they gave him a salary increase and hired another staff person to help with the load!

Expectations, Frustration, and Exhaustion

Pastors have expectations of people, people have expectations of pastors, the board has expectations of the staff, the staff has expectations of the board, husbands have expectations of their wives, wives have expectations of their husbands, and on and on it goes. The church is springloaded with expectations. Often there is a trickle-down impact. Pastors feeling the weight of excessive expectations may, in turn, bark at others about what they're doing or not doing—filling their proverbial backpacks with pressure and guilt. Unrealistic expectations breed unrealistic expectations. Jesus told the religious leaders, "You crush people with unbearable religious demands, and you never lift a finger to ease the burden" (Luke 11:46). Unrealistic expectations come loaded with shoulds and oughts. Depression, guilt, and frustration often follow, and spiritual-sounding legalism slithers in, choking and strangling the work of the Spirit. As a pastor, it's easy to lay heavy expectations on the people without understanding the pressure in their world.

When I launch my work with a church, I usually give a message entitled "What to Expect." This message is from Matt. 11:28–30 and Jesus's words about heavy burdens and light yokes. I particularly enjoy the way *The Message* paraphrases it "Are you tired? Worn out? Burned out on religion? Come to me. Get away with me and you'll recover your life. I'll show you how to take a real rest. Walk with me and work with me—watch how I do it. Learn the unforced rhythms of grace. I won't lay anything heavy or ill-fitting on you. Keep company with me and you'll learn to live freely and lightly." Just reading this slows my pulse and calms my nerves.

As I speak on expectations, I explain what they can expect from me (detailed later in the chapter). And I share my expectations of the congregation:

- Love the Lord your God and one another.
- Be responsive and obedient to the teaching of God's Word.

- Exercise your spiritual gift in serving one another.
- Financially support the ministry as the Lord enables you.
- Call me or someone in leadership if you're facing a crisis—health, finances, work, or family.
- Communicate concerns about the ministry directly to me or someone in leadership.
- Seek opportunities to share your faith and pray regularly for the leadership and ministry of the church.

I emphasize that it is not healthy to be at the church four or five nights a week. As a church, our priority is building families—not tearing them apart. Sometimes we equate being fully committed to Jesus with being at the church every time the doors open. This is unfortunate and erroneous.

Unrealistic expectations strangle spiritual life and create frustration, guilt, and bitterness. If messages are a constant barrage of start doing this and stop doing that, the people begin to feel hammered and helpless. As a result, some folks leave the church rather than endure the haranguing. Volunteer leaders typically balance their schedule with full-time work, so demanding church commitments shouldn't hijack marriage and family time. As pastors, we need to extend compassion and understanding to our leaders and the congregation and guard against overloading them with unrealistic expectations.

Pastors, too, often chafe under overloaded expectations. Excessive demands and overwhelming pressure are destructive, leading to resentment, burnout, and sometimes, leaving the ministry. In addition, a frustrated pastor is vulnerable to temptation—the menace of moral failure lurks close. An overworked and angry pastor will have unrealistic expectations of the staff, leadership team, and congregation.

With the desire to combat all of this, let's examine the expectations of a pastor and explore some solutions.

WHAT ARE THE EXPECTATIONS OF A PASTOR?

Dr. Thom Rainer is a leading resource for pastors and leaders in the church. Thom did a survey while pastoring in St. Petersburg, Florida. He asked his leaders to write down the minimum amount of time they thought he should spend on various pastoral duties each week. The result, when tallied, shows on the chart below.

EXPECTATIONS OF A PASTOR[1]

TASK	HOURS
Sermon preparation	18
Administration	18
Hospital and home visitation	15
Prayer	14
Worship/preaching	10
Outreach visitation	10
Counseling	10
Community activities	5
Denominational tasks	5
Church meetings	5
Miscellaneous	4
TOTAL HOURS WEEKLY	**114**

That amounts to 16-hour days, seven days a week. Why not purchase a cot and live at the church? One of the churches I served as a transitional pastor had a bed and shower in the pastor's office. He often worked all night. Tragically, though not surprisingly, he died of a heart attack.

When the expectations of people are not met, criticism begins to fly. Perhaps some pastors have tough skin to shield the pain of criticism, but most pastors, partly because of their sensitive and caring hearts for people, feel the pain of criticism very deeply.

Christian researcher George Barna said, "Our studies show that church-goers expect their pastor to juggle an average of 16 major tasks. That's a recipe for failure—nobody can handle the wide range of responsibilities that people expect pastors to master. ... The pastor who strives to meet everyone's demands and tries to keep everyone happy is guaranteed to fail."[2] Since George Barna doesn't list the sixteen tasks, I wrote my own list. While different pastors may have more or fewer tasks, I find that most senior or lead pastors juggle some combination of these responsibilities. This is particularly true for pastors of small or medium-sized churches.

Major Tasks of a Senior or Lead Pastor

1. Prepare messages, preach, and teach
2. Develop and communicate goals and vision for the church and all its ministries
3. Serve as the chief executive officer of a corporation
4. Structure worship services and deal with worship styles and music preferences
5. Lead, disciple, and train the church board or leadership team
6. Administrate the church and meet with committees
7. Serve as chief fundraiser
8. Create promotional materials and write articles for newsletters
9. Visit the sick in the hospital and at their homes
10. Resolve conflicts
11. Equip and train believers to exercise their gifts

12. Lead the staff and coordinate their efforts—deal with human resource issues
13. Train and baptize new members and new believers
14. Perform weddings and other ceremonies, dedicate children
15. Care for families during a time of loss and conduct memorial services
16. Recruit personnel for church ministries
17. Evangelize and develop community outreach plans and programs
18. Counseling—premarital, personal, marriage, and crisis intervention
19. Visit Bible studies and various ministries periodically, and attend church social events and special occasions for members such as graduations, birthday parties, and anniversaries
20. Respond to benevolence requests and care for the needy
21. Lead or participate in community and denominational activities

Some of these responsibilities occur every week, while others shove their way onto the priority list at random—usually inconvenient—times. Resolving conflict is an example that some assume is rare. Not so. Studies indicate that most pastors deal with conflict every month, if not more frequently. Sometimes they mediate a clash; at other times, they are personally involved in the dispute. In both instances, conflict resolution is exceptionally draining and challenging work.

A System Designed to Fail

Such relentless pressure dramatically increases the likelihood of a crash that no one intends. Everyone hopes for the best, but when it doesn't work out, the pastor takes the brunt of the blame while few realize they contributed to a system destined to fail. Why does this happen? While the pastor is madly trying to cover all the tasks, three priorities tend to slide to the bottom of the list.

22. Prayer and spiritual growth
23. Marriage relationship
24. Family time with the children

Sadly, these three priorities drift to a default setting below the seemingly more urgent demands. Everyone I know will argue vehemently that this shouldn't happen. But it does. It's inevitable with the scramble to meet all the expectations. This sets in motion the first of a swirling convergence of storms that can capsize the ministry boat.

In the corporate world, a chief executive officer takes on the enormous task of leading and administrating an organization. A teacher or public speaker has their hands full preparing materials, teaching, and relating to students. A full-time load for a professional counselor is fifteen to twenty appointments per week. In the lead pastor role, all three positions—chief executive officer, public speaker and teacher, and counselor/caregiver—merge into one position. George Barna rings the alarm when he says, "Many churches make a grievous mistake: They expect their pastor to be the master of all trades. The expectations set for most pastors doom them to failure before they begin their work."[3] Instead of altering the system of broken expectations, churches search far and wide for someone who can do it all.

The Search for the Super Pastor

When a church is without a pastor, a search committee usually conducts a survey of the congregation. From this, they develop a profile of the person they are looking for and their expectations for the new pastor. Unfortunately, there's a lot of idealism in the process. I've seen profiles and expectations five or six pages long. One group of elders asked me to review the senior pastor profile developed by their search team. I felt the church had a promising future with a multi-million dollar facility and a good location. I commended them for their hard work in developing the profile but mentioned it included far too many expectations. They continued the search process for three years, with one candidate after another turning them down. Meanwhile, people began leaving the church, and finally, the church gave up and closed its doors. Their unreasonable expectations killed the work God was doing.

Once a candidate is selected, almost messianic-like anticipation kicks in. I call it the NPC syndrome (when the "new pastor comes"), a ministry salve to solve most of the ills in the church. "When the new pastor comes, he'll get the lack of children's workers solved." "When the new pastor arrives, he'll bring unity despite this disruptive group." "I'm certain we will see a turn-around in the attendance and finances when the new pastor comes."

Finally, the pastor arrives. Anticipation is high, both from the congregation and the pastor. With a firm commitment to serve God and a strong desire to succeed, the pastor embraces the responsibilities with vigor and enthusiasm. The initial response is excitement and rewarding affirmation.

Here's what often happens. The first two or three years set a relentless pace. The pastor may have messages from a previous pastorate. If so, these don't require as much study as developing new materials. It works to pull one out on Saturday evening, pop it in the spiritual microwave, and serve it up on Sunday. With the scramble to fulfill major tasks, the pastor may shortchange his time alone with God.

With the urgent screaming for the pastor's attention, the spouse begins to feel isolated and neglected. Important events in the lives of the children may slip by unnoticed. The pastor offers assurances to his family: "Once we get through this initial time, things will settle down, and we'll have more time together." But somehow, the pace and expectations only increase.

Proverbs says pointedly, "The fool who provokes his family to anger and resentment will finally have nothing worthwhile left. He shall be the servant of a wiser man" (11:29 TLB). David was a great warrior, king, and songwriter, but his family was a royal mess. When Solomon penned these words, he may have thought back to the seething resentment that fueled the rebellions of his brothers, Absalom and Adonijah.

When spiritual growth, marriage, and family are neglected, disaster looms. It will all unravel—sooner or later. The wheels are going to come off the ministerial wagon. So what's the solution to avoid this crisis? It begins with a close examination of God's priorities for ministry.

What God Expects of a Pastor

I recently read through 1 and 2 Timothy, Titus, and other passages asking myself the question, "What does God expect of a pastor?" I jotted down every responsibility mentioned and grouped them. Rather than the list of twenty-one expectations listed earlier, God keeps it simple—five clear expectations for a pastor.

Priority One: Pray and study the Word of God.

High on the pastor's list of priorities is the importance of daily prayer and biblical study. Acts 6:4 says, "We will devote ourselves to prayer and to the ministry of the word" (NASB). Paul urges Timothy to pray for all people and lead the church in prayer (1 Tim. 2:1-8). Pastors devote themselves to studying Scripture to be approved by God as workmen who accurately handle the truth (2 Tim. 2:15). To be approved by people? No. Study to be approved by God. When pastors drift from regularly studying the Word, spiritual intimacy declines, and God's approval may be removed. A pastor only thrives while cultivating a vibrant relationship of listening, learning, and being led by God.

Priority Two: Teach and preach the Word of God.

Much like a court oath, Paul charges Timothy in the presence of God to preach the Word in and out of season (2 Tim. 4:1-2). Even if folks get "itchy ears" and want entertaining messages, pastors must preach and teach the Word. Whether the place is packed or the crowd is sparse, God commands pastors to preach and teach the Word. The pastor is to do this with love from a pure heart, a good conscience, and a sincere faith (1 Tim. 1:5). The pastor and elders are to guard the church against false teaching (Acts 20:28-29). Paul tells Timothy, and urges all pastors who follow him, "Focus on reading the Scriptures to the church, encouraging the believers, and teaching them" (1 Tim. 4:13). In other words, read the verse, teach the verse, and apply the verse. Paul also tells Timothy, "do the work of an evangelist" (2 Tim. 4:5 NASB). I have made it my practice to present the gospel in every message, regardless of the topic. Appendix 4 is "Three Simple Steps to New Life," a format I use to share the gospel.

Priority Three: Equip and train the believers.

Paul tells Timothy to teach faithful leaders who will teach others (2 Tim. 2:2). Rather than being a do-it-all, high-performance leader, the pastor invites the people to share in the ministry and equips them to exercise their spiritual gifts (Eph. 4:11-12).

Priority Four: Lead at home and in the church.

As an overseer (one who watches over), the pastor leads the church (1 Tim. 5:17; 1 Thess. 5:12) as well as their family (1 Tim. 3:4). The word used for *lead* in the church is the same word for leading in the home. This is *not* dictatorial ruling. When I received my master's degree, I told my wife and kids they should meet me at the door saying, "Master, master ..." while bowing slightly. It didn't work! The word *lead* means "to stand before" or "to care with diligence." Rather than lording it over, the pastor must lead willingly with love and eagerness (1 Pet. 5:2-3).

Priority Five: Be a shepherd for God's people.

The perfect pastoral model is Jesus, who "calls his own sheep by name" and "sacrifices his life for the sheep" (John 10:3, 11). Jesus cares deeply for the needs of people (1 Pet. 5:7). The pastor feeds, watches over, guides, and protects the flock (John 21:15-17; Heb. 13:17), sharing this responsibility with the elders.

The Battle Charge for Pastors

"Fight the good fight" (1 Tim. 1:18) is a straightforward summons from Paul, who later said, "I have fought the good fight" (2 Tim. 4:7). The pastor's job is indeed battle—welcome to spiritual warfare. A pastor must be prepared to suffer for the gospel (2 Tim.1:8) and suffer hardship as a good soldier (2 Tim. 2:3; 4:5) since anyone who desires to live a godly life will be persecuted (2 Tim. 3:12).

Repeatedly, the Bible remind pastors to live a qualified life (1 Tim. 3:1-7; Titus 1:5-9), to be an example in speech, conduct, love, faith, and purity (1 Tim. 4:12), to pursue righteousness, godliness, faith, love, perseverance, and gentleness (1 Tim. 6:11), and to keep themselves pure (2 Tim. 2:21-22). These requirements apply to other leaders as well.

A pastor needs a strong faith and a clear conscience (1 Tim. 1:5), which some have abandoned and so suffered shipwreck (1 Tim. 1:18-20). God calls pastors to lead disciplined lives (1 Tim. 4:7), to pay close attention to themselves and their teaching (1 Tim. 4:16), and to guard the treasure entrusted to them (2 Tim. 1:14). Pastors must flee from the love of money (1 Tim. 6:9-11). Leaders motivated by money will self-destruct.

God expects this from pastors. He issues a specific, but not restrictive, call—a pastor may be involved in many other things as long as the primary responsibilities come first. Appendix 5 is a sample Ministry Position Description for a senior or lead pastor.

Fine-Tuning Expectations

In light of what God expects, I recommend a careful examination of the church's expectations. Several steps can guide the process.

1. **Identify the pastor's gifts and strengths.**

What's their sweet spot? What are the areas that bring them great joy and satisfaction? What are their spiritual gifts and their areas of greatest effectiveness? Paul told Timothy, "Do not neglect the spiritual gift you received through the prophecy spoken over you when the elders of the church laid their hands on you. Give your complete attention to these matters. Throw yourself into your tasks so that everyone will see your progress" (1 Tim. 4:14-15). In his second letter to Timothy, Paul circled back to the same topic. "This is why I remind you to fan into flames the spiritual gift God gave you when I laid my hands on you" (2 Tim. 1:6). The Greek word *zopuron*, translated "fan into flame," comes from *zoas*, a "live coal," and *pur*, "to blow and kindle into flame." Imagine leaders gathered around a campfire, throwing another log on the fire with affirmation and fanning it into flame with encouragement. When pastors concentrate on their area of greatest giftedness, everyone benefits.

2. **Identify the major tasks that drain the pastor.**

In simple terms, there are three areas in a pastor's ministry: preaching, people, and planning. Most pastors are strong in two of the three. Rarely are they outstanding in all three. Is administration difficult and unfulfilling for your pastor? Does the pastor struggle to develop vision and goals for the church? Is hospital, home visitation, or counseling a greater strength for another leader, not your pastor? Excessive time spent in meetings? The Francis A. Schaeffer Institute of Church Leadership Development reports that 50 percent of pastors spend an average of 3 to 4 hours a week in needless meetings, and 25 percent spend more than 5 hours a week.[4] Every ministry position includes some unpleasant tasks but, by and large, minimizing these areas invigorates everyone.

3. **Identify areas other leaders can assume responsibility.**

The pastor must be willing to allow others to do some tasks. Pastors often feel the need to be all things to all people, and they frequently have a hard time letting go. Select an administrative assistant to work alongside the pastor if the pastor is more effective in meeting with people than doing administrative work. If counseling consumes significant chunks of time, arrange for professional counseling referrals or train lay counselors. If a pastor's presence is not essential for a meeting, other people can attend and give the pastor a phone call to report the details.

4. **Identify areas that are optional for participation.**

   Everyone knows it's a lot more fun to show up for something when you're not required to be there. As a pastor, I enjoyed attending birthday parties, anniversary celebrations, and graduations whenever possible, but expecting your pastor to be at all of these events becomes more of a burden than a joy. Releasing a pastor from some obligations can make participating in an all-church workday, popping in for a youth group event, or visiting a home Bible study delightful again.

5. **Move the most important things to the top of the list.**

   The most important priorities are prayer and spiritual growth, followed by a healthy marriage and family relationship. These form the foundation for effective ministry. "You husbands must give honor to your wives. Treat your wife with understanding as you live together. She may be weaker than you are, but she is your equal partner in God's gift of new life. Treat her as you should so your prayers will not be hindered" (1 Pet. 3:7). Did you catch that last phrase? "So your prayers will not be hindered." Someone articulated it like this: the sighs of the wounded wife come between the husband's prayers and the ears of God. It is impossible to build a God-honoring, healthy, vibrant ministry while ignoring needs at home. Most people nod their heads in agreement, but the practice often doesn't get past the platitudes.

   Next, explain to the congregation, "We want our pastor and spouse to have time together every week and go on a date at least once or twice a month. When their children have an important event, we want them to be there. We cannot build a healthy church without building healthy marriages and families." Don't be surprised when you make this announcement and see long-time member Bill elbow his wife Sonja and whisper, "Did he say go on a date? When did we last go on a date?" Now, you're teaching by example.

STOPPING THE LOSS OF SPIRITUAL LEADERS

Pastoring is difficult work. Widely recognized management expert Peter Drucker told Pastor Steve Sjogren, "You know Steve, over the years, I have made a career out of studying the most challenging management roles out there. After all of that, I am now convinced the two most difficult jobs in the world are these—one, to be President of the United States, and two, to be the leader of a church like yours and Rick's (Warren)—where you start it then lead it to serve others in greatness. This week, after spending some quality time with you all, I am convinced of this—*the most difficult job is being one of those kinds of pastors.*"[5]

The loss of pastors in the ministry should cause everyone great concern. "When an army loses its officers, disaster is just around the corner," according to Ken Sande, Founder of Peacemaker Ministries. He continues, "Even a madman like Adolph Hitler understood this. Just before he launched his attack against the Soviet Union in 1941, he arranged for Stalin to see forged documents that indicated his own officers were conspiring against him. Gripped by paranoia, Stalin executed or imprisoned 35,000 top officers—over half of the Russian officer corps. When Germany launched its attack, the Russian army was headless and helpless and suffered staggering casualties and defeats."[6]

We're like the Russian army—losing far too many effective leaders from the ranks. Unrealistic expectations contribute to this loss. The Francis A. Schaeffer Institute of Church Leadership Development research indicates 41.27

percent of pastors have seriously considered leaving the ministry, and 18 percent will leave the ministry for a less stressful job.[7]

Overloaded expectations contribute to burnout for many pastors. Burnout fries the emotional circuitry. The battery goes dead, and it won't take a recharge. Remember, one-third of pastors are currently at high or medium risk of burnout,[8] and 71 percent report experiencing burnout at some point in their ministry.[9] One survey indicates that 52 percent of pastors feel they are overworked and can't meet their church's unrealistic expectations.[10]

Let's look at the interplay between unreasonable expectations and a lack of understanding.

A Lack of Understanding and Unrealistic Expectations

Frustrations mounted. "We can't move forward because this guy doesn't get his stuff done." A highly motivated, performance-driven leadership team was growing impatient and angry because of the non-performance of one group member. He faithfully attended meetings but repeatedly failed to complete his assignments. The agitation had risen over the months, and now there was talk of asking him to resign. Then someone learned his wife was battling stage four cancer. His day started at 4 a.m. and continued until late at night as he cared for his wife and held down his job.

No one in the group knew of the burden this brother carried. Instead, they judged him for not doing his job while oblivious to the crisis he faced. When asked why he didn't share about his wife's cancer, he replied, "Well, this is a business meeting, and I didn't feel it was appropriate to talk about personal problems." Board meetings in the business world may function this way, but not God Meetings—we share our lives and care for each other.

Lack of understanding fuels unreasonable expectations.

We make assumptions without knowing the facts. We judge others without insight into the challenges in their life—this lack of understanding is evident in three areas.

First, we fail to understand each other's pressure. Most volunteer leaders live highly pressured lives, balancing work, family, and church. Many are business executives who work long hours, and they do church ministry in addition. Unfortunately, pastors often overlook this in their expectations of volunteer leaders.

When we enter a God Meeting, God knows what's going on in every life. We come as we are—energized or exhausted, rejoicing or discouraged. We're fragile, weak human beings. Unlike God, the team doesn't know the pressures everyone faces. To remedy this, the first part of the meeting should offer an opportunity to "unpack your bags" and to check in regarding life. This may be, "Please pray for me. My boss just chewed me out this afternoon." Or "We need prayer. Our teenager is wreaking havoc in our home." As discussed earlier, cohorts or prayer partnerships of two or three praying together are a great way to facilitate unpacking your bags. Events—good or bad—in the last month, week, day, or even the previous two hours impact everyone's mindset. Leaders having difficulty paying their own monthly bills may struggle to consider a costly visionary venture for the church. A leader scarred by childhood sexual abuse may advocate a more stringent policy to prevent sexual abuse, and opposition may trigger a strong emotional reaction.

Second, we fail to understand each other's perspectives. Chuck Swindoll commented, "Pastors typically possess a theological or biblical perspective, a problem-solving method that they probably picked up in seminary. Board members tend to solve problems more pragmatically, using a tried-and-true method they learned in the business world.

It's the idealism/realism rub."[11] Ken Eichler stated, "Pastors should not expect board members to think like them, feel what they feel, or know what they know." How true.

Third, we fail to understand each other's passion. The CoreStrengths assessment tool discussed in Chapter 3 is simple to understand, but the ramifications are far-reaching. People usually have primary motivation in one of three areas: people, performance, and process. The people person is passionate about caring for the needy and may have difficulty understanding the process person who focuses on research and statistics. The performance person may be impatient with the process-motivated person who seems to overanalyze a decision, while the process person may resist the passionate plea of the people person unless backed with substantiated evidence. When presenting a proposal to a people-driven person, I talk about caring for the needs of people; for the performance-driven person, I talk about objectives and goals; for the process-driven analyzer, I bring statistical research on the topic. These are important bridges of understanding.

Turning Expectations into Expectancy

You've undoubtedly heard the phrase, "You have to believe in yourself." I tried that—what a disappointment. Solomon wisely cautioned, "A man is a fool to trust himself!" (Prov. 28:26 TLB). Miles Stanford observed, "To be disappointed with yourself is to have believed in yourself."[12] Expectations, whether of ourselves or someone else, rely on human performance, so expect a letdown. This is quite different than anticipating what God will do. Leslie Eichler, friend and Standing Stone Shepherd, wrote, "Take all of your expectations of what could be, should be, or will be, and set them at the foot of the cross. Then pick up the 'spirit of expectancy' and cover your minds and hearts with that. ... When you set aside your preconceived ideas of what *could have been*, or what *should have been*, or *what will be* in the future, you are creating space for the Lord to work in your life."[13]

The spirit of expectancy anticipates what God will do. If you hold unrealistic expectations of yourself, your spouse, or leaders in the church, disappointment lurks in the shadows. Set these down at the cross. Even with realistic expectations, you may be disappointed. On the other hand, expectancy anticipates and relies on God, looking forward in faith to what he will do.

Breathe deep of Jesus and remember his yoke is easy to bear, and his burden is light.

Live with surrendered expectations.

And you'll find rest for your soul. So will those around you.

REFLECTION AND DISCUSSION

Quick Recall

- What three priorities in a pastor's life tend to become numbers 22, 23, and 24?

- What is the NPC syndrome?

- What are the five things God expects of a pastor?

    Priority One: _____
    _____.
    Priority Two: _____
    _____.
    Priority Three: _____
    _____.
    Priority Four: _____
    _____.
    Priority Five: _____
    _____.

Thinking It Through

1. Do you feel the pressure of unrealistic expectations? How does this make you feel when you come up short?

2. Refer to the list of major tasks for a senior or lead pastor. How does this compare to the duties assigned to the lead pastor in your church?

3. What steps need to be taken to protect and prioritize spiritual growth and family health for your pastor? What about for each person on the leadership team?

4. What do you expect from your pastor's spouse? Is it realistic and appropriate?

I solemnly urge you in the presence of God and Christ Jesus, who will someday judge the living and the dead when he comes to set up his Kingdom: Preach the word of God. Be prepared, whether the time is favorable or not. Patiently correct, rebuke, and encourage your people with good teaching.

For a time is coming when people will no longer listen to sound and wholesome teaching. They will follow their own desires and will look for teachers who will tell them whatever their itching ears want to hear. They will reject the truth and chase after myths. (2 Tim. 4:1-4)

—12—

STORM NO. 2: UNREALISTIC SCHEDULE

PREVENTING BURNOUT AND FAMILY BREAKDOWN

Bright, gifted, driven leaders are crashing, bringing pain to themselves, their families, and their ministries. A frightening number of flameouts occur due to unchecked busyness. An unrealistic pace of life precedes danger.

Sometimes this relentless pace of life is imposed by others, like the church or the leadership team. But more often than not, the internal drive of the leader propels them. Ministry happens 24/7, and spiritual leaders often feel guilty—"I can't do enough"—which gets translated, "I'm not good enough." This restless, submerged pressure and fear fuels drivenness. A by-product of drivenness is shallowness since there is little time to cultivate intimacy with God and others. Being *driven* is quite different than being *directed* by the Holy Spirit.

In *Overwhelmed,* Perry Noble speaks candidly about his unrealistic pace of life while building a megachurch.

He started NewSpring Church with 115 people in the first service. Three years later, three thousand attended, and thirteen years later, it was recognized as number two on America's Fastest-Growing Churches list. Perry worked up to eighty hours per week while functioning on four to five hours of sleep. Outwardly, he was a fantastic success; inwardly, he was falling apart. A friend warned him, "Your pace is unsustainable. You are going way too fast." Perry quickly replied, "The devil never takes a day off." His friend wisely countered, "I'm not sure the devil is supposed to be your example." With his life spinning out of control, Perry finally acknowledged his condition.

- Some nights I couldn't sleep … even with the assistance of medicine. And as I lay awake, I would worry and obsess over things that were completely out of my control.
- I began to distance myself from people who were close to me.
- I thought about leaving everyone and everything behind and starting all over again.
- I couldn't recall the last time I'd had fun.
- I sank into a deep depression and began having panic attacks.
- Worry became my go-to emotion.
- Everything that happened to me had a dramatic impact on my emotions, whether positive or negative. Emotionally speaking, I was a roller coaster.
- I kept telling myself that what I was going through was simply a season and that once my schedule became less hectic and my responsibilities decreased, I would be fine.[1]

Things didn't change. The frantic pace of ministry continued as Perry's inner life unraveled. During this time, a counselor told him, "The Bible calls those who will not work lazy, but it calls those who will not rest disobedient."[2] He admits hating the word rest. His troubles deepened as alcoholism gripped his life, and he and his wife separated. The church leaders lovingly came alongside, but Perry refused their recommended corrections. Finally, he was dismissed from NewSpring Church, leaving behind a debt load of $47 million. Two years later, the church leaders amended the bylaws to reflect that Jesus Christ is the senior pastor over a team-led church model, consisting of four lead pastors and three teaching pastors.[3] Perry Noble started a new church, appropriately named Second Chance Church.

I understand Perry Noble. I was raised to be a workaholic, and I didn't disappoint. My addiction settled in early and has trailed me ever since. I grew up thinking Labor Day was a workday since my dad always announced, "It's Labor Day. It's time to go to work." So I was honestly surprised to discover families went swimming and had picnics and backyard barbeques on Labor Day. I honor my father for many things I learned from him, though I regret never having a close relationship. For Dad, work spelled worth—or so it seemed. He worked from early morning until late at night and expected a hot meal, whether he came in at 7, 9, or 11 p.m. There must have been times when the entire family shared an evening meal and relaxed together in the living room, but I don't recall any. Like father, like son, I learned a driven lifestyle and carried it with me for many years. Many pastors grew up in homes like mine.

Turbocharged

This I-can't-get-it-all-done worry plagues many leaders. Thankfully, the Bible provides no shortage of teaching on this subject. Luke's gospel describes Martha as a there's-so-much-to-do person. In Luke chapter ten, we read of

Martha preparing the meal for Jesus, the disciples, Mary, and probably Lazarus—sixteen or more people. No small task. As Martha fretted about the fixin's for the meal, frustrated that her sister didn't help more, Jesus lovingly pressed in: "My dear Martha, you are worried and upset over all these details! There is only one thing worth being concerned about. Mary has discovered it, and it will not be taken away from her" (Luke 10:41-42). Was Mary lazy, shirking her duty? Jesus wouldn't approve of that. In translating this, the text makes it clear Martha's sister Mary *also* sat at Jesus's feet (Lk. 10:39). The word *also* is the Greek word *kai*, meaning "and or in addition to." This gives us a clue that Mary helped out in the kitchen and also sat with Jesus. I think Martha may have been in a tizzy over unnecessarily elaborate details.

The Greek word, *merimnao*, translated *worried* in this passage, means "to split the mind." A similar modern statement might be, "I have a splitting headache." A worried mind darts about like a heat-seeking missile, attaching to things that have to get done, with little discernment between the urgent and the unimportant. Worry stokes a fire of fear inside—what if I can't get it all done? Jesus tells Martha she is upset, using the Greek word *turbazo*, the source for our English word *turbocharged*. It's one thing to turbocharge your car, but quite another to turbocharge your emotional system. It's like Jesus is saying, "Martha, you're revving your engine. Take your foot off the pedal."

Life in the Fast Lane

I always liked sports cars, since my dad was a small-town Chevy dealer, and I rushed into schooling and ministry like a turbocharged Corvette entering the racetrack. Working to earn my way through Biola University, the schedule was an adrenaline-driven addiction. I went to class in the morning, painted houses or other jobs in the afternoon, served on the student council every year, and studied nights at Denny's restaurant near the school, spending the entire night a few times. With all the coffee I drank, I didn't sweat—I percolated. Friends thought I was so wired I could jump-start a car without booster cables. Later, I joked that I should have invited the Denny's staff to my graduation—I would never have made it without them.

My college buddies decided to have a Saturday morning Bible study. After an exhausting week, you'd think we'd sleep in and meet at 9 a.m. But, no, we scheduled it for Saturday mornings at 6 a.m. to prove our spirituality, self-discipline ... and stupidity. The first half-hour was a lot of crowing about how exhausted and short on sleep we were. One morning after our cawing, my brother, Carl, who was usually quiet and observant, read the verse, "It is senseless for you to work so hard from early morning until late at night, fearing you will starve to death; for God wants his loved ones to get their proper rest" (Ps. 127:2 TLB). A stunned silence descended—as if someone had gone through the room and popped every ego balloon.

Joanne and I married when she had two years to complete the nursing program at Biola, and I had one more year of college and three years of seminary. To our delight and surprise, our daughter, Julie, was born thirteen months after our wedding. I was going to school full time, helping with the baby, working nights loading trucks to pay the bills, and speaking in churches and camps. I didn't have the good sense to take my seminary training at a slower pace.

Looking back, I see how dysfunctional and out-of-balance my life was. I recall my two-year-old daughter, Julie, sitting at my little manual typewriter so grown-up-like. As she was pretending to type, she turned her head and announced, "Don't bother me. I'm busy!" I knew where she'd learned that.

I was talking recently with one of my friends, a medical doctor. I said, "You know, the way we were trained is a contradiction. The brightest and best young men and women are sent to the finest medical or ministry schools that require studying hard, sleeping little, living highly stressed lives, eating fast food on the run, so they can graduate and teach others how to control stress, slow down, eat right, be healthy, exercise, and live a balanced life." He nodded his head in agreement.

Once I started my first ministry position, I continued the pace I was accustomed to, while pursuing additional graduate studies. If there was an unscheduled evening, I remember feeling anxious and guilty. How could I sit home doing nothing? At the very least, I should be making phone calls or planning my schedule. I was driven and restless.

I tell you all this to reveal that I played the game. I also know the pain. I was away far too many evenings because of a "crisis in the ministry." I would give anything to redo those years. My two daughters have chosen to follow the Lord, but that is by God's grace—not because I was there for them when they needed me. My eyes grow moist, and my heart breaks as I write this.

In my first ministry position, the pastor training me was more driven than I was. He thought nothing of speaking on Sunday morning and evening and then teaching five or more Bible studies a week while doing marriage counseling for fifteen to twenty hours a week. He shared his philosophy with me. "I've told God that I'll take care of the church, and he will have to take care of my children since I'm doing his work." Bad advice.

My advice to every ministry or lay leader: busyness never glorifies God. As pastor and theologian Dallas Willard put it, to follow Christ you must ruthlessly eliminate hurry from your life.[4] Are you ready for that?

An Unrealistic Schedule

A pastor's schedule is an anomaly. Their week is a combination of a job and ministry in one package. Surprisingly, many people expect the pastor to be in the office from 9 a.m. to 5 p.m., even though the pastor has evening meetings and weekend responsibilities. Few pastors survive working nine to five plus four or five nights a week and weekends while on-call 24/7. This chapter intends to prompt a healthy discussion at the leadership level.

Recently, a Christian leader told me that one of his very vocal board members insists he should work eighty to ninety hours per week. The board member says if you love Jesus and are committed to the cause, how could you do anything less than give your all? I'd ask, "At what cost?" Consider the story of Bob Pierce.

Bob Pierce was an energetic, driven man out to evangelize the world. His philosophy was to "burn out, not rust out," for God. In 1947, Pierce visited China, and thousands came to Christ during four months of evangelistic meetings. Everywhere he turned, impoverished people fought hunger and the threat of communism. This gripped him deeply. China soon closed, but Pierce continued his crusade, toting a camera across Asia to show the pictures of starving children to Christians in America. His cause was incorporated in 1950 as World Vision. In his Bible, Pierce wrote these words: "Let my heart be broken with the things that break the heart of God."

Bob impacted thousands for Christ, but in caring for the children of the world, he neglected his own children. One of my early writing coaches, Tim Stafford, writes,

> The same intensity led to his downfall. He had an ungoverned temper and frequently clashed with the World Vision board, particularly over his insistence on

making financial commitments on the fly. He traveled as much as 10 months of the year, and his family suffered. "I've made an agreement with God," he said, "that I'll take care of his helpless little lambs overseas if he'll take care of mine at home." In 1963 he had a nervous breakdown. For nine months he almost disappeared, preferring to travel the world rather than return home. In 1967 he resigned from World Vision, bitter at those whom he felt interfered with his organization. On a 1968 good-bye tour of Asia, his daughter Sharon reached him by phone. She asked if he could come home, but he refused, saying that he wanted to extend his trip to Vietnam. His wife, Lorraine, started home immediately, but by the time she arrived, Sharon had tried to commit suicide. Later that year, she tried again and succeeded.

By then Pierce was hospitalized in Switzerland. He would stay there for a year, treated with insulin and other drugs. The following year, he took over a small hunger organization that became Samaritan's Purse. In 1970 he legally separated from his wife. His daughter Marilee wrote that his memory was "badly crippled" and his mind "frequently unclear." Just once, in September 1978, the family was able to gather for an evening of reconciliation. Four days later, Pierce died.[5]

An unrealistic schedule is the second of a swirling convergence of storms that bring shipwreck.

Investing Time Wisely

Time is one of our most valuable gifts from God, and, like everything else in our lives, it belongs to him. David prayed, "Lord, remind me how brief my time on earth will be. Remind me that my days are numbered—how fleeting my life is. You have made my life no longer than the width of my hand. My entire lifetime is just a moment to you; at best, each of us is but a breath" (Ps. 39:4-5). James echoes much the same thought, "How do you know what your life will be like tomorrow? Your life is like the morning fog—it's here a little while, then it's gone" (James 4:14). My friend, motivational speaker Willie Jolley, shared this with me.

> I have only a minute, only sixty seconds in it.
> Forced upon me, can't refuse it.
> Didn't seek it, didn't choose it.
> But it's up to me to use it.
> I must suffer if I lose it.
> Give account if I abuse it.
> Just a tiny little minute, but eternity is in it.[6]

Of course, every minute is valuable, but how does this relate to being a driven workaholic? How can we not be turbocharged when there is so much to do?

Paul precedes the classic section on being filled with the Holy Spirit with this instruction, "Therefore be careful how you walk, not as unwise men but as wise, making the most of your time, because the days are evil" (Eph. 5:15-16 NASB). At first glance, this would seem to support the driven, turbocharged mindset. Not so. There were two words for time in the Greek language. One was *chronos*, a *quantity of time*—months, weeks, days, hours, minutes. The word used for *time* in Ephesians 5:16, however, is *kairos* which emphasizes the *quality of time*. Chronos is a measure of time; kairos is the value of a moment in time. We don't have an equivalent word in English for kairos, but opportunity comes closest. In Greek mythology, the Greek god Kairos is pictured as "running swiftly, balancing on a razor's edge, bald but with a lock of hair on the forehead."[7] To capture Kairos, you had to grab the tuft of his hair as he streaked by, or he was gone. It reminds me of the plight of baldness, "It's hair today and gone tomorrow." Kairos is the fleeting moment of opportunity that comes and passes in the blink of an eye.

Chronos is living by the clock. Kairos is capturing the moment. The workaholic may be driven to use every minute (chronos) and miss the strategic opportunity (kairos). There have been times when I was so chronos driven that I missed a kairos moment to care for someone. The chronos person is obsessive. The kairos person is opportunistic—focused but flexible. One lifestyle is rushed anxiety; the other is relaxed availability. It's the difference between being guilt driven or led by the Spirit.

When your children are young, priceless kairos opportunities quickly slip by. A kairos moment hangs in the balance when your son or daughter asks to shoot some baskets in the backyard or help bake cookies. A kairos mindset allows you to set work aside and walk hand-in-hand with your spouse in the park or at the beach. Bumping into someone you know in the grocery store while you're rushing to get your shopping done could be a kairos moment. Paul said, "Therefore, whenever we have the opportunity [Grk. *kairos*], we should do good to everyone—especially to those in the family of faith" (Gal. 6:10 bracketed insert mine). Capturing the kairos moment means giving full attention to the person in front of you. Coming alongside a hurting person with a tender touch and a warm smile reveals kairos priorities. Sharing your faith with someone who asks, "How do you cope with life?" provides a kairos opportunity—an open door for a brief moment. Don't let it slip by.

Is chronos, then, our enemy? By no means! The New Testament never identifies chronos and kairos as mutually exclusive. Chronos is the larger and more inclusive term and embraces all kairos moments, but not conversely. A healthy outlook balances chronos and kairos. The wise person will guard their time (chronos) to achieve certain goals while being alert to the unexpected opportunities (kairos) God brings their way. Being filled with and listening to the Holy Spirit (Eph. 5:18) is the key to balancing the two.

The Chronos-driven, Chin-down Leader

Losing perspective of the big picture usually accompanies an overloaded schedule. If you run from one crisis to the next, you have little time to step back, observe, and discern. When rushed, we're prone to misread a subtle comment or fail to notice the hurt look on a person's face. People tense up around a chronos-driven person because the conversation is difficult with someone who's constantly revving their engine to get more done. According to *Fortune* magazine "A chindown manager has his chin so buried in today's emergencies that he does not have time to raise his head to look around."[8] Sadly, we all know people like this.

Exhausted leaders make others tired just watching them. The chaos impacts everyone in the organization and conflicts follow, further compounding the chaos. The out-of-control leader then loses perspective of the pressure others face—the struggle to fit their schedule around the mania of the leader's schedule—and resentment, frustration, and a lack of respect multiply.

Instead of chin-down management with a frown, practice chin-up leadership with a smile by wandering about, intentionally greeting people, and observing the ministry. It's a great opportunity to encourage others, and you'll learn a lot by listening.

Twenty-one Units in a Week

Many years ago, I had breakfast with Jay Kesler, then President of Youth for Christ (YFC). Our conversation landed on ministry priorities and schedules. He revealed, "YFC leaders charge into ministry with little sense of balance. They think nothing of being out five or six nights a week. As a result, they run themselves ragged and damage their marriages." And then he said something that stunned me. "We tell our YFC staff there are three parts to the waking portion of the day: morning, afternoon, and evening. You owe two of the three to your job, and you owe one to growing in your relationship with God and your family. In other words, if you're out in the evening, you need to be home during the morning or afternoon. If you don't practice this, you will crash and burn in ministry." I had never heard such a concept, and I certainly wasn't practicing it.

Armed with Jay Kesler's wisdom, I hit on a new way to build accountability and balance into a pastoral schedule. Since that time, I have used this in my own life, trained staff members to employ it, and shared it with many pastors, leadership teams, and congregations. When I share this, I see the lights of understanding come on. This mindset brings new freedom to the ministry and provides a practical way to manage a schedule often misunderstood. Even though I'm speaking about full-time ministry leaders, I hope volunteer leaders will find this tool helpful to assess and balance their schedules as well.

Building on the principle of two parts of the day to your work and one part to growing in your spiritual relationship with God and your family, how does this take shape in a pastor's week? There are twenty-one units in a week, seven mornings, seven afternoons, and seven evenings. I call it a Balance 21 Schedule. The following sample schedule of a senior or lead pastor shows how easily, and severely many pastors' lives careen out of balance.

Pastor's Sample Weekly Schedule on Overload

Time	Sunday	Monday	Tuesday	Wednesday	Thursday	Friday	Saturday
M O R N	Sunday Worship Services	Office	Staff Meeting & Prayer	Study	Study	Scheduled Day Off Hospital Emergency	Men's Breakfast Hospital Visit
A F T	Lunch & Hosting Missionary Family	Office	Office Staff App'ts.	Office	Office	Home & Family	Crisis Marriage Counseling
E V E	Leading Small Group	Home & Family	Leadership Team or Other Comm.	Prayer Group & Worship Team	Home & Family	Church Event & Dinner	Study and Prayer

This pastor works eighteen of a possible twenty-one units, leaving the family with leftovers—three units or blocks of time. There is little time for quiet and reflective intimacy with God. This schedule is destructive to long-term ministry health and the family of the pastor—a predictor of potential disaster. You will notice the pastor scheduled a day off, but was it? He may not have been in the office, but he got a call regarding a hospital emergency, so he spent most of the morning at the hospital. He zoned out at home for a while in the afternoon, but a church event consumed the evening. It was a Sabbath gone sour.

What has been squeezed out of the pastor's life in this schedule? The good part. Back to Jesus's words to Martha about her sister, "Mary has chosen the good part" (Lk. 10:42 NASB). The word *good* also means best or excellent. What Mary chose was the sumptuous, extravagant portion of the meal—the main course! Mary made room for what matters most. What was that? Time to worship at Jesus's feet. Without it, we have nothing of substance to give others, let alone survive ourselves. As leaders, how can we lead and care for the souls of others when our soul is empty? Not well.

A Kairos Schedule with Margin

Using the Balance 21 Schedule planner, let's look at a pastoral schedule with margin on the next page.

Pastor's Sample "Balance 21" Weekly Schedule with Margin

Time	Sunday	Monday	Tuesday	Wednesday	Thursday	Friday	Saturday
M O R N	Sunday Worship Services	Sabbath Day of Rest	Study	Study	Study	Study	Shepherds' Meeting (1x/mo) / Home Maint. & Projects
A F T	Lunch with Friends / Rest	Reading and Recreation	Staff Meeting & App'ts.	Office App'ts. & Planning Meetings	Margin for Urgent Needs	Hospital Emergency / Office Counseling Marriage in Crisis	Son's Baseball Game
E V E	Leading Small Group	Date with Spouse	Home & Family	Leadership Team or Worship Team	Home & Family	Dinner with Close Friends	Study and Prayer

I recognize this is idealistic—very few weeks fit this pattern perfectly. Caring for people is often messy and unpredictable, and it's impossible to anticipate everything that will come up Sunday to Saturday. This schedule preserves margin, which "is the space between our load and our limits. It is the amount allowed beyond that which is needed. It is something held in reserve for contingencies or unanticipated situations. Margin is the gap between rest and exhaustion, the space between breathing freely and suffocating. Margin is the opposite of overload. If we are overloaded, we have no margin."[9] A schedule helps but expecting the same things to work every week is a setup for frustration. Robert Thune, son of my life-long friend Bob, described one of his weeks as a pastor.

> Last week, a young woman in our church slept with her non-Christian boyfriend, then took the "morning-after" pill. She is wracked with guilt and shame. A couple plagued by infertility finally got pregnant, only to experience a miscarriage. They are grieved and angry with God. A homosexually-tempted man who recently came to know Jesus overdosed on crystal meth—for the second time this month. He is needy and confused. An older couple got a phone call that their twenty-something son had been thrown in jail on drug and alcohol charges. They are unsure how to respond. And this is just in the past seven days![10]

This is emotionally draining stuff. Ministry is unpredictable. Carefully guard your time alone with God and your family and go with the flow allowing the Holy Spirit to guide and direct.

Using the schedule on the previous page for illustration, let's imagine this is lead Pastor Joshua and his wife, Sophia, a registered nurse. They have two boys and a girl, ages twelve, nine, and six. Rather than working eighteen units, Joshua works eleven or twelve units. The Saturday morning meeting with the leadership team is once a month, allowing time for yard work, paying bills, or household repairs on the other Saturdays. Sometimes emergencies come up, and it becomes thirteen or fourteen units. He has his hands full, keeping up with church ministry along with his growing family.

There are three relational areas for a healthy ministry: relationships with God, family, and people. All three are essential, and maintaining a balance between the three is not easy. As you analyze the schedule above, look for the time invested in the three areas.

Time with God. As the preaching pastor, Joshua has wisely set aside the morning hours during the week to study and pray. This nourishes his soul, ignites his spiritual fire, and allows God to speak and direct him. The amount of time to prepare a message will vary from one pastor to another, though fifteen to twenty hours seems to be the norm for most. All leaders—senior pastors, associates, ministry directors, and volunteer leaders—need thirty minutes to an hour, preferably at the beginning of the day, to cultivate their relationship with God.

Time with family. Pastor Joshua has a Sabbath rest on Monday and enjoys a date with Sophia in the evening. Yeah! While his week is full and busy, he also makes time for his son's baseball game on Saturday. Wise father. There are also evenings available to meet with people, including friends, extended family, or a neighbor.

I spotted a cartoon showing the pastor and his wife sitting on a couch reviewing his packed calendar. She says, "God loves you … and everyone has a plan for your life." It's easy to allow others to fill your calendar rather than making time for what is most important. Years ago, in my first year at a church, I went to twenty-three Christmas events in twenty-one days leading up to Christmas. Everyone expected their new pastor to attend their group event, and, of course, every occasion featured festive food. When Christmas arrived, I was exhausted and felt like the gospel blimp. I struggled with a month of depression following this and learned a hard lesson.

Joanne and I intended to have weekly dates, but the calendar would fill up somewhat like osmosis. So we now schedule our time together in advance and write it in our calendars. When someone calls, I say, "I'd love to, but I'm scheduled for that time." However, we're not rigid about this. If the request is vitally important, we talk it over and reschedule our time together. We limit the number of evenings away from home for our balance and healthy home life.

Time with people. Pastor Joshua isn't isolated from people. Some pastors hibernate, preparing sermons for thirty-five to forty hours a week, and spending little time with people. Their messages may be superb, but the sheep begin to feel distant from their shepherd. Shepherds know their sheep and the sheep know them. People need a shepherd who spends time with them, communicating care and personal concern. When someone asks if I have a few minutes to talk, I sometimes reply, "I was just looking for something to do." And I sincerely mean it. This is a kairos response, and it communicates a relaxed availability. In Bangor, Wales, shepherds who prefer warming themselves by the fire have developed an electronic beeper attached to the sheep to track their wanderings. It's called the Bangor Orange Position Estimating Equipment for Pastures or BO PEEP for short.[11] I admit this is a unique invention for a lazy shepherd, but biblical shepherding is far more than beepers, tracking devices, and databases. There is no substitute for face-to-face involvement with the flock.

Being an accessible and relational pastor matters to God. Paul identifies the three-fold work of shepherds: "We request of you, brethren, that you appreciate those who diligently labor among you, and have charge over you in the Lord and give you instruction" (1 Thess. 5:12 NASB). Notice the phrase "among you." This is being available and approachable. It's rubbing shoulders, interacting, and working together.

There are dozens of variations for the Balance 21 Schedule. I invite you to discover the flow that works best for you. When life gets out of balance, and we don't make time for the restoration of mind, body, and soul, we cannot perform at our best.

God's Gifts for a Healthy You

God also has three wonderful gifts for you to stay refreshed and balanced.

1. God's Gift of Soul Care

Where do you find rest in a restless world? I heard a speaker who chose "Come Apart and Rest" from Mark 6:31 for his message title. The thought crossed my mind that many are practicing the first two words—they are "coming apart." Their marriages are coming apart, their families are coming apart, their careers are coming apart, and their health is falling apart. But where is the rest?

Soul-satisfying rest comes from one source and only one. "You have made us for yourself, O Lord, and our heart is restless until it rests in you," Augustine concluded after his futile search of hedonistic pleasure and other religions.[12] God promises that he "gives power to the weak and strength to the powerless. Even youths will become weak and tired, and young men will fall in exhaustion. But those who trust in the LORD will find new strength. They will soar high on wings like eagles. They will run and not grow weary. They will walk and not faint" (Isa. 40:29-31).

Why do we become tired? God could have designed us perpetually energized; instead, we tire often—daily. The next time you're exhausted, *remind yourself tiredness is God calling you to himself.* Connect your soul with your Creator like a child who crawls into daddy's lap at the end of an exhausting day. Tiredness is a constant reminder of your need for soul care.

The soul is the home of everything in me—my mind, feelings, desires, people, events, disappointments, fears, and dreams. The soul is who I am—the intersection of my past and present and the birthplace of my future.

Self-care, a word familiar to the secular world, is caring for your physical, mental, and emotional needs. Soul care is spiritual self-care—taking time to care for your inner spiritual well-being. When you spend time alone with God—reading, listening, meditating, and praying—your spiritual battery recharges. God heals the wounds, calms the storms, and clarifies the perplexities of life. Like water to a desert wanderer, soul care satisfies the inner thirst for peace and purpose.

Sermon preparation is not the same as soul care. Preparing a weekly message was a pressure I lived with every week. Sometimes it flowed easily, but most of the time, it was intense and demanding work. So while message preparation includes time in the Word and prayer, it's different than soul care—private time with God. Soul care and sermon preparation are not mutually exclusive, but the purpose is different. Sermon preparation is for others; soul care is personal. Sermon preparation has a deadline; soul care is unhurried. Sermon preparation is highly important; soul care is what matters most.

2. God's Gift of Sleep

Remember those college days when we pulled all-nighters, cramming for a final? Now we know we were probably making it harder on ourselves to remember and concentrate on the exam. Joanne, as a psychiatric nurse, writes this section.

Medical science has come a long way in understanding what happens when we sleep and when we don't. Not only does sleep bring rest to our bodies, but it also impacts our emotional stability and mood. Poor sleep disrupts the amygdala in combination with the prefrontal cortex, creating mood swings and erratic behavior. As a result, 50 to 90 percent of the roughly forty million American adults who suffer from depression and anxiety suffer from sleep deprivation. In addition, 75 percent of people with ADHD have insomnia.[13]

The Center for Disease Control has identified medical diseases such as diabetes, cardiovascular disease, obesity, elevated blood pressure, memory loss, an increase in beta-amyloid in the brain, and metabolic changes (with weight gain) as outcomes of sleep deprivation. "Beta-amyloid is a metabolic waste product that's found in the fluid between brain cells (neurons). A buildup of beta-amyloid is linked to impaired brain function and Alzheimer's disease."[14]

An essential part of your weekly schedule includes adequate rest, which science tells us is seven to nine hours a night. You may feel it's impossible to get everything done in the fifteen to seventeen hours remaining, but you may be surprised how much more focused and pleasant you are to be around when your brain has done its work overnight.

However, sleep and rest are not necessarily the same thing. We generally think of rest as getting enough sleep, but it's so much more than that. Sometimes after a good night of sleep, you awaken still exhausted—emotionally drained, lacking creativity and energy. This is an accumulation of long hours, high-stress living, and emotionally draining events or relationships. God has a solution to refresh and renew every week.

3. God's Gift of the Sabbath

What day is the Sabbath for a pastor? Some folks think it's Sunday. I assure you, Sunday is not a day of rest for a pastor. The biblical word Sabbath means simply "rest, a cessation from labor."[15] This is a God-given principle for health and well-being. I know from personal experience that when I fail to take a Sabbath day of rest, I begin to malfunction on the tenth or eleventh day. I spin my wheels on projects, my creative edge to write or study is gone, and I get grumpy and irritable. Research by Baylor University shows the rate of obesity rises to nine out of ten for those who work more than seventy hours per week and do not take a Sabbath day of rest.[16] God created the Sabbath rest for our benefit.

Jesus said, "The Sabbath was made to meet the needs of people, and not people to meet the requirements of the Sabbath" (Mk. 2:27). A day off is not necessarily a Sabbath. The day off may include mowing the lawn, fixing the leaking sink, or shopping. But the Sabbath is different. The Sabbath is a multifaceted gem, a day of rest and refreshment, a wonderful gift from God. There are at least six dimensions to Sabbath rest: spiritual, physical, mental, emotional, relational, and sensory.

The first dimension of the Sabbath is *spiritual rest.* "So there is a special rest [a Sabbath rest] still waiting for the people of God. For all who have entered into God's rest have rested from their labors, just as God did after creating the world. So let us do our best to enter that rest. But if we disobey God, as the people of Israel did, we will fall" (Heb. 4:9-11). While the believer experiences daily rest by walking in faith and obedience, the word for *rest* at the beginning of verse 9 is a different Greek word meaning specifically a Sabbath rest—ceasing work on the seventh day as God did after completing creation. It is a day of surrendering our anxieties, replacing push and panic with peace, striving with serenity. Slow your system and breathe deeply of God's grace.

There is a place reserved for you at God's banquet. The Sabbath day celebrates completion—we are complete in him (Col. 2:10), lacking nothing. "God has given us everything we need for living a godly life" (2 Pet. 1:3). Practicing the Sabbath is an act of faith that demonstrates you believe God will help you get your work done without working on that seventh day. Failing to enter into rest sets us up for a fall (Heb. 4:11). We're more vulnerable to temptation. We're more prone to be grumpy, lose our temper, overeat, entertain lustful thoughts, and worry when we fail to enter God's rest.

Okay, it's your Sabbath, and there's a spiritual feast waiting. What's on the menu? First, it's spiritual rest and refreshment. That means time to listen to God and read his Word. It's a day of adoration and praise, singing and meditating, confessing sin, and renewing your spiritual commitment. But the Sabbath also includes **physical rest**. Cease your labor. Give your body and mind a break. Set aside the projects, both at home and work. Rest may be active as well as passive. If you work in an office all week, do something different. Part of your Sabbath may be getting outdoors for a hike or a bike ride. If you do hard physical labor all week, enjoy a snooze in your recliner. What is restful for one person may be quite the opposite for someone else. Discover what refreshes you.

Keep in mind, a truly restful Sabbath doesn't happen without preparation. I attempt to wrap up my work projects the day before the Sabbath, clean out my email and texts, and assign things pressing on my mind for the following week. When Joanne was young, her family planned for their Sabbath by dividing and conquering. It was all hands on deck as mom shopped and baked for the Sunday meal, the girls took on the housecleaning, and dad and brother washed the car and completed outdoor chores. Shoes were shined, and shirts were pressed. Those were simpler days, but you get the gist. You have to plan to make it happen.

In addition to spiritual and physical rest, the Sabbath offers **mental and emotional rest.** Step aside from the things that cause mental and emotional fatigue in your life. Journaling is a good way to release the emotions from the week and an effective way to talk with God about the future. If the news makes you anxious, take a break from it and read a book that is uplifting and encouraging.

Few think of this, but you also need **relational rest.** Some relationships are draining while others are restoring. Discern the difference between the two. Do you need time alone? Or perhaps time with a special friend will bring refreshment to your soul.

Another dimension of Sabbath rest is **sensory rest**, that is, refreshment for your five senses: sight, sound, smell, taste, and touch. "Sensory rest is about giving your senses a break. People need sensory rest when they overwhelm their senses with constant stimuli. ... Unplug. Spend some time away from your electronics."[17] Perhaps you can go for a drive or spend time in a park or arboretum enjoying the quiet and refreshing sights, sounds, and smells. God has a front-row seat reserved for you in his theater.

CARING FOR THOSE WHO CARE FOR YOU

Pastors need pastors. Shepherds need shepherds. Pastors faithfully serving God are going to take hits—usually every week. Attacks may take the form of an unresolved conflict, underhanded criticism, or a feeling of personal despair and depletion. Who does your pastor talk to? Easily 80 percent of the hits a pastor takes can't be discussed with the congregation, and many of them are off-limits to share with other leaders. Solomon said, "By yourself you're unprotected. With a friend you can face the worst" (Eccl. 4:12 MSG). Standing Stone Shepherds are veteran pastors and ministry leaders who come alongside pastors and spouses, providing a completely confidential relationship. While they never charge for their service, this is one of the best insurance policies you can have for your pastor. Every pastor needs a pastor. Even Billy Graham realized his need for a pastor. Don Wilton served in this role. "During his weekly visits with the Grahams (and, after Ruth died, with Billy alone), the two men spent a lot of time together. 'There were countless times when we would sit together in the kitchen or on the lawn overlooking the Smoky Mountains,' Wilton said. On other occasions, 'we would laugh our heads off.'"[18]

This chapter intends to invite healthy discussion at the leadership level. Spend a session with your pastor discussing the pressure points in their schedule. Is it balanced? Is there sufficient time for God? For family? If there are misunderstandings, this is an excellent opportunity to discuss and work them through. This is often a sensitive area, so provide a friendly dialogue with ample understanding and acceptance. Avoid being rigid and dogmatic. Ultimately a pastor must follow the leading of the Holy Spirit regarding the investment of their time.

For volunteer leaders, how are you handling the demands placed on you? Most of you walk a tight rope of long hours in your work, church responsibilities, and time for personal growth and family. As a shepherd, the lead pastor needs to promote a balanced margin for staff and volunteers.

It's helpful if the leadership team communicates the Balance 21 Schedule to the congregation with a very general flow of the pastor's schedule. Help them understand why the Sabbath day of rest is essential, along with soul care and family time. It's very difficult for a pastor to explain this without coming across as defensive or self-serving.

Here's a bonus idea that will pay long-term dividends. For churches committed to keeping the pastoral marriage relationship strong, let me suggest you allow the pastor and spouse to have a weekend to themselves every fifth Sunday. Arrange for a guest speaker or another member of the staff to preach. This should not count toward their annual vacation. Many people in the congregation have Saturday and Sunday away from their work every week. In contrast, a pastor and spouse rarely have two full days away from the pressure.

As leaders, let me also encourage you to provide a Standing Stone Retreat for your pastoral couple. Some churches are sending their entire ministry staff, one couple at a time. Standing Stone Retreats are led by a couple who understand the pressures of ministry. Each day there is a discussion of an important topic: marriage and family, strengths, balance, life journey, personal hurt or disappointment, and an entire day spent dreamstorming. Most couples discover a road map for their lives and ministry for the next five to ten years. The goal is to help the couple feel listened to and exclusively cherished. As a result, the couple and the retreat shepherds develop a lasting bond and ongoing relationship for years to come. Check it out at www.standingstoneministry.org.

Balance Instead of Busyness

It's time to break the trend and return a sensible balance to doing the Lord's work by caring for our spiritual well-being and families. Scripture says, "God's promise of entering his rest still stands" (Heb. 4:1). Stephen W. Smith said,

> The Chinese word for "'busyness" means "heart annihilation." We are literally killing ourselves through the speed in which we are living and all that we are trying to accomplish. Many leaders run their lives on empty—believing that inner emptiness is all there is. Wrong. We are doing way too much, and what's worse, we don't know how to stop or live within our limits. A busy leader often lives in fifth gear, having stripped their soul of all the lower gears. It's as if you can almost smell the burnt odor as fretful leaders move around town. The nonstop, ever busy, and burned-out soul of a leader's life is a clear sign that dark clouds are brewing.[19]

I need that reminder.

I think I'll shift into a lower gear and do some slow-moving meditation on my bike. The wonders of what God created leave me breathless ... as does the bike ride!

REFLECTION AND DISCUSSION

Quick Recall

- There are three parts to the waking portion of the day: morning, afternoon, and evening. You owe _____ to your job, and you owe _____ to growing in your walk with God and your family.
- Chronos is a _____, kairos is the _____.
- The Chinese word for *busyness* means _____.

Thinking It Through

1. Ask your pastor: Where and when is the best time to study and pray? Is the church office conducive to this? What is needed to protect this time from interruption?

2. What are the major pressure points for your pastor? What are the pressure points for each member of the leadership team?

3. Does your pastor have margin in their schedule?

4. Is it possible for another leader or staff member to be on call for emergencies on the pastor's day off?

Therefore be careful how you walk, not as unwise men but as wise, making the most of your time, because the days are evil. (Eph. 5:15-16 NASB)

—13—

STORM NO. 3: UNREALISTIC PRESSURE TO SUCCEED

PREVENTING FEELINGS OF FAILURE IN A SUCCESS-SATURATED CULTURE

A sense of panic settled in among the leadership of this once-flourishing movement. The ministry was tanking, going down fast. The boat was leaking and in danger of sinking. What was wrong? Had the leader lost his appeal and charisma? Was he oblivious to what was taking place? Why did he keep saying things that irritated the crowd? Some thought he had lost his mind. People were leaving in droves.

From its small beginning of a dozen, the crowd had soared to over ten thousand enthusiastic followers. It was quite a sensation, a mega success. The popularity of the movement was capturing the attention of religious and political leaders alike. Some were curious; others were jealous. But then the tide turned, and the numbers began to plummet. Disillusioned crowds exited at an alarming rate. There was grumbling in the ranks and disagreements. When the leader asked the crowd to stop complaining, it did little good.

With the crowds abandoning the cause and folks scurrying for their homes, Jesus turned to his disciples and asked, "Are you also going to leave?" (John 6:67). It was a pivotal moment in the numerical collapse of a once successful ministry. Most leaders would be fired from their jobs at this low point. Not Jesus—he was crucified.

A Success-Saturated Culture

Diminishing numbers hardly fit with our concept of success. Early in life, we're fed the idea that success has to do with popularity, power, and possessions. The dictionary defines success as "the attainment of wealth, favor, or eminence."[1] Jesus doesn't play by these rules. Just as he overturned the tables of money changers in the temple, Jesus now capsizes the twisted values of our success-saturated culture. Rather than advocating large bank accounts, Jesus teaches, "Store your treasures in heaven" (Matt. 6:20). Instead of fretting about food and clothing, he commands, "Seek the Kingdom of God above all else" (Matt. 6:33). When it comes to leadership, Jesus flips the success ladder upside down. "Many who are the greatest now will be least important then, and those who seem least important now will be the greatest then" (Mark 10:31).

Worldly success and godly success are often confused. A person may be successful in the eyes of the world and a failure before God. There is also a difference between public and private success. Some achieve great things that win applause in the public arena, while their personal and family life is in shambles. *New York Post* columnist Cindy Adams said, "Success has made failures of many men."[2]

Writing more than a century ago, William James called the worship of the "goddess of success" our "national disease."[3] How insightful. Blind ambition has ruined health, marriages, careers, and churches.

When the world's criteria for success—numbers, notoriety, appearance, possessions, money, and other measurements—are applied to the work of God, they create unrealistic success. It is success ill-defined. Godly success gets twisted, distorted, lost in the picture, and in some cases, abandoned. What God values is pushed aside in the pursuit of people-pleasing success. This unrealistic pressure to appear successful elevates status and statistics as the primary indicators of a successful ministry. The approval of people is addictive. The applause of the crowd is misleading. Adulation is confused with authenticity, charisma with godly character. Is this success?

Stephen W. Smith claims one of the storms capable of toppling a spiritual leader is "a success intoxicated leadership culture." He writes, "Leaders constantly need to redefine 'success.' Numerical success is shallow, and not long-standing when there is no solid foundation to stand on. As we grow and mature, our understanding of success should morph because we learn to view people, life, God, and money in different ways."[4] Christian leaders pumped up on the world's version of success create a toxic culture. All too often, fleshly techniques become the tools to make things happen instead of humble dependence on the Spirit.

Let me clarify. The job of pastor is not without pressure. Ministry is a race, a fight, a battle to be won (2 Tim. 4:7). Run from sin, run to win, and live a disciplined life (1 Cor. 9:24-27). Endure suffering like a soldier, train like an athlete, and work hard as a farmer (2 Tim. 2:3-6). A faithful—and successful—servant of God lives with a compelling drive to care for God's people and reach the lost. Coasting is not the calling of God. Unfortunately, some pastors rarely break a sweat, doing just enough to get by. Biblical success is pressing on "toward the goal for the prize of the upward call of God in Christ Jesus" (Phil. 3:14 NASB)—quite different than the unrealistic success of numbers, notoriety, and money.

Playing the Numbers Game

Most pastors feel an unrelenting pressure to produce numerical growth. I've heard board members say, "If our church isn't growing ten to fifteen percent a year, something is wrong." These board members often judge success based on attendance, the amount of money in the church's bank account, and the popular programs of other churches. By comparing themselves to other churches, they may conclude their church is failing.

Research by the Barna Group indicates one out of every seven adults changes churches each year. In addition, one out of every six adults attends a carefully chosen handful of churches on a rotating basis.[5] If this accurately reflects your church, it means you have to grow 14 percent yearly to stay even. To increase overall attendance, you have to add 14 percent plus 5 to 10 percent. Of course, for any church to see 20 percent conversion growth would be thrilling, but much growth (and decline) is migration and shopping around—people moving from church to church—not conversion.

Lyle Schaller, a recognized church specialist, writes: "The loyal member born before 1940 is upset and baffled when a longtime member becomes dissatisfied and quietly departs to worship with a different congregation in that same community. The younger member, who was reared in a culture overflowing with choices, shrugs off that departure as normal and completely acceptable."[6] Brand loyalty has all but disappeared, whether it's your grocery store, gas station, or internet provider. With each passing year, this has become increasingly true regarding allegiance to a particular church or denomination.

When people leave, those who remain tend toward hand wringing and blame casting while giving the pastor the brunt of the criticism. Some pastors are effective Bible teachers, strong leaders, and greatly loved by the people, but when the numbers go down, they are forced to resign. It's a classic example of playing the numbers game.

In a large church on the East Coast, a visionary junior high pastor set a goal of thirty-five baptisms for the upcoming year. What an exciting and challenging goal. However, at the end of the year, he had baptized only thirty-two—three short of the thirty-five baptisms. The senior pastor called the executive pastor into his office and insisted that he fire the junior high pastor for no other reason than his failure to achieve the goal of baptizing thirty-five. The junior high pastor was dismissed and wounded deeply.

A decline in numbers may be cause for concern but never for panic. Leadership's knee-jerk reactions occur too often—making radical changes or firing someone just because numbers dip. Churches should expect some yearly fluctuation. Indeed, if cantankerous people leave, it may prove a "blessed subtraction" for your congregation.

While a decline in numbers can be disappointing, a far greater danger lurks in the shadows, and few realize it. Attitudes change. Fear and worry take over as a gloomy pessimism settles in. The pastor seems a little downcast, and people bark at one another instead of blessing each other. There may be an atmosphere of suspicion in leadership meetings. When there is a loss of people, and income suffers, leaders and people tend to get "owly and growly."

This attitude of pessimism, accusation, and fear boomerangs and kills joy and love, the very fruit of the Spirit that attracts people to your fellowship. It's a double whammy. This decline of joy and caring relationships hurts a church more than the loss of a few people. It takes maturity to deal with losses while maintaining a spirit of love and rejoicing, but this is our godly charge. "Rejoice in the Lord always; again I will say, rejoice!" (Phil. 4:4 NASB).

God may use a drop in numbers to redirect your efforts. I learned this roughly fifty years ago, but the story took time to unfold. It started when *Christianity Today* ran a feature describing the Sunday evening service at Peninsula Bible Church in Palo Alto, California. "It happens every Sunday night. Eight hundred or more people pack into a church auditorium designed to seat comfortably only 750. ... The gathering is called a Body Life Service, a time for members of the body of Christ to fulfill the function of edifying one another in love."[7] I attended one of these services in Palo Alto, and the church was alive—joyous singing, spontaneous sharing, praying for each other, and practical Bible teaching.

During this time, I served as a pastor with John Wimber, who later led the Vineyard. Our Sunday evening service at Yorba Linda Friends Church was similar to Body Life at Peninsula Bible Church. For two hours, there was singing, testimonies from the audience, praying for one another, Bible teaching—and no one seemed concerned about the length of the service. It topped out at about five hundred in attendance but then began an alarming decline. It dropped to four hundred, then three hundred, and finally two fifty in attendance. We prayed and agonized over what we were doing wrong, and we tweaked various elements attempting to revitalize what was lost. I took the decline personally and felt like a dismal failure. When it reached about a hundred twenty-five people, we moved the service into the social hall, and it never regained its spark. People seemed to prefer being in their small group rather than coming out on Sunday evening.

Years later, I invited Bob Smith, an Associate Pastor at Peninsula Bible Church, to speak at an adult retreat at Mt. Gilead Bible Conference Center. At lunch, I asked Bob how things were going. He sighed, "There were the days when the Body Life Service was eight hundred, and then it began to decline. Ray Stedman and I agonized over what was happening. We changed things, but despite our efforts, it plummeted from eight hundred to about a hundred fifty people. Finally, we moved the service into the fellowship hall. This was very discouraging for us. After all, we were known nationally for the Body Life Service."

I'm sure my jaw hung slack as I asked, "What did you discover through the process?" Bob replied, "It finally became clear to us that Body Life—people sharing their lives, praying for one another, and being taught the Word—never stopped. It just changed locations. Rather than Body Life happening in a large audience, God moved it into small groups, which continue. It took us a long time to see the hand of God in declining numbers."

It took me a decade, but I finally realized God directed the numerical decline in our Sunday evening service so that our small group ministry could increase. God may use a decrease in numbers to redirect efforts at your church too.

Does God Want Every Church to be a Megachurch?

What is God's favorite size of church? Small, medium, and large. Jesus loves the church in all its variety, and one size doesn't fit all when it comes to people.

Some folks wouldn't think of attending a megachurch. "Too much like the parking lot at Disneyland. I'd be lost in the crowd." But the large church will reach people the small church won't and vice versa. I have often thought if I were an unbeliever wanting to check out Christianity, I would prefer to slip in unnoticed to a large church where I could observe and listen while deciding if Christianity was for me.

My friend, Karl Vaters, wrote *The Grasshopper Myth: Big Churches, Small Churches, and the Small Thinking that Divides Us*. Karl is not opposed to the megachurch, and in fact, he celebrates the work they do. But he's concerned about small churches and their pastors who may suffer from grasshopper thinking (a la the spies' mindset after encountering the giants in the Promised Land). "We're so small and insignificant. We can't do much. We're limping along." This is grasshopper thinking. Instead, Karl Vaters says, "Do small great." Megachurches, Vaters writes, can be compared to the giant cruise ships in the harbor, but small churches can be like the speed boats, zipping around getting things done while having a ton of fun doing it.

In America, small churches form the vast majority. According to *Christianity Today*, most churches "have fewer than 100 people attending services each Sunday (57%), including 21 percent who average fewer than 50. Around 1 in 10 churches (11%) average 250 or more for their worship services."[8] In other words, a whopping 89% of churches are 250 and under. To put this into perspective, "Half of all Christians in America and far more than half of Christians worldwide attend a Small Church, not because they lack options, but—shockingly, they go to a Small Church *because they want to!* ... The next time you're tempted to get frustrated about how many people are driving past your church to attend a megachurch, realize that there are more people who drive past megachurches to attend a Small Church."9 Vaters reveals approximately 4,000 megachurches (with weekly attendance over 2,000) worldwide care for about 100 million people every week. Small church pastors care for about one billion people weekly—ten times more than megachurches do. Over one billion people!10

The prophet Zechariah heard the people's frustration regarding a small start on rebuilding the temple. "This new temple won't compare to the glory of Solomon's temple," they grumbled. God went straight to the heart of the matter, "For who has despised the day of small things?" (Zech. 4:10 NASB). Does your perspective on size and numbers need a holy adjustment?

My home church in Murdo, South Dakota, had an enormous impact with only fifty or sixty people. More than twenty from this little church have gone to Bible schools, and a significant number serve as pastors and missionaries. I had the opportunity to lead worship services and preach in high school—experiences I wouldn't have had in a large church. Don't despise small things. Whether it's your Sunday service, life group, or youth ministry, *do small great!*

How Large Were Churches in the New Testament?

As I've stated earlier, numbers in the Bible were neither ignored nor promoted. Someone said, "Those opposed to statistics usually have none to report." I'm not against numbers and statistics properly used. The book of Acts records the phenomenal growth of the early church. In Acts 2:41, there were about 3,000 added to the church. Fifteen nations, provinces, or ethnic groups were represented, so many returned to their homes. Still, the Jerusalem

Church instantly became a megachurch. By Acts 4:4, the church had grown to 5,000 men (including the women and children, the total could have been 15,000 or 20,000). Acts 6:7 says the number of disciples greatly increased. Acts 21:20 refers to "thousands of Jews" who believed. The Greek word translated thousands here, *murias,* means "10,000s" (plural), sometimes used in a general sense to indicate a large number. Revelation 5:11 refers to myriads (10,000) times myriads (10,000) plus thousands of angels. Millions of angels? Wow! Worship in heaven is going to be exciting beyond anything we can imagine.

Looking at all these numbers, perhaps you think bigger is better in God's eyes. But what size was the church in Ephesus, Thessalonica, Phillipi, Laodicea, Rome, and other places? We don't know. Maybe that's on purpose. Other than the Jerusalem Church, we have no indicator of any church's numerical size. Gene Getz, writing in *Elders and Leaders,* states, "Archeologists have discovered residences in some locations in the Roman Empire that could actually seat up to five hundred people in the garden room alone. This may describe a family complex owned by a well-to-do man like Cornelius in Caesarea or Philemon in Colossae."[11] If the home of a wealthy person was available, some of the churches might have had several hundred people. However, many of the churches may have been under fifty in size or smaller. If the home of Aquila and Priscilla was small, I don't think they had seven services on a Sunday in their home. It's more likely, as numbers increased, they met in multiple homes.

The silence on numbers is significant. In evaluating the seven churches in Revelation, Jesus never mentions church size. The Lord measured a church's love, faith, service, patience, purity, and perseverance in suffering. He rebuked churches for losing their first love, tolerating false teaching, having a reputation of being alive but actually being dead, and being lukewarm. Admittedly, these things are more challenging to measure, but a church's numerical size clearly wasn't Christ's priority. Why should it be any different for us? A healthy and vibrant church of fifty pleases God infinitely more than a church of five thousand, entertaining crowds and compromising the gospel.

De-emphasizing numbers never justifies a church becoming ingrown or losing its evangelistic fervor. Whether large or small, our mission remains the same: "Go therefore and make disciples of all the nations" (Matt. 28:19 NASB). First-love Christianity needs frequent rekindling.

Forget fretting about what size your church is and focus on impacting your community and world with the love of Jesus. As a pastor, I acknowledge sometimes riding a weekly emotional roller coaster depending on the attendance. It was a foolish mindset to be self-evaluating my performance and worth based on numbers. If I were to do it again, I would spend less time agonizing over and analyzing the numbers. I wouldn't ignore statistical data, but rather than examining it weekly, I would review the statistical trend quarterly.

The Pressure to Produce

The church growth movement came into prominence between forty and fifty years ago and continues today. It focuses on increasing churches' numerical size through evangelism, research, demographic studies, sociological principles, and marketing strategies. While the movement has brought numerical increase for some churches, it has also generated frustrations and feelings of failure for those who do not experience the same results. As the pressure to grow numerically ramped up and numerical growth became the predominant evaluation of a congregation, church health suffered. There has been a correction of this to some degree, but I still see pastors put out to pasture simply because attendance isn't steadily increasing. This assumes the pastor is the reason for growth or decline and fails to consider the large number of factors that influence numerical increase or decrease. The following eight characteristics must be considered when assessing numerical growth or decline.

1. **The community surrounding the church**

Fast-growing suburbs with new housing developments have far greater potential for growth than rural, inner-city, or long-established communities. Changing demographics, cost of housing, and people moving impact growth or decline. If the community population is spiraling downward and the median age is rapidly rising, the church will struggle to grow.

2. **The capacity and condition of the facilities**

Inadequate or unkempt worship and educational facilities are a detriment to adding new people. Peeling paint and smelly bathrooms are like a flashing exit sign. Facilities need to be warm, inviting, and clean. Those who attend the church regularly become oblivious to what visitors see on their first visit. During my years as a senior pastor, I phoned every new person who visited the church to welcome them. I also sent a brief survey asking for their opinion about the facilities, friendliness of the people, music, and message. I learned a great deal and was sometimes surprised by the fresh perspective of the new person.

3. **The condition of the hearts of people**

Jesus mentions four types of soil—hardened, rocky, thorny, and good—summarized as follows.

The Soil of Human Hearts
Matthew 13:3-23; Luke 8:5-15

The Soil	Condition	Human Life
Hard soil	Hard, indifferent	Hardened life
Rocky soil	No root, tempted, easily falls away	Shallow life
Thorny soil	Choked by worries, riches, pleasures	Worldly life
Good soil	Tender toward God and others	Fruitful life

People rarely take this into account when assessing church growth. Are the hearts of the people in the community (including the church) hardened to spiritual truth or choked with the world's worries, riches, and pleasures? Imagine a community with 25 percent hardened soil (atheistic, agnostic, or hostile to Christianity), 65 percent thorny soil (gripped by materialism, pleasure, hedonism), and 5 percent rocky soil (shallow beliefs, Christian in name only). Good soil, where the seed of the Word will grow, makes up only 5% of this community. This is a tough mission field, and no growth strategizing will fix this. No pastor, no program, no projections can change the soil of the human heart. God alone changes hearts. Churches plant the seeds and pray for God to change hard, rocky, and thorny soil into good soil. As Hosea said, "Plant the good seeds of righteousness, and you will harvest a crop of love. Plow up the hard ground of your hearts, for now is the time to seek the LORD, that he may come and shower righteousness upon you" (Hosea 10:12).

4. **The leadership gifts of the pastor**

Some pastors are at their best caring for fifty to two hundred people, while leading two thousand would be overwhelming. Other pastors thrive on delegating responsibilities and leading the large church. Put them in a small church, and they may be frustrated with the multi-tasking required. The gift set needed for leading a small or medium-sized church differs from a large church.

5. **The attitude of the people toward newcomers**

This is a huge factor. Some churches are a network of long-established, closed social relationships. These churches tend to stay about the same size. Someone shrewdly observed, "You can't grow this type of church, and you can't kill it either." They often think of themselves as very friendly because they warmly greet new people. But they don't go out of their way to include the new person in their social network. As a result, new people leave feeling excluded rather than included.

6. **Few relationships with neighbors**

My wife, Joanne, directed the women's ministry at our church. She recalls the frustration of planning an outreach event for pre-believers and having only believers attend. The problem was not an unwillingness to invite. Instead, she discovered few of them had friends who were unbelievers. So, rather than promoting busyness at church, we encouraged people to build relationships in the neighborhood—block parties, baking bread, bike rides, golf, shopping with unbelievers. Perhaps your church needs similar encouragement.

7. **The style of ministry**

Music, attire, decorations, length of services, and types of sermons positively or negatively impact new people. Some of your church practices may feel strange to a new person. Unfortunately, churches often hang on to stylistic things and cling to traditions that need a decent burial. Without compromising the message, examine the practices that may repel the new person and change things.

8. **The spiritual condition of the church**

If petty jealousies, long-standing feuds, grumbling, complaining, hypocrisy, or bitterness have infected a church, a new person will pick up these signals faster than you think. No one wants to join a church marred by infighting. A church like this needs repentance more than growth.

WHO AND WHAT GROWS THE CHURCH?

While there are many verses in the Bible on sharing the faith and leading people to Christ, leaders are often surprised when I tell them there are only three passages in the Bible that mention church growth. Two of these tell *who* is responsible for church growth, and the other section explains *what* grows the church.

First, who grows the church? Paul says, "I planted, Apollos watered, but God was causing the growth. So then neither the one who plants nor the one who waters is anything, but God who causes the growth" (1 Cor. 3:6-7 NASB). Who takes full responsibility for the growth of the church? Twice it says *God causes the growth*. Don't expect a person to produce what only God can do. Jesus assumes full responsibility for building his church. "I will build my church, and all the powers of hell will not conquer it" (Matt. 16:18). While writing my doctoral dissertation on the topic, "The Reproducing Cycle of Church Growth," I read every book on church growth in print at that time. I learned things that helped me in my ministry, but I also encountered an inescapable fact: growth is not a mechanical thing, something programmed into a computer. It doesn't fit a formula like a 5:1 ratio of sharing the gospel and people responding to the message. Spiritual growth is not a by-product of entertaining speakers and slick advertising. Growth is a God-thing. We are God's garden, and God takes ultimate responsibility for what grows there. You can cultivate the soil in your backyard, plant seeds, and water them, but ultimately, it is God who causes a tiny seed to germinate, sprout, and finally pop out of the ground.

Second, what grows the church? In Ephesians 4:11-16, we find another crucial passage regarding church growth. Apostles, prophets, evangelists, and pastor-teachers equip believers for the work of the ministry, thereby building up the body of Christ. As a result, "the whole body, being fitted and held together by what every joint supplies, according to the proper working of each individual part, *causes the growth of the body* for the building up of itself in love (Eph. 4:16 NASB emphasis supplied). Did you notice what causes the growth? The healthy functioning of every believer. We need to equip all believers to exercise their God-given spiritual gifts. "As each one has received a special gift, employ it in serving one another" (1 Pt. 4:10 NASB). No spiritual unemployment in God's family. If 10 percent of the people do 90 percent of the work (which is quite common), make changes. Some faithful ten percenters need encouragement to let go of long-standing responsibilities. Challenge them to train someone new to do what they do. The goal is 100 percent of the people do 100 percent of the church's work. I say it this way, "The spiritual impact of the church is directly proportionate to the mobilization of every believer to be filled with the Spirit and exercise their spiritual gift toward a clear God-given mission and vision." God will take care of the growth.

Growth in quality or quantity? Hopefully both. Maturity and multiplication. Growth in the fruit of the Spirit and growth in new followers of Jesus. Growth is a by-product of a healthy organism. When assessing growth, start with the question, "Is the church healthy?" A great resource to develop a healthy church is Natural Church Development (NCD). This assesses the church's health in eight areas: empowering leadership, gift-oriented ministry, passionate spirituality, functional structures, inspiring worship service, holistic small groups, need-oriented evangelism, and loving relationships. NCD identifies the factors impacting ongoing growth and multiplication, regardless of culture. More than seventy thousand churches on all six continents have used this biblically-based tool. The health of the church is the focus rather than numerical goals. The health and vitality of the eight factors are the keys to ongoing growth and multiplication.

You've probably heard the statement, "All healthy living organisms grow." True, but that doesn't mean all healthy organisms grow to the same size. The beautiful flowers my wife plants in our backyard grow and blossom, but I would think it quite strange if the flowers grew to the height of our evergreen trees. I believe God wants churches of different sizes in his garden, all blossoming with the fruit of the Spirit and seeking to lead others to Christ.

THE FALLOUT FROM THE PRESSURE TO APPEAR SUCCESSFUL

In the scientific world, fallout refers to the airborne particles from a nuclear explosion, industrial accident, or volcanic eruption. It's dangerous stuff. The fallout from an unrealistic success mentality is equally hazardous and toxic. Ruined careers, families, and churches are strewn across the landscape of Christianity. Several times a month, Joanne and I come alongside a pastor or spouse among the walking wounded. Either they have been discarded because they didn't measure up or have imploded from their own drivenness for unrealistic success. The pressure to appear successful creates hazardous fallout.

Along with unrealistic expectations and an unrealistic schedule, the pressure to appear successful—unrealistic success—is the third of the swirling convergence of storms that can shipwreck the relentlessly driven leader.

The Danger of Celebrity Status

There are a growing number of young, ambitious, multi-gifted pastors who achieve rapid numerical success. They are usually nontraditionalists meeting in schools, theaters, and shopping centers. Some of these leaders have little formal training, but they make up for it with passion and drive combined with an exceptional ability to communicate with a younger generation. "Trading traditional suits and clerical robes for skinny jeans and untucked shirts, using plugged-in musicians in place of choirs, and displaying virtuoso homiletic skills, these pastors began rapidly adding new members even as large traditional churches were losing them."[12] Their message resonates, the crowds grow, and many come to Christ, which brings me nothing but joy. But I am grieved and heartbroken when I see too many of these young leaders unravel—failed marriages, moral failure, burnout, and sometimes suicide. A closer look reveals many of them are adept at developing quasi-celebrity status with their fans but have few intimate friends. Their followers speak of them like celebrities or rock stars. What happened? "One of the dangers in today's leadership culture is that leaders who achieve 'success' quickly can become intoxicated by their own egos. They can develop an overinflated idea about who they are and what they can do."[13] Pride is an elusive sin, noticed by others but rarely apparent to the person carrying the virus. There is a subtle danger of ministry slippage with expanding influence and unchecked power. The church "often celebrates the success of a church leader over their character, and their influence over their integrity. The Bible does the opposite."[14]

I've found many quasi-celebrity pastors measure their staff and leadership teams against a painful double standard. They want the expectations adjusted and personal time increased for themselves, yet they're demanding and pushy toward their team. Pastor Scott Thomas, who previously served as President of Acts 29, a coalition of over seven hundred churches, wrote, "I watched an intelligent church leader self-destruct over enviousness, boastfulness, arrogance, and manipulative bullying. He had extraordinary success in ministry, but his spiritual immaturity capsized it. After years of browbeating his staff, church officers, and members, the church board finally enacted disciplinary actions against him. The church removed him, and it left a mess. I wish this were an isolated case."[15]

However, there are many faithful, God-honoring leaders with a high profile in the public arena. Not all who become well-known pastors or evangelists fall prey to the pride trap. I pray for them and thank God for their ministry.

The Danger of Shallow Relationships

The pressure to perform and appear successful makes it difficult to have close, personal relationships. Being in the spotlight is a lonely place. Leaders put up walls to protect their image and the prestige of their position. Deep within, they may wonder if they're good enough or doing enough—if they have what it takes to keep up the relentless pace and the public persona. Too often, the leadership culture surrounding them applauds the strong and implies that weakness is for losers. Pain and struggle are not comfortable topics to talk about. To share personal inadequacy or weakness feels too risky. They have no place to talk about fears and struggles. How unfortunate. This isolation sets a leader up for ministry catastrophe.

Paul knew better. He wrote openly about feeling weak, crushed, and overwhelmed beyond his ability to endure. He asked for prayer. He invited help. He loved deeply and was loved in return. Vulnerability drove him to stop relying on himself (2 Cor. 1:8–9). Inadequacy forced him to draw on God's strength to make it through (2 Cor. 3:4–6). Paul describes himself as a clay pot—unattractive and fragile. He wanted everyone to know the power came from God, not him (2 Cor. 4:7). Paul was pressed with troubles on every side, perplexed, persecuted, and knocked down but not knocked out (2 Cor. 4:8–9). The power in Paul's ministry was directly related to his personal weakness. "So now I am glad to boast about my weaknesses, so that the power of Christ can work through me. That's why I take pleasure in my weaknesses, and in the insults, hardships, persecutions, and troubles that I suffer for Christ. For when I am weak, then I am strong" (2 Cor. 12:9–10).

Leaders, drop your guard and be real with those around you. Cultivate genuine friendships. Share your struggles and weaknesses. Pray for each other. If you're afraid, say so. If you're tempted, admit it. If you're drained and exhausted, acknowledge it. I explore this topic in more depth in *Your Winning Edge: God's Power Perfected in Weakness*. Success should never equal shallow relationships.

The Danger of Excessive Drivenness to Achieve

This point is pointed right at me. Whenever I take a personality evaluation, achieving is always my highest score, but an unhealthy drive to succeed nearly ruined my health, family, and ministry. I often denied it, but underneath there was the need to produce the numbers that would affirm my worth and value. This verse gets under my skin every time I read it. "Are you seeking great things for yourself? Don't do it!" (Jer. 45:5). Scott Thomas shares this honest reflection, "When I first became a lead pastor thirty years ago, I pushed myself and others to achieve *my* goals for the church. I led the church with the business and marketing principles I knew. I emphasized numerical growth at the expense of spiritual growth. It wasn't until I discovered a consistent thread in the Bible of gospel-shaped leadership that I had a new perspective on how to lead. I regret not finding it earlier."[16] Success-seeking, self-seeking pastors leave churches with massively destructive fallout.

The Danger of Catering to the Crowd

We tend to be impressed by numbers and wowed by big crowds. There is an excitement and adrenaline rush in speaking to a large crowd. Singing with a full house is exhilarating, and the lure to build a bigger crowd is powerful. The ministries of Dwight L. Moody, Billy Graham, and many others testify to the power of the gospel proclaimed to large crowds of people. I pray that all Bible-believing, gospel-preaching churches will be filled and overflowing. However, if there is an unrealistic pressure to pack the house, it may compromise the message. Rather than delivering the Word of God, the temptation may be to preach on popular topics without digging into the Scriptures or presenting the cross and the gospel. Crowds swelled around Jesus, but he never catered to their quest for the spectacular. When multitudes showed up, Jesus intentionally zeroed in on the cost of discipleship (Luke 14:25-30)—not exactly a way to pump up the numbers. He didn't trust the crowd because he knew what was in people's hearts (John 2:23-24). Amazingly, Jesus never lost sight of the person in pain while teaching thousands (Matt. 9:36; 11:28-30).

Like a sports coach who is a hero one day and a bum the next, crowds can be fickle and unpredictable. A crowd cheered at the triumphal entry of Jesus (Luke 19:36-40), and a few days later, the mob shouted "crucify him" (Luke 23:18-25). Catering to the crowd is dangerous.

The Danger of Comparison

Many unreasonable expectations that demoralize and discourage are rooted in the unbiblical practice of comparison. "When we compare ourselves to others, we agree with the plans of the enemy for our lives. Comparison is the thief of joy and the stretcher of truth. Comparison says, 'I am ill-equipped for the task at hand.' The truth is God has given me everything I need for the plans he has set before me."[17] Paul was being compared and responded, "For we are not bold to class or compare ourselves with some of those who commend themselves; but when they measure themselves by themselves and compare themselves with themselves, they are without understanding" (2 Cor. 10:12 NASB). I'm learning that I'm the very best me when I am just me—under the control of the Holy Spirit.

The Danger of Power and Greed

Early in my ministry, I was trained by a high-flying corporate consultant whose résumé included some of the largest corporations in America. He was a Christian who could quote reams of Scripture, and I received some valuable training from him, things I still use today. However, along the way, I found my thinking skewed by his pompous love of wealth and power. A short time after my training with him, he was convicted on eleven counts of securities fraud with the church he served. The Lord used this event to open my eyes to the danger of his love for money. Later, he and his wife were divorced, and ten years after that, he and the secretary he was living with were indicted as the masterminds behind a real estate investment scheme that stole investors' funds. He was charged with twenty-two counts, including racketeering, securities fraud, perjury, and theft—a sad story and a solemn warning.

In many cases today, pastors and leaders learn theology in Bible schools and seminaries but turn to the corporate world to learn to lead. This trend is not all bad since there is much we can learn from business leaders. Some corporations have committed believers at the helm who lead from a servant's heart, but these leaders are rare. What about learning from a corporate leader who has no use for God and lives an immoral lifestyle? I'm concerned that in too many cases, they're teaching pastors how to lead ... *and* how to behave. Often, they're living an opulent lifestyle of yachts and private jets, sexual affairs and mistresses, and financial fraud. It's a slippery slope to learn leadership principles from a godless corporate leader without falling prey to their lifestyle of greed and power. Jesus made it clear the "student who is fully trained will become like the teacher" (Lk. 6:40).

Jack McCullough, writing in *Forbes*, identifies CEOs who crave power and dominant positions but "are also chameleons, able to disguise their ruthlessness and antisocial behavior under the veneer of charm and eloquence." One CEO would "fire anyone who challenged him, explaining there was no reason to second-guess him because he was always right and needed people to execute his vision rather than challenge it."[18] Intelligent and charming, they also are manipulative, lack empathy, and treat others ruthlessly. Thankfully most executives are not like this, but I am deeply concerned about this pattern increasing among pastors and ministry leaders. When this happens, ministry leaders are more like CEOs than shepherds, board meetings mimic the corporate model, and business meetings mirror stockholder meetings. Where is the biblically faithful shepherd burdened with the well-being of every one of the sheep, caring and compassionate for the wounded, laying their life down to protect the flock from danger, and often receiving minimal compensation?

In an eye-awakening article, "The Modern Evangelical Church is Sick. Here's Where It Fell Apart," Pastor Darvin Wallis laments that we hire corporate experts to train pastors to lead the church. He has seen the raw side of this. He served under three megachurch pastors who followed the corporate executive pattern of leadership. All three had moral failures. Darvin summarizes his concern with this stinging statement.

> The leadership system we currently have in place is churning the church through continuous moral scandals. We are hypocrites for valuing the bottom lines of church attendance and revenue over the character of our church leaders. We are hypocrites for identifying and forming church leaders not by their faith, but by their dominance. We are hypocrites for becoming more interested in organizational growth than discipleship. We are hypocrites for adopting corporate level leadership norms, and expecting not to have corporate level scandals. And the true tragedy is that our hypocrisy is resulting in millions of people being turned off to faith in Jesus.[19]

As we step back from the fallout and toxicity of unrealistic success, let's examine this crucial question.

What Matters Most?

What defines success and failure in the ministry? I often pose this question to pastors who feel like they have failed. Do you think Isaiah, Jeremiah, Ezekiel, and the other prophets were successful in God's eyes? Absolutely! They endured horrific persecution while delivering an unpopular message. They served without visible success or statistics to report. The prophet with the greatest numerical success—Jonah—was defiant, rebellious, and an emotional mess.

Some pastors and missionaries serve in relative obscurity, working long hours for little or no pay. Many are bi-vocational because their flock is small. They faithfully proclaim the gospel and love people but have minimal visible results. No one identifies their work as heroic, though God knows it is. They receive little, if any, public applause as the enemy subtly whispers, "You haven't accomplished much with your life." One of the pastors I care for shared his inner turmoil. "I've led the church from a hundred twenty in attendance to less than a hundred. I guess I'm a failure." Really? He has faithfully cared for the people, taught the Word of God, and championed caring for the persecuted church worldwide. Considering the community's changing demographics, I think he has done well to keep the church steady.

Bottom line: Success and failure aren't always what we think. Failure is not falling short of one or more of your goals. Effective leaders don't achieve every objective. A plateaued church or numerical decline doesn't necessarily mean you have failed. Being forced out does not mean you're a failure in God's evaluation.

Failure is an affair with the church secretary. Failure is embezzling funds. Failure is plagiarizing sermons off the internet rather than doing the hard work of study and preparation. Failure is abusing people and the power of the pastoral position. Failure is berating the sheep rather than lovingly leading them. Failure is when pastors and board members behave as if they own the church that belongs to Jesus. Failure is promoting self rather than seeking the glory of God.

When the applause ends, the lights are turned down, and the crowd has gone their way, what really counts? Is it having a church of fifty, five hundred, or five thousand that really matters? How do you measure success?

Success is having an eternal impact on people ... one person at a time. Success is a cup of cold water or a warm blanket to a needy person in the name of Jesus. Success is a faithful witness to your community and world. Success is hard work and perseverance. Success is lifting up Jesus.

Faithful shepherds receive an "unfading crown of glory" (1 Pt. 5:4). In Paul's time, victorious athletes received a crown of flowers that wilted quickly. Applause, notoriety, and earthly recognition are earthly crowns that wilt like yesterday's flowers. The crown for a faithful shepherd is eternal.

Ultimately, success comes down to one word: *faithfulness*.

Faithfulness to God, faithfulness to the Word of God, faithfulness to your calling, faithfulness to love people, faithfulness to your family, and faithfulness to share the faith—this is what matters.

Did Jesus say, "Well done, my good and successful servant"? No.

"The master said, 'Well done, my good and faithful servant. You have been faithful in handling this small amount, so now I will give you many more responsibilities. Let's celebrate together!'" (Matt. 25:23).

Be successful—be faithful!

Reflection and Discussion

Quick Recall

- Research by the Barna Group indicates one out of every _____ adults changes churches each year.

- What is grasshopper thinking?

- Who takes full responsibility for church growth? __
_____

Thinking It Through

1. After reading this chapter, how do you view unrealistic success in the ministry? In your opinion, what is the fallout of a toxic success mindset?

2. How would you describe success in the ministry?

3. Why is your church health more important than numerical growth?

4. How do you measure church health? What is the health of your church? What could be done to improve this?

The master said, "Well done, my good and faithful servant. You have been faithful in handling this small amount, so now I will give you many more responsibilities. Let's celebrate together!" (Matt. 25:23)

—14—

STORM SURVIVAL GUIDE: A PLAYBOOK FOR THE TEAM

PREVENTING PROBLEMS AND RESOLVING CONFLICTS

The Great Peace March for Global Nuclear Disarmament left from the steps of Los Angeles City Hall on March 1, 1986, with 1,200 marchers and 6,000 supporters cheering them on. The goal was to press for the elimination of nuclear weapons. The plan was to march across the country to Washington, D.C., spreading their message to 65 million along the way and creating a national and international demand for global disarmament. The march organizers anticipated thousands would line the streets of America's towns and villages to welcome them and visit Peace City—their movable, solar-powered, environmentally-friendly model community with educational murals—while Hollywood celebrities entertained the crowds. They counted on others joining them en route, and finally, one million strong, they would march into Washington, D.C., on November 14 to present their ultimatums. The march organization, PROPeace (People Reaching Out for Peace), would call for massive civil disobedience before continuing the march overseas, demanding world peace.[1]

There was trouble from the start. According to the *Los Angeles Times*, the marchers were a divisive conglomerate—the employed taking a leave of absence from their work, retirees, as well as "unkempt, strung-out, at times immodestly dressed, people from the fringes of society and beyond."[2] Bernie May, President of Wycliffe USA, in a letter to supporters, wrote,

> A newspaper in Huntington Beach carried the report of a group of peace marchers making their way across the United States demonstrating against nuclear arms. Headline: "Participants Bickering Every Step of the Way on Great Peace March." The board of directors called for a dress code. A lot of the marchers rebelled. Some of the men started wearing dresses to protest the rules and regulations. Then the board, saying they were falling behind schedule, increased the number of miles the group would walk each day.[3]

The marchers rebelled since board members rode in cars and vans. Some dropped out, and others went home to pick up their cars. Undercurrents of exasperation, flare-ups about equipment and tents, and demands to know what happened to the money led to more desertions. With the ranks thinned, they spent a day trudging nine miles through mud in pouring rain.[4]

Los Angeles Times reporter Kathleen Hendrix wrote, "Ask who's in charge and watch them laugh. The marchers bucked attempts at authority and insisted on consensus for decision making in tortuous meetings that go on for days in uncomfortable surroundings." One marcher said, "Peace

City is *some* place to live. It's harder than the march. We can't agree on anything except to knock at the Porta-Potty."[5]

And then, just two weeks into the march, PROPeace declared bankruptcy and canceled the Great Peace March. Many left for home.[6] Those remaining were stranded on the edge of the Mojave desert, with numbers and supplies dwindling. Amazingly, the stalwarts regrouped, and four hundred completed the entire walk across the country.

Reading the Great Peace March archives brought to mind the Israelites squabbling and complaining as they wandered in the wilderness for forty years. Sometimes Christians are like participants on a great peace march, bickering every step of the way.

What is the solution to prevent problems and resolve conflicts before they become destructive? As we've seen, God Meetings give leaders a renewed mindset for working together, but this doesn't eliminate differing viewpoints. Conflicts are an inevitable part of life because God designed us with unique wants, desires, and perspectives. Most people dread the thought of conflict, but it isn't always bad. Conflict has the potential to be destructive or constructive, unnerving or invigorating. The seeds of great benefit are waiting to bloom from conflict managed correctly, including preventing problems instead of cleaning up messes.

What follows are lessons learned—a playbook to deal with some of the gnarly issues in ministry. Make these plays your modus operandi—the DNA of your leadership and staff.

Your Playbook

In high school football and basketball, the coach handed out a playbook at the start of the season with the instruction, "Memorize the plays before our first practice." Playbooks at the high school level were fairly simple. Not so for professional sports. The playbook for the typical NBA team is roughly a hundred ten pages with about a hundred plays. And forget the myth about NFL players not being too bright. The playbook developed by Super Bowl Champion Coach Al Saunders was eight hundred pages in length ... and growing.

In sports, playbooks facilitate quick and intuitive thinking. When a situation arises, teammates know the plays so well that they respond automatically rather than reacting emotionally. A godly leadership team can operate in a similar manner. Thankfully, the playbook for God's team in this chapter is refreshingly simple. So huddle up, and let's get started.

Play No. 1: Show up.

It's that simple. Half of being used by God is being there. Make an in-the-flesh, real live appearance. Unless there are extenuating circumstances, be there and be on time. Can you imagine a basketball player who regularly shows up halfway through the first quarter and expects to play? Absence and tardiness demoralize a group. And remember, teams have a way of giving undesirable assignments to absentees.

Play No. 2: Do an attitude check.

Paul said, "Devote yourselves to prayer, keeping alert in it with an *attitude of thanksgiving*" (Col. 4:2 NASB emphasis supplied). William James offered this insight, "It is our attitude at the beginning of a difficult task which, more than anything else, will affect its successful outcome."[7] Ted Engstrom, who was at the helm of Youth for Christ and World Vision, observed, "The higher you go in any organization of value, the better the attitudes you will find."[8] Attitude is a choice, so cultivate a thankful heart.

Attitude always impacts your work. Half-hearted performance affects others and demoralizes the team. In the final analysis, your work is presented to God. "Whatever you do, do your work heartily, as for the Lord rather than for men; knowing that from the Lord you will receive the reward of the inheritance. It is the Lord Christ whom you serve" (Col. 3:23-24 NASB).

Play No. 3: Be diligent to preserve the unity of the Spirit.

Oneness, work together, be of the same mind, live in harmony, pursue peace, agree with and love one another—hundreds of verses in the New Testament echo this theme. Paul told the Corinthians, "I appeal to you, dear brothers and sisters, by the authority of our Lord Jesus Christ, to live in harmony with each other. Let there be no divisions in the church. Rather, be of one mind, united in thought and purpose" (1 Cor. 1:10). Jesus said, "Your love for one another will prove to the world that you are my disciples" (John 13:35). Sadly, our actions often prove otherwise. Chuck Swindoll expressed a deep burden over this.

> There's not a more divided church on any continent or in any era of church history than there is in the United States today. It's nothing short of tragic. Every city has its own stories of church splits—some of them are legendary. Towns and villages have pastors that won't talk to each other, much less support or encourage one another. As believers committed to walking in a manner worthy of our calling, we should all cry out, "What a shame!" Because when unbelievers observe our disregard for unity, they think, "What a sham!"[9]

Francis Schaeffer also pointedly observed, "We cannot expect the world to believe that the Father sent the Son, that Jesus's claims are true, and that Christianity is true unless the world sees some reality of the oneness of true Christians."[10] Let that sink in.

Regardless of age, color of skin, education, social standing, style of worship, denomination, or affiliation, seven essentials unite all believers. This is a straightforward command from the Apostle Paul.

> Therefore I, a prisoner for serving the Lord, beg you to lead a life worthy of your calling, for you have been called by God. Always be humble and gentle. Be patient with each other, making allowance for each other's faults because of your love. Make every effort to keep yourselves united in the Spirit, binding yourselves together with peace. For there is one body and one Spirit, just as you have been called to one glorious hope for the future. There is one Lord, one faith, one baptism, one God and Father of all, who is over all, in all, and living through all. (Eph. 4:1-6)

These verses read like a doctrinal statement in an abbreviated form. To summarize ...

SEVEN ONES OF THE FAITH
Ephesians 4:4-6

ONENESS
of the Triune God — reflected in the ⟶ **ONENESS**
of Who We Are

ONE GOD AND FATHER
ONE LORD
ONE SPIRIT

ONE FAITH built on the foundation of God's inspired Word

ONE BODY uniting every believer globally

> Being diligent to preserve the unity of the Spirit. (Eph. 4:3 NASB)

ONE BAPTISM identifying externally the internal reality of the Spirit

ONE HOPE anticipating Christ's return and certainty of eternal life

These seven statements are the essentials. Non-negotiables. While some promote bringing everyone together under one ecumenical tent, catastrophic danger follows casting aside one or more of the seven pillars for oneness.

It's like riding on a bus missing one or more of its wheels. The seven ones are foundational for unity, and we preserve unity by adhering to the clear teaching of Scripture.

While there is a danger of subtracting ones (compromising the faith), adding ones is also dangerous. Some well-intentioned Christians become dogmatic and sometimes downright ugly, adding ones and insisting others conform. Additions have included one version of the Bible, one style of music, one style of preaching, one political alignment, one way of serving communion, one set of non-biblical rules for Christian living, etc. When these become conditions of fellowship, the body of Christ is divided.

There are seven ones—not three or five, not eleven or twelve. Based on the seven ones, "Be diligent to preserve the unity of the Spirit" (Eph. 4:3 NASB)

How does your leadership team apply this? When a difference of opinion or potential conflict arises, ask yourself, *Is this one of the seven nonnegotiables? Is this worth "going to the wall" to fight for?* If the issue pertains to the inspiration of Scripture, the deity of Jesus Christ, or another major biblical issue, fight for it. But if it's the brand of the copy machine, the color of the youth room walls, taking the offering before the sermon or after, or hundreds of other issues, express your thoughts, spend a reasonable amount of time debating pros and cons, but don't damage relationships for it.

Play No. 4: Make decisions based on core values.

When you're sitting across the table from other team members discussing a thorny issue, these foundational values will be your compass. In Appendix 6, I have included a sample of core values.

Play No. 5: Develop ministries with an effective game plan.

Wise leaders encourage a culture of creativity. It's healthy for new ideas to flow and new ministries to be imagined and launched. I've seen churches discourage this through negative scrutiny and lengthy procedures that rival acts of Congress. Creativity is strangled. It's no wonder these churches die a slow death. Rather than tightly controlling future developments, leadership needs to be alert to where God is at work and encourage ministry opportunities to sprout effectively. Guide the process with strategic thinking and prevent the idea from fizzling or creating problems.

This principle applies to established ministries as well. During my pastoral ministry, I developed a one-page planner for new and existing ministries to establish direction. See Appendix 7, the Charting the Course Ministry Planner. We kept this intentionally simple, but it helped launch ministries with an effective game plan.

Play No. 6: Don't ramrod proposals and plans.

A ramrod is a rod for ramming home the charge in a muzzle-loading firearm.[11] In other words, a ramrod sets up an explosion. Leaders who ramrod their ideas through the leadership team can expect an explosion sooner or later. "Bullies push and shove their way through life. Careful words make for a careful life; careless talk may ruin everything" (Prov. 13:2-3 MSG). Proposals presented with powerful driving forces automatically create equal or greater resistance forces. Sometimes it's not resistance to the idea—it's resistance to the way it was presented. Defuse resistance forces with intentional listening. Be open to ideas and suggestions. "Fools think their own way is right, but the wise listen to others" (Prov. 12:15).

How do you become more persuasive? Solomon had wise words about this: "Pleasant words are persuasive. ... From a wise mind comes wise speech; the words of the wise are persuasive" (Prov. 16:21, 23). Ben Franklin, a wise man, gifted at persuading others, suggested this method: "The way to convince another is to state your case moderately and accurately. Then scratch your head, or shake it a little and say that is the way it seems to you, but of course, you could be mistaken about it; which causes your listener to receive what you have to say, and as like as not, turn about and try to convince you of it, since you are in doubt. But if you go at him in a tone of positiveness and arrogance, you only make an enemy of him."[12]

Even with the best approach, changing things can be dicey and sometimes explosive. Attempting to control the outcome, some leaders make the mistake of not allowing others to give input, and then they wonder why they encounter opposition. Always keep in mind, people place their enthusiasm behind things they have a part in creating. When I've taken the time to listen, allowing the Holy Spirit to work, I've often watched God bring others to the same conclusion. I've also been changed by listening to others. When you seek the advice and perspective of others, you make your change their change. "Plans go wrong for lack of advice; many advisers bring success" (Prov. 15:22). Don't push, don't rush, take your time. This play will pay significant dividends.

Play No. 7: Hold each other accountable to your ministry integrity statement.

This is a crucial preventative measure. Unfortunately, shame and disgrace have brought devastation to pastors and ministries too often. Moral and ethical failure make the headlines while the world shakes its head in disbelief and mockery.

Despite being intensely scrutinized, Billy Graham's ministry spanned decades without scandal and garnered the admiration and respect of believers and nonbelievers alike. In November of 1948, Billy Graham saw several evangelists whose ministries fell due to moral, ethical, and financial scandals. While the team was staying in a hotel in Modesto, California, Billy called his associates together to establish preventative measures. They developed what became known as "The Modesto Manifesto," consisting of these four areas.

> **Money**: It was common practice among evangelists to put a lot of emotion and flourish into taking love offerings. This could bring unnecessary criticism—and temptation. The men vowed not to emphasize the offering. To avoid criticism they would always have the local campaign committees oversee the offerings and disbursements of funds—they would accept a straight salary regardless of how high the offerings were.
>
> **Immorality**: Religious leaders especially those who traveled were regularly falling to this temptation. The men agreed continually to pray for God to guard them from it. They also set up some rules to follow. They would never allow themselves to be alone with women—lunches, counseling sessions, or rides to auditoriums or airports. And they would always get their hotel rooms close together as another safeguard.
>
> **Exaggeration**: The phrase evangelistically speaking has been coined to label exaggerated figures of the number attending meetings or the number saved. The men vowed not to fall to this practice. If numbers were mentioned they were the ones generated by the local police, fire departments, or arena managers.
>
> **Criticism**: Often evangelists would criticize local pastors and churches from pulpits. The men vowed not to do this, nor would they ever criticize pastors who openly criticized them.[13]

In Appendix 8, I have included a "Commitment to Ministry Integrity." I urge you to review, revise, and adapt it for your ministry. Then make it your standard and hold each other accountable. I also suggest sharing it with the congregation. By doing so, you will encourage the people of your church to practice accountability in their own lives.

I also urge leadership to establish a firm policy to prevent child sexual abuse. Sadly, child sexual predators exist, and no church or ministry is immune from this problem. Predators often look for an opportunity to get involved in the youth or children's ministry or serve as camp counselors. Brotherhood Mutual recommends the following safeguards for churches.

1. **Use the Six-Month Rule**

    Don't give any volunteer worker the opportunity to be involved in a nursery or children's or youth work until he or she has been associated with your church for at least six months.

2. **Screen All Workers**
    - Investigate prior church membership and volunteer work.
    - Check references.
    - Develop an application form and have your attorney review and modify it.

3. **Use the Two-Adult Rule**

    On or off premises, always have at least two, unrelated adults supervising each room, vehicle, or other enclosed space—even if only one or two children need care.

4. **Other Preventive Measures**
    - Discourage the use of teenagers as nursery workers.
    - Increase supervisors for large groups.

- Prohibit situations in which one adult is alone with children in changing areas or restrooms.
- Develop a "claim check" procedure so that children are released only to a parent, guardian, or other authorized person.
- Don't permit participation in off-premise events, especially when they involve overnight stays, unless an adequate number of adult workers will be present.[14]

Play No. 8: Check communication with the five questions.

Is it true? Check the facts. Is it only hearsay? So often, we hear one side of the story and assume it to be true. Dig for the facts, hear the other perspective. "Fools have no interest in understanding; they only want to air their own opinions. ... Spouting off before listening to the facts is both shameful and foolish" (Prov. 18:2, 13).

Is it kind? Not every truthful word is kind, and not every kind word is truthful. "Speak the truth in love" (Eph. 4:15). Before sharing information, think through how it will make others feel and whether it might place someone in an awkward, embarrassing situation. "Do not let kindness and truth leave you; Bind them around your neck, Write them on the tablet of your heart" (Prov. 3:3 NASB). Wear kindness and truth like a beautiful necklace.

Is it confidential? Confidential information is to be shared only with someone who is either a part of the problem or a part of the solution. "A gossip goes around telling secrets, but those who are trustworthy can keep a confidence" (Prov. 11:13).

Is it appropriate? Should this be discussed with the person in private? If you need to discuss a concern that may be embarrassing to a team member, don't bring it up in the group setting. Set a time to meet alone and share your concern. "Some people make cutting remarks, but the words of the wise bring healing" (Prov. 12:18).

Is the source identified? Part of maturity is learning to be responsible for the words we speak. Paul identified the source when he brought up church concerns (1 Cor. 1:11). Before sharing a concern or criticism from congregants, make certain they are willing to have their names attached. If they prefer to remain anonymous, then don't pass it on. "Fire goes out without wood, and quarrels disappear when gossip stops. A quarrelsome person starts fights as easily as hot embers light charcoal or fire lights wood. Rumors are dainty morsels that sink deep into one's heart" (Prov. 26:20-22).

I've had several "egg on my face" blow-ups in the ministry. Here's one riveted in my memory bank. Fresh out of seminary, I had two of the leading ladies in the church approach me with concerns about one of the church secretaries, recently divorced and in her mid-thirties. "We don't think it's right that a male college-age intern is at her home at midnight. What's going on? We also think this secretary is not dressing appropriately for the church office, wearing low necklines and short skirts. Since you're her supervisor, we think you should talk to her about this." I thought to myself, *Where's the manual on how to talk to a woman about inappropriate attire?* Every indication pointed to an affair between her and the college-aged intern, but both denied it vehemently. Not knowing what else to do, I called the secretary in and launched into the issues. At first, it seemed she was taking things pretty well; then she asked the pointed question, "Where did these accusations come from?" I hadn't asked permission to name the two ladies who had the concern, so I said, "Let me talk to them." I went to the two women, and they both said, "We don't want anything to do with this. Don't mention our names." I was trapped. Hurt and angry, the secretary exploded about the cowardice of the two women who wouldn't talk to her face-to-face.

To make things more complicated, the secretary's ex-husband, a brilliant psychiatrist, was attending one of our Bible studies. Young women would attend the group, several making a decision to follow Christ, and then they'd abruptly stop attending. Strange? After investigating, we discovered he was sexually preying on the young women in the Bible study. We started church discipline, but he was crafty and slick. Understandably, the accusers felt intimidated by this psychiatrist, but how could I confront him without their evidence?

Meanwhile, the two women who didn't want to be identified kept asking, "When are you going to deal with this? We see the car of this college-aged intern at her house in the early morning hours." They were spying. The secretary was brimming with hostility, the intern was defiant, the morally twisted psychiatrist was claiming his innocence, and the two women making the accusation were fuming mad that I wasn't doing my job. The issue spilled over to other people, some taking sides without knowing the facts. The problem festered for months without a resolution in sight. Finally, the secretary and the intern left the staff and the church; the psychiatrist also withdrew. I was beaten up and depleted by the time it was over.

I learned never to allow anonymous grievances. Now, when someone launches into a tirade about another person, I recommend they make an appointment to talk face-to-face with them. Often the response has been, "You're the pastor. I think you need to talk to them." I say, "No, expressing your concern is your responsibility. If you need support in doing this, I will go with you." It's amazing how many issues are dropped at this point. For more serious concerns—like the sexual impropriety and predatory behavior I just described—the presence and support of a pastor or spiritual leader who will follow Matthew 18 principles can make all the difference.

Play No. 9: During a conflict, seek to understand rather than demand to be understood.

This play requires listening more than talking. Listen for the hurt that may lie below the surface. When you speak, choose your words carefully and lower the volume of your voice. A raised voice stirs anger and decreases the effectiveness of what you're saying. Anger is often fueled by faulty facts, so slow things down and seek clarification. Leave room for possible missing information while giving the person the benefit of the doubt. Avoid using sarcasm. Hot-headedness does not accomplish God's work. "A gentle answer deflects anger, but harsh words make tempers flare" (Prov. 15:1). "You must all be quick to listen, slow to speak, and slow to get angry" (James 1:19). Pointing out where someone is wrong to justify your position only adds fuel to the fire. Instead, admit where you're wrong or how you've inflicted pain and ask forgiveness.

Play No. 10: Refrain from talking *against* a member of the team ... talk *to* them.

Siblings can pick a fight even into their eighties! The leadership triad—Moses, Miriam, and Aaron—had a squabble late in their ministry game. "Then Miriam and Aaron spoke against Moses because of the Cushite woman whom he had married (for he had married a Cushite woman)" (Num. 12:1 NASB). Here are several observations about this incident.

First, they spoke against instead of speaking to Moses. The Bible tells us that Miriam was afflicted by the Lord with leprosy after grumbling against her brother, Moses (Numbers 12:10), an indication of the seriousness of her sin. Why did Miriam break out with leprosy but not Aaron? Numbers 12:1 uses a feminine singular verb, indicating Miriam led the criticism. Weak-kneed Aaron seemed to jump on the criticism bandwagon, going with the flow much like he did when he accommodated the request of the people to make a golden calf (Exod. 32). We'll never know what might have happened if Miriam and Aaron spoke directly to Moses, but we know their complaints behind his back led to a serious reprimand from the Lord.

Second, the issue was not the issue. Miriam and Aaron criticized Moses because he married a Cushite woman, that is, a non-Hebrew woman from the area we call Ethiopia. This was a smokescreen for the smoldering ember under the surface—the green-eyed monster jealousy. They complained, "'Has the LORD spoken only through Moses? Hasn't he spoken through us, too?' But the LORD heard them" (Num. 12:2). The real issue was bitter envy, an emotion often camouflaged. Here's an insight. When someone is upset, be alert to the potential of a deeper, underlying issue. If an individual is critical of the pastor's sermon, they may be concerned about the sermons or disappointed that the pastor didn't support their pet project. In addition to the surface issue, always look for a potentially deeper issue.

Third, the Lord heard them. God listens to every word we speak—a reality that should command our attention and lead us to a reverent fear of his holiness. James says, "Don't grumble about each other, brothers and sisters, or you will be judged. For look—the Judge is standing at the door!" (James 5:9). I know this verse refers specifically to the coming of Christ, but I also picture Jesus standing at the door, listening to my conversation.

Fourth, the Lord called for a face-to-face meeting. God confronts the problem directly. "Suddenly the LORD said to Moses and Aaron and to Miriam, 'You three come out to the tent of meeting.' So the three of them came out" (Num. 12:4 NASB). It's like the Lord was saying, "You three. In my office—now!" Problems are best dealt with face to face. Indeed, I believe most issues can be resolved when direct communication takes place. Your team's best play is face-to-face conflict resolution, so speak *to* people, not *against* them.

Play No. 11: Speak up when you feel misunderstood, hurt, or wounded.

Passivity isn't the answer when you have been misunderstood or wronged. If you bury your feelings, they will fester inside and eventually leak out. Choose the right setting and bring it up. Rather than making accusations, explain your own feelings in an honest and straightforward manner. "An open rebuke is better than hidden love! Wounds from a sincere friend are better than many kisses from an enemy" (Prov. 27:5-6).

Play No. 12: Do correction and performance reviews in private.

Public correction is a setup for hurt and embarrassment. Performance reviews must be done in private. Church staff members, including the senior or lead pastor, deserve to have someone sit down with them to talk through their work, commend them, and identify areas needing improvement. Whenever I did a private yearly review of the staff, I turned it into as positive an experience as possible. Appendix 9, a

Staff Review and Excellence Planner, can help your team with this.

Before meeting with staff members, I asked them to complete the review as they perceived their performance. They were usually tougher on themselves than I was. While noting areas needing improvement, I identified bright spots where their performance was exceptional and outstanding. After adding my evaluation, we talked about goals for personal development and excellence.

Following this, we read through their Ministry Position Description (MPD) point by point to ensure this accurately reflects their current responsibilities. Assignments often shift in an organization, so the MPD should also be revised for their protection. Following this, I asked what I could do to help them be more effective or aid in their personal growth and development. I also checked that they had the right equipment to be effective—computer, software, desk, chair, workspace, etc. And then we prayed together.

The review process does not need to be a dreaded experience. Handled in the right way, it can be uplifting and encouraging while corrective as needed. There may be a time when a person's performance needs to be discussed by the entire leadership team. Conversations with the person in private should precede this. Personnel matters must be kept confidential, in a locked file or password-protected computer. Privacy honors and protects everyone on the team.

Play No. 13: Confront sin and carry out biblical discipline when Scripture calls for it.

Four times in my ministry, I've been involved in a situation requiring church discipline. Truthfully, I would rather have a root canal. There is nothing easy about confronting sin. Here are some things I've learned. Before taking any action, spend several days in prayer, allowing God to give you a broken heart of compassion for the person as well as perception of what's going on in their life and what may be driving their behavior. Then, make an appointment to meet in private. Rather than being accusatory, express grief and concern for their well-being. Allow them to explain themselves with the awareness that you may be wrong. Always offer hope. The goal is not punishment but restoration. Not every sin requires discipline, so reserve it for situations that bring shame and damage to the family of God. I've included a list of sins requiring discipline according to Scripture on the flow chart in Appendix 10. This will help guide you in this difficult process.

Play No. 14: Encourage, encourage, encourage!

"Encourage one another day after day, as long as it is still called "Today," so that none of you will be hardened by the deceitfulness of sin" (Heb. 3:13 NASB). One of Satan's sharpest tools is discouragement. When hope fades and obstacles loom, discouragement moves in like an evening fog. Enthusiasm weakens, dreams dim, and pessimism takes over. No one is immune from discouragement. Some bouts of discouragement may be short-lived, while more severe episodes may linger for weeks or months. The potency of discouragement in the devil's arsenal is pictured in this imaginative illustration.

> It was announced that the devil was going out of business and would offer all tools for sale to whoever would pay the price. On the night of the sale, they were all attractively displayed, and a bad looking lot they were: Malice, Hatred, Envy, Jealousy, Sensuality, Deceit, and all the other implements of evil were spread out, each marked with its price. Apart from the rest lay

a harmless-looking wedge-shaped tool, much worn and priced higher than any of them.

Someone asked the devil what it was. "That's Discouragement," was the reply.

"Why do you have it priced so high?"

"I can pry open and get into a man's heart with that when I could not get near him with any of the others, and once inside, I can use discouragement in whatever way suits me best. It is worn well because I use it on everybody I can, and few people even know it belongs to me."[15]

If possible, I attempt to encourage someone every day. Encouragement is an antidote to the poison of discouragement and a preventative inoculation. Run play no. 14 all the time. Practice godly encouragement frequently so the devil doesn't get a foothold.

Play No. 15: Choose to be committed to the team.

It may be that more ministries fall apart from internal divisiveness than from any other cause. When you join a team—whether it is becoming an elder, serving as a deacon or deaconess, becoming part of the staff, or taking on another ministry role—it's easy to overlook some realities. We all have weaknesses. Everyone has a flat side. Some of these characteristics may not be immediately apparent, but as you work together, flaws will surface. This will test your commitment. As a team, make the deliberate choice to commit to each other. If you reach the point that you're unable to remain committed to the members of the team, it may be time for you to move on. I suggest everyone in the group sign something similar to the "My Commitment to the Team" tool found in Appendix 11 and renew the commitment from time to time.

Great job, team. You've read through God's playbook for a winning team. Now it's time to put things into practice. Appendix 12 provides a quick-reference guide summarizing the fifteen plays.

STAND TOGETHER

"Reese and Robbie," by Jack Doyle, is a heart-warming story about Jackie Robinson, the first black player to break into major league baseball. Branch Rickey, the owner of the Dodgers, told Robinson he would be insulted and denigrated beyond anything he could imagine when he joined the team. He was right. Robinson endured relentless verbal abuse, hate mail, racist obscenities, and death threats. Jackie replied to critics with his play on the field and was named Rookie of the Year in 1947. In 1949, he led the league with a .342 batting average, 37 stolen bases, and 124 runs-batted-in to be named National League MVP. The Dodgers won six pennants and the 1955 World Series with Jackie Robinson.

How did Jackie Robinson survive the attacks and not fall apart? Enter Pee Wee Reese, who grew up in segregated Louisville, Kentucky. Though he rarely had contact with blacks, Reese had a childhood memory of his father showing him a tree used for lynchings. Early in 1947, the Dodgers players drew up a petition refusing to take the field with a black man, but it fizzled when Pee Wee Reese refused to sign it. When Jackie Robinson joined the Dodgers later in the year, Pee Wee was the first Dodger to walk across the field and shake his hand. He later said, "It was the first time I'd ever shaken the hand of a black man."[16] Pee Wee endured insults and threats because of his association with Jackie. Reese and Robbie ate together in restaurants and roomed together when they were on the road. Reese's friendship during those dark days helped Robinson endure the hate mail and death threats.

The movie *42* and a statue in Brooklyn, New York, commemorate an incredible moment in history. And not just Reese and Robinson's history, but *all* history. On April 15, 1947, the Dodgers played in Cincinnati's Crosley Field against the Cincinnati Reds.[17] Prior to the game, Robinson had received death threats, and Cincinnati fans taunted him with racial slurs during the pregame infield practice. When the Dodgers took the field with Robinson at first base, the stands erupted with the ugly venom of racial hatred. Roger Kahn's classic book, *The Boys of Summer*, describes the scene. "Reese raised a hand. Then he walked from shortstop to first base and put an arm around the shoulders of Jackie Robinson. He stood there and looked into the dugout and into the stands, stared into the torrents of hate, a slim white southerner, who wore number 1 and just happened to have an arm draped in friendship around a black man, who wore number 42. Reese never said a word. The deed was beyond words."[18]

Fifty years later, at the funeral for Pee Wee Reese, Joe Black, an African American player who helped integrate baseball, paid tribute to Reese's support for Robinson. "When Pee Wee reached out to Jackie, all of us in the Negro League smiled and said it was the first time that a white guy had accepted us. When I finally got up to Brooklyn, I went to Pee Wee and said, 'Black people love you. When you touched Jackie, you touched all of us.' With Pee Wee, it was No. 1 on his uniform and No. 1 in our hearts."[19]

Since 1997, every team in baseball has retired Jackie Robinson's number 42, and on April 15, every major league player wears number 42 in Robinson's honor.

The day may come when an innocent teammate falls under attack. Others have abandoned them. They're standing alone against a barrage of insults and accusations.

And this is your moment.

Put an arm on their shoulder and stand with them.

No words needed.

Reflection and Discussion

Quick Recall

- What are the five questions to check communication?

    Is it _____?

    Is it _____?

    Is it _____?

    Is it _____?

    Is the _____

    _____?

- One of Satan's sharpest tools is _____

    _____.

Thinking It Through

1. Someone approaches you with a criticism of a church staff member. How do you handle this?

2. When you have a brilliant idea, how would you go about winning others over to adopt it?

3. What would you include in your "Commitment to Ministry Integrity" statement? Why?

4. What play would you add to the playbook?

Always be humble and gentle. Be patient with each other, making allowance for each other's faults because of your love. Make every effort to keep yourselves united in the Spirit, binding yourselves together with peace. (Eph. 4:2-3)

—15—

STORMS AND STANDING STRONG

PREVENTING DISASTER BY DEVELOPING DEEP ROOTS AND AUTHENTIC RELATIONSHIPS

Why do some ministry leaders stand strong for decades while others fall?

Consider a parable.

When the Santa Ana winds howl through Southern California, it's a common sight to see eucalyptus trees topple over. While these trees sometimes grow to a height of a hundred fifty to two hundred feet, shallow root systems put them at risk. About 90 percent of a eucalyptus tree's roots grow in the top twelve inches of soil. As a result, the taproot of the eucalyptus must extend at least six feet into the ground for it to stand. Even so, the tree may not withstand a strong windstorm.[1]

In contrast, the giant redwood and sequoia trees in Northern California last for centuries. My close friend,

Dale Haskins, was a forest ranger at California's Armstrong State Park, the sanctuary for some of the tallest trees in the world. The giant Parsons Jones tree in Armstrong State Park stands 310 feet in height—equivalent to a football field standing on end. Some redwoods date back to the time of Christ. So how do these gigantic trees withstand the storms of centuries? Redwoods intertwine with other redwoods—sometimes extending their roots a hundred feet from the trunk. They thrive in thick groves where the roots weave together and fuse. Connected through their massive root systems, redwoods derive incredible standing strength—withstanding high winds and raging floods. Try uprooting a redwood tree, and you have to deal with all his buddies close by.

THE ROOT OF THE PROBLEM

If we look at the ministry landscape as a forest, moral failure and burnout are toppling too many leaders, leaving disarray and confusion for the churches they served. Followers fall away. Some never return. Though there are other reasons, two primary factors cause ministry leaders to fall: shallowness and isolation.

Shallow Roots

Like a eucalyptus tree, if a ministry leader's root system is shallow, toppling over is inevitable. What makes the difference between shallow or deep roots? According to Jeremiah, roots deepen near water. "Blessed are those who trust in the LORD and have made the LORD their hope and confidence. They are like trees planted along a riverbank, with roots that reach deep into the water. Such trees are not bothered by the heat or worried by long months of drought. Their leaves stay green, and they never stop producing fruit" (Jer. 17:7–8). Note the phrase, "roots that reach deep into the water."

A friend told me after visiting a megachurch and listening to a well-known pastor and popular speaker, "He was a good speaker, very entertaining, but his message seemed to be about an inch deep. There was nothing to nourish the soul." About a year later, this well-known pastor was removed from the ministry because of moral failure.

As we've already observed, busyness and unrealistic expectations leave too many ministry leaders drained dry. With little time to extend their roots by the stream and drink deeply of the living God, cracks develop in their "bark"—and their "bark" develops a "bitter bite." They become irritable, difficult to work with, critical, and cranky. They live in the shallows—there is a noticeable lack of depth in their ministry.

Pastors have struggles, fears, and discouragements, and sometimes, they feel downright cynical. When tangling with cantankerous people, ministry leaders may struggle not to return the same. They're not beyond bitter feelings. Pastors are shepherds, but they are also sheep. They get depleted and exhausted. Many leaders run on empty, unable to give others what has been drained from their souls. Pushing for bigger programs and greater numbers when exhausted is dangerous. Effective leadership only flows from a repeated cycle of giving and refueling.

> Studies show that pastors experience anxiety and depression at a rate that is disproportionately high compared to the rest of the population. Because of the unique pressures associated with spiritual warfare, unrealistic expectations from congregants and oneself, the freedom many feel to criticize and gossip about pastors with zero accountability (especially in

the digital age), failure to take time off for rest and replenishment, marriage and family tensions as a result of the demands of ministry, financial strain, and self-comparison, pastors are prime candidates for relational isolation, emotional turmoil, and moral collapse.[2]

Ministry leaders must develop deep roots to prevent a fall. They must likewise guard against another root issue.

Isolated Roots

It's ironic. The isolated pastor is surrounded by people every day, but the relationships tend to be one-sided. Ministry leaders may be highly acclaimed and respected. They may appear to have it all together, with hundreds of followers and fans hanging on their every word and snapping up their best-selling books. But the applause of the crowd and approval of people is elusive and deceptive, masking the deep need for a few loyal friends who know them well, accept them when they're down, and speak truth into their life. Isolation is one of the most significant predictors of ministry failure. Instead of placing pastors on pedestals, we need to recognize they're not invincible or beyond human weakness. Only Jesus deserves to be on the pedestal.

We all have a dark side—weaknesses we're not proud of, pain we're reluctant to share, and our unique vulnerability to temptation. The poet Mary Oliver wrote, "The heart has many dungeons? Bring the light! Bring the light!"[3] The human heart harbors many secrets—deep feelings of inadequacy, lurking lust, woundedness, and disappointment. When the storm hits and the tempter attacks, isolated pastors have no one to turn to for help. Often, they can't share their pain with the congregation, the board, or staff. After all, they're supposed to be "the strong one." So, they isolate lest someone sees their cracks. Without someone to share the inner turmoil, personal disappointments, and inevitable tensions of the ministry, temptation beckons and invades, taking down the leader who has every conviction to the contrary. With few exceptions, moral failure is preceded by relational isolation, which is rarely identified as the cause. There is a solution. With a close confidant, a leader can "bring light" to hidden wounds, bitterness, and lurking temptations before they metastasize into ministry-threatening cancer.

How many pastors are going it alone? Far too many. This is what we're committed to preventing through Standing Stone Ministry. Our shepherds are trained, veteran pastors and missionaries who provide safe, confidential, and caring relationships. If every one of the Christ-centered, Bible-loving pastors in America had a shepherd, a confidant, a trusted friend, we'd see far fewer flameouts and a great deal more fruit for the kingdom. We'd march rather than limp. There'd be less shame and more spiritual success.

My friend, Gary Tangeman, was part of a group of pastors in the Seattle area who met together for seven years. During the group's monthly gathering, one of the pastors (I'll call him Dan) announced he wanted to retire. This abrupt change of plans took everyone by surprise. It seemed totally out of place. As they inquired further, they discovered Dan was depleted, burned out, and felt unable to continue. He acknowledged going off his medication for depression, deepening the problem. The group listened and cared for this exhausted servant of God, and then they asked if they could meet with the elders of Dan's church. He consented, and the elders warmly received them. When the group described the burnout Pastor Dan was experiencing, the elders gave Dan a three-month sabbatical, and the pastors from his group rotated to fill the pulpit in his absence. Dan returned renewed and energized. Without other pastors surrounding and intervening on his behalf, Dan very likely would have left the ministry.

Joanne and I meet monthly with four other pastoral couples to share two things: a meal and our lives. It's not a Bible study, though the Bible is woven into everything we share. It's not a prayer group, though we pray for each other. It's life sharing. Support for each other. Encouragement. It's a safe place to talk about what's heavy on our hearts. During our time together, we've worked through the loss of employment, end-of-life issues, depression, church conflict, back problems, eye surgeries, asthma, issues with our children, coronavirus, loss of a home, grieving ministry loss, and more. We laugh more than we cry—but we do shed tears. And it's okay to shed tears and acknowledge being lower than a whale's belly. As a group, we fight isolation. We extend our roots, growing deeper by the stream and wider as we get entangled in each other's life. Together we're stronger.

Storms on the Horizon

Discouragement, criticism, opposition, sickness, betrayal, personal failure—storms will come. Like a category four or five hurricane, the storms can rip apart our lives and leave a path of destruction. God allows the tempests to sharpen his servant, but Satan seeks to destroy us. As leaders, our roots had better be deep and strong.

Satan hates the church and the cause of Christ, and he is doing everything possible to obliterate it. So, like Paul, let's focus our spiritual eyes on the invisible spiritual battle raging around us. "For we are not fighting against flesh-and-blood enemies, but against evil rulers and authorities of the unseen world, against mighty powers in this dark world, and against evil spirits in the heavenly places" (Eph. 6:12).

Satan has an imaginary "bull's eye" on your chest if God is using you. He studies your weaknesses, aiming to take you down. As ministry leaders, we are engaged in a going-for-the-jugular, life-and-death fight to the finish. To the glory of God, the enemy is only given enough rope to hang himself.

Satan's Sifting

Luke records Jesus eating the Last Supper with his disciples. For some senseless reason, they reignite an old argument about who's the greatest. Jesus uses this opportunity to teach them about serving one another, the true path to greatness. And then he turns to Peter and addresses him, but the warning is for all the disciples as indicated by the inclusive language. "Simon, Simon, Satan has asked to sift each of you like wheat. But I have pleaded in prayer for you, Simon, that your faith should not fail. So when you have repented and turned to me again, strengthen your brothers" (Luke 22:31–32). Noting three things Jesus reveals about sifting can help you—and other ministry leaders—develop deep, strong roots.

First, Jesus calls Peter by his former name, Simon. Why didn't Jesus call him Peter? After all, Jesus gave him that name. Peter means "rock," but Simon is sinking in quicksand at this moment. I believe "Simon, Simon" calls to mind the headstrong, I'll-do-it-my-way fisherman of the past. Peter is reverting to his old ways and relying on the flesh. Rejecting the pull of the flesh and our former ways of life strengthens and deepens our roots.

Second, Jesus unmasks Satan's strategy to destroy Peter's faith. These days sifting wheat uses modern equipment, but in the time of Jesus, sifting was a hands-on, two-part process. The first step, threshing, loosened the outer shell, called the chaff, from the edible grain. The wheat was spread on a stone floor and beaten with a flail, a wooden handle attached to a shorter stick that would swing freely. Threshing involved crushing, pounding, and beating the wheat. The second step was winnowing. The wheat and the chaff were thrown into the air, and the very light chaff was blown away by the slightest wind. The wheat would fall back to the ground. As a biblical symbol, chaff represents the unbeliever blown away by the latest fad or philosophy. David declared the ungodly "are like worthless chaff, scattered by the wind" (Ps. 1:4). Satan hoped to destroy Peter's faith with shame and self-recrimination. He wanted Peter to deny his identity as a follower of Jesus. The prince of demons connived to sift Simon, hammering him with grief and guilt, then tossing all his hopes and aspirations in the air, hoping Peter's faith would vanish in the wind. Thankfully, the story didn't end here.

Finally, Jesus prayed for Peter that his faith would not fail. I think back to times when I felt beat up, disappointed in myself, and ready to quit the ministry. I know Jesus was praying for me. Jesus knew precisely why sifting was necessary and what he planned to accomplish in my life through it. He used the pounding and breaking. Being sifted precedes being lifted to serve in God's strength.

Be aware that Satan strategizes to sift ministry leaders—to deliver a pounding and beating that will blow them out of the ministry. Jesus didn't give up on Peter, and we should never give up on the ministry leaders around us. We help by praying for and encouraging those being sifted. The sifting of the shepherd is necessary to crush the outer shell of pride, blow away frivolous, fleshly efforts, and bring a ministry harvest. J.C. Metcalfe said,

> It is more than comforting to realize that it is those who have plumbed the depths of failure to whom God invariably gives the call to shepherd others. This is not a call given to the gifted, the highly trained, or the polished as such. Without a bitter experience of their own inadequacy and poverty, they are quite unfitted to bear the burden of spiritual ministry. It takes a man who has discovered something of the measures of his own weakness to be patient with the foibles of others.[4]

Ministry isn't about impressive credentials, a polished personality, and winsome communication skills. It's the broken vessel that releases the sweet aroma of Jesus. Pastor and author Neil Anderson made this observation. "Those who come to an end of themselves have transformational ministries; those who don't simply share information and coordinate programs."[5]

For over thirty years, I served as a senior pastor and now have a better understanding of the sifting that was going on in my life. I often felt like a failure, and I feared others would discover what I knew about myself. And I acknowledge going it alone during many of those years. I had no one to turn to. I cried in solitude, internalized fuming anger, tried to bandage my own wounds, struggled with bouts of depression, and frequently asked God why there was no one to care for me. Desperately I needed a close confidant, a shepherd with an arm around me, a friend to breathe encouragement in my loneliness.

Thank God there were exceptions to this loneliness when I had a like-minded friend who spoke truth into my life. Let me mention one of several: Pastor Avery Powers. Our relationship was like Jonathan and David, deep love and respect between two men. I knew he wanted the best for me, but he wasn't afraid to tell me what I needed to hear. A small faction—less than a handful—in the church worked tirelessly to undermine my leadership. They wanted me and others on the staff gone. But, nearly every week, Avery and I met, sharing our lives. He propped me up when I was ready to quit, and he ran interference with those who wanted to tan my hide.

One morning, as we discussed frustration with how boards operate, I blurted out, "Wouldn't it be great if we had 'God Meetings' instead of 'board meetings?'"

Avery said, "I was thinking the same thing as I drove here this morning." It was the spark behind the book you hold in your hand.

Sifting is not the problem. It's shallow roots and isolation that beget ministry failure. Listen to the weathered, imprisoned veteran of the faith, Paul, who goes to his knees in prayer:

> I pray that from his glorious, unlimited resources he will empower you with inner strength through his Spirit. Then Christ will make his home in your hearts as you trust in him. Your roots will grow down into God's love and keep you strong. And may you have the power to understand, as all God's people should, how wide, how long, how high, and how deep his love is. May you experience the love of Christ, though it is too great to understand fully. Then you will be made complete with all the fullness of life and power that comes from God. (Eph. 3:16-19)

The storms will come, and they will be ferocious, shaking the foundations of your faith and faithfulness. Count on it.

Pastors and leaders, a golden opportunity lies before you. If you allow God to weave your personalities, experiences, personal callings, and Christlike passions together, your team will become like the mighty redwoods. You will not fear or be devasted when facing the strong winds of powerful storms. Instead, the strength of working together and your commitment to each other will weather the storms and bring glory to God. You'll also develop great confidence in being a member of a Spirit-led team.

Stand strong—like the giant redwoods. Deepen your roots daily beside the stream of living water and extend your roots in deep, authentic relationships.

And do more than survive.

Thrive!

REFLECTION AND DISCUSSION

Quick Recall

- In order to withstand storms, the roots of redwood trees intertwine with the roots of other trees up to _____ feet away.

- There are two root problems that cause ministry leaders to fall: _____ roots and _____ roots.

- If you're being used by God, Satan has an imaginary _____ on your chest. He studies your _____, aiming to take you down.

Thinking It Through

1. Discuss the dangers of shallow roots and isolated roots.

2. How do you support and care for a spiritual leader who is being "sifted"?

3. Develop and share a personal plan to deepen your spiritual roots.

4. Share your personal plan to grow in healthy, authentic relationships.

Blessed are those who trust in the Lord and have made the Lord their hope and confidence. They are like trees planted along a riverbank, with roots that reach deep into the water. Such trees are not bothered by the heat or worried by long months of drought. Their leaves stay green, and they never stop producing fruit. (Jer. 17:7–8)

ABOUT THE AUTHORS

DAVE AND JOANNE BECKWITH

One week after their wedding in 1969, Dave and Joanne began their journey in pastoral ministry. And what an adventure it has been—some thrilling joys and successes along with many struggles, pain, and setbacks.

Dave's ministry experience includes youth and camp ministry, church administration, and senior pastor for over thirty years. Joanne has been an active partner in the ministry, working alongside Dave while leading women's ministries, mentoring, and teaching.

Currently, Dave and Joanne serve as shepherds with Standing Stone Ministry, caring for spiritual leaders. Dave is also the Western US Volunteer Director for Standing Stone. In 2007, Dave was named senior pastor emeritus for Woodbridge Community Church in Irvine, California, where he served as senior pastor for twenty years. He also serves as a lead pastor for churches going through transitions.

Dave and Joanne are both graduates of Biola University. Joanne received her BS degree in nursing. Professionally, she has worked in alcohol and drug rehab and psychiatry. Dave received his BS degree in business administration at Biola and did his seminary work at Talbot School of Theology. Additional graduate studies have included an MA in biblical studies, DMin in organizational leadership, and a PhD in church and family ministry. Other books by the authors include *I LOVE THE WORLD—It's People I Can't Stand* and *YOUR WINNING EDGE: God's Power Perfected in Weakness*.

Dave and Joanne love to hike, bike, and travel. They are blessed with two married daughters, Julie and Tami, four grandchildren, and ten great-grandchildren.

God has given them a heart for those who hurt and a shared life mission to help others discover God's power in their weakest moments. They'd love to connect in person or by phone or zoom. You may contact them for speaking, consulting, or leader care at:

STANDING STONE MINISTRY
National Headquarters
2340 S. El Camino Real, Suite 3
San Clemente, CA 92672
(970) 264-9329

dave.b@standingstoneministry.org
www.standingstoneministry.org
www.booksbybeckwith.com
www.pastorbiker.weebly.com

Date: _____

GOD MEETING

"My thoughts are nothing like your thoughts," says the Lord. "And my ways are far beyond anything you could imagine. For just as the heavens are higher than the earth, so my ways are higher than your ways and my thoughts higher than your thoughts." (Is.55:8–9 NLT)

Trust in the Lord with all your heart; do not depend on your own understanding. Seek his will in all you do, and he will show you which path to take. (Prov. 3:5–6 NLT)

6:30 p.m. *Surrender* Before God

Prepare your hearts to listen to God. Pray together in prayer partnerships of two or three, and/or read the Word followed by adoration, praise, and confession.

7:00 p.m. *Report* What God is Doing

Review the minutes from the previous meeting. Schedule a report from one of the ministries. Look for what God is doing and where he is leading. Gather around to pray and affirm those bringing a report.

7:30 p.m. *Discover* the Will of God
   Address agenda items for discussion and action. Make certain proposals have been thoroughly researched in advance. Pray before making major decisions and move forward with a sense of oneness.

8:45 p.m. *Do* the Work of God
   Make specific assignments for action items with due dates. Note these in the minutes and review them the following month during the reports.

9:00 p.m. *Sing* a Song of Praise and Close in Prayer

© 2021 *God Meetings*, Dave and Joanne Beckwith. Permission granted to reproduce for ministry leadership.

BIBLICAL QUALIFICATIONS FOR LEADERSHIP

Elder-Pastor-Overseer	**Deacon and Deaconess**
1 Tim. 3:1-7; Titus 1:5-9; Gal. 5:22-23; James 3:17-18	1 Tim. 3:8-13; Acts 6:3; Gal. 5:22-23; James 3:17-18

Personal Character

• Above reproach and well thought of	• Well respected and good reputation
• Good reputation and respectable	• Clear conscience
• Self-controlled and clear-headed	• Self-controlled and clear-headed
• Sensible and wise	• Faithful in all things
• Lover of what is good	• First tested and carefully examined
• Just and fair	• Not a heavy drinker or substance abuser
• Disciplined with a good grip on self	• Not dishonest with money
• Free from the love of money	• Honesty, integrity, not double-tongued
• Not self-centered	• Not sharp-tongued or a malicious gossip
• Not a heavy drinker or substance abuser	
• Not dishonest with money	

Family Life

• Faithful and committed to marriage partner	• Faithful and committed to marriage partner
• Well-managed home and obedient children	• Manages household and children well

Relationships with People

- Gentle, patient, kind, and not pushy
- Hospitable, enjoys guests in the home
- Good reputation outside the church
- Good reputation, full of the Spirit and of wisdom (Acts 6:3)
- Not hot-headed and quick tempered
- Not violent or attacking others
- Not quarrelsome and contentious
- Characterized by God's wisdom (James 3:17-18)
- Characterized by God's wisdom (James 3:17-18)

Spiritual Maturity

- Growing in the qualities of a Spirit-filled life (Gal. 5:22-23)
- Growing in the qualities of a Spirit-filled life (Gal. 5:22-23)
- Committed to the Word of God
- Committed to the mystery of the faith
- Apt to teach, encourage, or correct error
- Not a new convert
- Devout and dedicated to God

© 2021 *God Meetings*, Dave and Joanne Beckwith. Permission granted to reproduce for ministry purposes

Appendix 3
A CHEERFUL GIVER

Key principles to practice and experience the joy of giving!

1. *Giving is first giving your life to God* (2 Cor. 8:5).

2. *Giving is not to help God out.* He already has unlimited resources (Hag. 2:7-8; Ps. 50:10-12). Giving is not God's way of raising money ... it is God's way of raising children.

3. *Giving is to be done cheerfully—not in response to pressure.* "Each one *must do* just as he has purposed in his heart, not grudgingly or under compulsion, for God loves a cheerful giver" (2 Cor. 9:7 NASB).

4. *Giving is a wise, safe, and secure investment with immediate and long-range benefits.* "Don't store up treasures here on earth, where moths eat them and rust destroys them, and where thieves break in and steal. Store your treasures in heaven, where moths and rust cannot destroy, and thieves do not break in and steal" (Mt. 6:19-20 NLT). The eternal returns are beyond comprehension (Mt. 19:29).

5. *Giving affects your heart attitude.* "Wherever your treasure is, there the desires of your heart will also be" (Mt. 6:21 NLT).

6. *Giving is to demonstrate love—not law.* "I am not speaking *this* as a command, but as proving through the earnestness of others the sincerity of your love also. For you know the grace of our Lord Jesus Christ, that though He was rich, yet for your sake He became poor, so that you through His poverty might become rich (2 Cor. 8:8-9 NASB). Giving to the Lord's work must be voluntary, not compelled. "What percentage should you give? 5, 10, or 20 percent?" The biblical tithe is 10 percent, and this is

a good starting point. However, it is far more important to allow the Holy Spirit to direct the amount you give.

7. *Giving is to be done in faith.* The Bible tells of those believers who gave "according to their ability and beyond their ability" (2 Cor. 8:3 NASB). The Philippians sent a sacrificial gift, and Paul encouraged them that God would supply all their needs according to his glorious riches (Phil. 4:18-19).

8. *Giving is to be done quietly—not for show* (Mt. 6:3-4).

9. *Giving is God's means of blessing you financially.* Giving is not a give-to-get gimmick, but it is God's way of blessing and providing for the believer in special and surprising ways. Jesus said, "Give, and it will be given to you; good measure, pressed down, shaken together, running over, they will pour into your lap. For by your standard of measure it will be measured to you in return" (Lk. 6:38 NASB). Proverbs says, "The generous will prosper; those who refresh others will themselves be refreshed" (11:25 NLT), and "Honor the LORD from your wealth, and from the first of all your produce; so your barns will be filled with plenty, and your vats will overflow with new wine" (3:9-10 NASB). Many struggle financially without realizing that giving is God's way of blessing them with a better financial future.

10. *Giving is to be prayerfully planned and regularly practiced.* Paul instructed the believers in the New Testament to set aside an amount on the first day of every week (1 Cor. 16:2). In other words, prayerfully establish a plan and practice giving on a regular basis.

© 2021 Dave Beckwith, *God Meetings*.

THREE SIMPLE STEPS TO NEW LIFE

Beginning the Christian life is as simple as the ABCs backward. Today you can begin the most thrilling adventure of your life as a follower of Jesus Christ. Here's how.

Confess your sins. You may have lived a good, moral life, but the Bible says, "Everyone has sinned; we all fall short of God's glorious standard" and "the wages of sin is death, but the free gift of God is eternal life through Christ Jesus our Lord" (Rom. 3:23, 6:23 NLT).

The Bible also says, "God showed his great love for us by sending Christ to die for us while we were still sinners" (Rom. 5:8 NLT). Jesus Christ shed his blood on the cross to pay the penalty for your sins and to provide complete forgiveness. Confess your sins and ask Christ to forgive your sins. God "is patient toward you, not wishing for any to perish but for all to come to repentance" (2 Pet. 3:9 NASB).

Believe in Jesus Christ as your Savior and Lord. When a religious man asked Jesus how to get to heaven, Jesus told him, "For God loved the world so much that he gave his one and only Son, so that everyone who believes in him will not perish but have eternal life" (John 3:16 NLT). Believing in Jesus Christ is a simple choice and a step of faith. "If you confess with your mouth that Jesus is Lord and believe in your heart that God raised him from the dead, you will be saved" (Rom. 10:9 NLT).

Accept Christ into your life. The Bible says, "To all who believed him and accepted him, he gave the right to become children of God. They are reborn—not with a physical birth resulting from human passion or plan, but a birth that comes from God" (John 1:12–13 NLT). By accepting or asking Christ into your life, he now lives within you. "This is the secret: Christ lives in you" (Col. 1:27 NLT).

Dear God,

I confess my sin. Thank you that you forgive every sin because of Christ's death on the cross.

I believe in Jesus Christ. I place my faith and trust in him. He proved himself to be God through his miraculous life, his death on the cross, and resurrection from the dead.

I accept Jesus Christ into my life. By your Spirit, I invite you to live within me. Thank you that you make me into a new creation and give me eternal life.

Signed: _____

Date: _____

© 2021 *God Meetings*, Dave and Joanne Beckwith. Permission to reproduce for leadership training is granted.

SENIOR OR LEAD PASTOR MINISTRY POSITION DESCRIPTION

POSITION TITLE: SENIOR OR LEAD PASTOR
Name: _____

DIRECTLY RESPONSIBLE TO: Leadership Team

QUALIFICATIONS: 1 Timothy 3:1-7 and Titus 1:5-9; Galatians 5:22-23; James 3:17-18

TIME PRIORITIES: To build a healthy ministry, we affirm that it begins with a deepening spiritual life and a healthy home life. As a church, we want to ensure you have sufficient time for private prayer, meditation, and reading the Word, as well as other reading for your personal spiritual growth and message preparation. We also want to make certain that you and your spouse have time to deepen your relationship and invest in the lives of your children. We encourage going on a date with your spouse once or twice a month and being present for the important events in your children's lives.

SPECIFIC RESPONSIBILITIES

- **TEACHING AND SHEPHERDING**
  (1 Peter 5:2; Acts 20:28; John 21:15-17)
  1. Daily prayer for people and their needs (Acts 6:4)
  2. Diligent study from the Word of God (2 Tim. 2:15; 3:16-4:2)
  3. Preaching and teaching the Word of God (2 Tim. 4:1-4)
  4. Guarding the flock against danger and false teaching (Acts 20:28-30)
  5. Equipping believers for effective service and ministry (Eph. 4:12)
  6. Responding to requests for counseling, hospital ministry, visitation, and prayer for the sick (James 5:14)

7. Baptizing believers, serving communion, officiating at weddings, baby dedications, funerals, and other special occasions
8. Witnessing, leading individuals to Christ, and welcoming new people (2 Tim. 4:5)

- **LEADING** (1 Tim. 5:17; 1 Thess. 5:12; Heb. 13:17)
    1. Communicating the church vision, values, ministry plans, and successes
    2. Leading and planning for congregational worship (1 Tim. 4:13) and oversight of anything included in the worship services
    3. Supervising and directing the work of all members of the staff
    4. Sensing needs, overseeing, planning, and coordinating the general ministry of the church according to biblical principles (1 Pet. 5:1-4)
    5. Seeing that things are done properly and in an orderly manner (1 Cor. 14:40)
    6. Working with the Leadership Team in the development of ministry plans that are consistent with the vision and values of the church

GENERAL RESPONSIBILITIES FOR ALL STAFF

- **SUPERVISOR INSTRUCTIONS:** Respond promptly and thoroughly complete all instructions from your supervisor. If unable to complete a specific assignment, inform your supervisor as to why it could not be completed, and clarify what alternate steps need to be pursued.
- **PHONE CALLS, E-MAILS, MEMOS**: Promptly return and respond to phone calls, text messages, and e-mails from staff, leadership, and the congregation.
- **COMMUNICATION:** Talk directly to the person when a misunderstanding develops, a clarification is

needed, a concern is brought to your attention, or you see something that is not right.

- **SCHEDULE:** Communicate schedule to your supervisor and other members of the staff on a regular basis. If away from the office, be available by phone or text.
- **FINANCIAL:** Follow all financial procedures by monitoring budget areas, turning in receipts for expenses, exercising caution and conservatism in spending church funds.
- **INTEGRITY:** Carefully follow all financial, moral, verbal and ethical guidelines specified in Principles for Ministry Integrity.
- **DILIGENCE:** Perform all responsibilities with excellence and wholeheartedness (Col. 3:23).
- **CONSTITUTION, BYLAWS, AND POLICIES:** Carefully follow all procedures specified in these documents.

STARTING DATE OF MINISTRY: _____

EFFECTIVE DATE OF MPD: _____

©2021 *God Meetings*, Dave and Joanne Beckwith. Permission to reproduce for leadership training is granted.

CORE VALUES

- *We value CHRIST as the Head of the Church.* We adore and honor him and yield our will, control, and ownership of the church to him.

- *We value the WORSHIP of God, who is present among us.* Our ultimate priority is to love God with our entire being and with all our strength every minute of every day and to gather regularly to worship him.

- *We value the BIBLE as God's inspired Word.* The Bible is the core content of all our teaching and daily guide for practical living.

- *We value PRAYER as God's plan for a personal relationship with him.* Prayer empowers us, unites us, and changes lives. We pray about everything.

- *We value PEOPLE and changed lives as our mission.* Only Christ brings permanent change and transformation of a life. Property, facilities, and financial resources are of secondary value to the eternal worth of a human life.

- *We value lifelong DISCIPLESHIP for spiritual maturity.* New life in Christ is immediate, but growth to Christlikeness is a process requiring time and patience—not spiritual shortcuts or quick formulas.

- *We value COMMUNITY through small groups and personal relationships.* We extend love, grace, forgiveness, acceptance, and encouragement to each other.

- *We value SPIRITUAL GIFTS given to every believer.* Pastors train and equip each believer as ministers. Our spiritual impact is directly proportionate to the mobilization of every believer to be filled with the Spirit and exercise their spiritual gift toward a clear God-given mission and vision.

- *We value TELLING OTHERS about the love and forgiveness of God through Christ.* We are in partnership with believers all over the world to grow the family of God.

© 2021 Dave Beckwith in *God Meetings*. Permission granted to reproduce for ministry leadership. Developed by the Leadership Team at Woodbridge Community Church in Irvine, CA 92604

CHARTING THE COURSE MINISTRY PLANNER

Worksheet for existing ministries and the launch of new ministries

1. Give a brief statement of WHY this ministry is important and WHAT the ministry hopes to accomplish. How does this contribute to the vision and purpose of the organization?

2. Identify WHO the ministry will reach, and WHO is responsible to lead and how many people are needed to carry out the work (identify specific positions and responsibilities). What are the minimum qualifications for someone serving in this ministry?

3. WHAT are the resources needed to accomplish this ministry? Meeting space, curriculum, publicity, budget, etc.

4. WHAT safety factors need to be considered? Background checks, insurance, adult supervision, transportation, etc.

5. HOW are other ministries impacted? Think laterally of how others will be affected by this ministry.

© 2021 Dave Beckwith in *God Meetings*. Permission granted to reproduce for ministry leadership.

COMMITMENT TO MINISTRY INTEGRITY

Financial

- When handling church funds, it is best to have others involved with you to protect your integrity.
- Carefully account for all church expenses with accurate records and receipts.

Moral

- Guard against being alone with a member of the opposite sex other than your spouse or a family member.
- Choose to not eat out or travel with a member of the opposite sex without others present.
- It is best for men to counsel men and women to counsel women. Exceptions to this should include others present in the office at the time, a window in the office, or a door propped open.

Verbal

- Practice letting your yes be yes and your no, no!
- Develop a reputation for dependability, reliability, and accessibility. Return phone calls, emails, and text messages.
- When reporting statistics or ministry reports, use accurate, conservative numbers.
- When using the work of others, be careful to give appropriate credit.
- Carefully guard and protect information shared with you in confidence.

_____   _____

Signature   Date

© 2021 Dave Beckwith in *God Meetings*. Permission granted to reproduce for ministry leadership.

STAFF REVIEW AND EXCELLENCE PLANNER

There are 4 underlying principles for this review:

1. **Excellence is a process of continual learning and sharpening.**
   Observe people who are good at their work— skilled workers are always in demand and admired; they don't take a back seat to anyone. (Prov. 22:29 MSG)

2. **Commendation and correction are both of great value.**
   Appreciate those who diligently labor among you, and have charge over you in the Lord and give you instruction, and that you esteem them very highly in love because of their work. Live in peace with one another. (1 Thess. 5:12-13 NASB)
   If you ignore criticism, you will end in poverty and disgrace; if you accept correction, you will be honored. (Prov. 13:18 NLT)

3. **Spirit-filled attitudes are God's will.**
   Rejoice always; pray without ceasing; in everything give thanks; for this is God's will for you in Christ Jesus. Do not quench the Spirit. (1 Thess. 5:16-19 NASB)

4. **Wholeheartedness is the minimal standard for our work.**
   Whatever you do, do your work heartily, as for the Lord rather than for men, knowing that from the Lord you will receive the reward of the inheritance. It is the Lord Christ whom you serve. (Col. 3:23-24 NASB)

KEY

A = Awesome, exceptional, and outstanding
G = Good work, satisfactory, and meets acceptable standards
W = Work on this, improvement needed

ATTITUDE

___ Appropriate cheerfulness and positive outlook

___ Quickly apologizes and asks forgiveness when others are hurt or wronged

___ Communicates that others are important and shows respect for the opinions of others

___ Talks directly to the person involved if there is a misunderstanding or concern, a clarification is needed, or a personal hurt

___ Compassion and concern for others

___ Demonstrates flexibility and cooperation

___ Considerate of others and tactful in comments

___ Friendly and warm to new people and church members alike

___ Frequently encourages others and expresses genuine appreciation

___ Seeks positive solutions to problems

___ Responds to authority

___ Demonstrates calm, patience, and control of temper when under pressure

___ Radiates an attitude of well being and confidence

___ Receives advice and correction without becoming defensive

___ Quickly acknowledges when wrong

Aptitude
Professional Skills

___ Cleanliness of work areas

___ Promptness for meetings and events

___ Completion of all aspects of Ministry Position Description (MPD)

___ Demonstrates a willingness to take steps of faith and believe God to provide

___ Thorough clean-up of a meeting area up after every use

___ Alertness to listen to others and perceive needs

___ Responds promptly to voice mail, email, and written communication

___ Presents plans with enthusiasm but without pushiness or manipulation

___ Performs required amount of work in a timely fashion

___ Accuracy of work and careful attention to details

___ Follows all policies and procedures

___ Manages budget area carefully and keeps accurate records and receipts

___ Seeks new and improved ways of doing things

___ Spends church funds with caution and shops for the best value

___ Communicates with everyone directly or indirectly impacted by a decision or change

___ Actively seeks the success of other members of the team

___ Follows all staff guidelines in interaction with the opposite sex

___ Consistency of office schedule and communication of schedule to other staff

MINISTRY SKILLS
(complete for pastors and ministry directors)

___ Diligently studies and prepares for teaching and preaching

___ Regularly reaches out to new people and seeks to lead others to Christ

___ Regularly sets aside time for personal and ministry prayer

___ Equips others to serve in the area of their spiritual gifts and seeks to pass ministry on to others

___ Gives appropriate credit when using the work of others

___ Responds promptly to requests for hospital visitation or counseling

___ Designs and distributes attractive promotional materials

___ Actively involved in mentoring others

___ Communicates all calendar events to the secretarial staff

___ Confronts unpleasant situations as needed and when appropriate

Notes and Goals for Personal Development and Excellence

_____
Signature of Employee

_____
Signature of Supervisor

_____
Date

© 2021 *God Meetings*, Dave and Joanne Beckwith. Permission to reproduce for leadership training is granted.

The Ministry of RESTORATION

WHEN IS RESTORATION NEEDED?

When a person engages in a continual, ongoing, unrepentant practice of "sexual sin, or is greedy, or worships idols, or is abusive, or is a drunkard, or cheats people" (1 Cor. 5:11 NLT), divisiveness, creating factions (Rom. 16:17-18; Titus 3:9-10), false teaching (Gal. 1:7-9; 1 Tim. 1:19-20; 2 Tim. 2:17-18), sorcery and occult practices (Deut. 18:10-11; Gal. 5:19-21).

WHAT IS THE ATTITUDE FOR RESTORATION?

"... if anyone is caught in any trespass, you who are spiritual, restore such a one in a spirit of gentleness; *each one looking to yourself*, so that you too will not be tempted." (Gal. 6:1 NASB)

WHAT IS THE RESTORATION PROCEDURE?

"If another believer sins against you, go privately and point out the offense. If the other person listens and confesses it, you have won that person back. But if you are unsuccessful, take one or two others with you and go back again, so that everything you say may be confirmed by two or three witnesses. If the person still refuses to listen, take your case to the church. Then if he or she won't accept the church's decision, treat that person as a pagan or a corrupt tax collector." (Mt. 18:15-17 NLT)

"Do not listen to an accusation against an elder unless it is confirmed by two or three witnesses. Those who sin should be reprimanded in front of the whole church; this will serve as a strong warning to others." (1 Tim. 5:19-20 NLT)

With repentance, begin the process of restoration which includes forgiveness and comfort (2 Cor. 2:5-11).

```
One person          2 or 3 talk          Church
talks to     -->    with the     -->    is informed    -->   D-I-S-C-I-P-L-I-N-E
them alone          person
        If sin              If sin              If sin
        continues           continues           continues
```

If the person repents and makes restitution and amends as needed, forgiveness is extended and restoration begins.

HOW TO FORGIVE AND RESTORE

1. **Offer hope.**
   "'For I know the plans I have for you,' says the LORD. 'They are plans for good and not for disaster, to give you a future and a hope.'" (Jer. 29:11 NLT)

2. **Extend forgiveness and protect the reputation of the person.**
   "... if any among you strays from the truth and one turns him back, let him know that he who turns a sinner from the error of his way will save his soul from death and will cover a multitude of sins." (James 5:19-20 NASB)
   "He who conceals a transgression seeks love, but he who repeats a matter separates intimate friends." (Prov. 17:9 NASB)
   "Most important of all, continue to show deep love for each other, for love covers a multitude of sins." (1 Pet. 4:8 NLT)
   Love "...keeps no record of being wronged." (1 Cor. 13:5 NLT)

3. **Establish a process of restoration, prayer partnership, and accountability.**
   "Confess your sins to each other and pray for each other so that you may be healed. The earnest prayer of a righteous person has great power and produces wonderful results." (James 5:16 NLT)

© 2000, 2021, Dave Beckwith from GOD MEETINGS

MY COMMITMENT TO THE TEAM

I am committed to Jesus Christ and to highly effective team ministry. I thank God for placing me with others who also love the Lord and desire to serve him.

I recognize that we are flawed human beings, and I expect that there will be different perspectives. Knowing God often uses irritations, disagreements, disappointments, and struggles to mold and shape character, I look for how God is using these things in my life and the lives of others on the team. As Christ has accepted me, I choose to accept my partners in ministry.

To preserve the oneness we share in Christ, I will give my support, encouragement, and commitment to each member of the team. I choose to give a good report to others, and if this is not possible, I will speak privately and work together to seek a solution.

- May God, who gives this patience and encouragement, help you live in complete harmony with each other, as is fitting for followers of Christ Jesus. Then all of you can join together with one voice, giving praise and glory to God, the Father of our Lord Jesus Christ. Therefore, accept each other just as Christ has accepted you so that God will be given glory. (Rom. 15:5-7 NLT)
- Set a guard, O LORD, over my mouth; keep watch over the door of my lips. (Ps. 141:3 NASB)
- May the words of my mouth and the meditation of my heart be pleasing to you, O LORD, my rock and my redeemer. (Ps. 19:14 NLT)

- Do not speak against one another. (James 4:11 NASB)
- I am in them and you are in me. May they experience such perfect unity that the world will know that you sent me and that you love them as much as you love me. (John 17:23 NLT)

With all this in mind, I choose to support, encourage, and be committed to the other members of this team to the glory of God.

_____   _____
Signed   Date

© 2021 Dave Beckwith in *God Meetings*. Permission granted to reproduce for ministry leadership.

Playbook for God's Team

Winning plays to work together and prevent problems

Play No. 1: Show up

Play No. 2: Do an attitude check

Play No. 3: Be diligent to preserve the unity of the Spirit

Play No. 4: Make decisions based on core values

Play No. 5: Develop ministries with an effective game plan

Play No. 6: Don't ramrod proposals and plans

Play No. 7: Hold each other accountable to your ministry integrity statement

Play No. 8: Check communication with five questions—is it true, kind, confidential, appropriate, and is the source identified?

Play No. 9: During a conflict, seek to understand rather than demand to be understood

Play No. 10: Refrain from talking against a member of the team … talk to them

Play No. 11: Speak up when you feel misunderstood, hurt, or wounded

Play No. 12: Do correction and performance reviews in private

Play No. 13: Confront sin and carry out biblical discipline when Scripture calls for it

Play No. 14: Encourage, encourage, encourage!

Play No. 15: Choose to be committed to the team

© 2021 Dave Beckwith in *God Meetings*. Permission granted to reproduce for ministry leadership.

ENDNOTES

Chapter One

1. Personal story of Dave and Joanne Beckwith, *Your Winning Edge: God's Power Perfected in Weakness* (Plymouth, MA: Elk Lake Publishing, 2019), 153-154, 181-182.
2. Gary McIntosh, "Building Board Unity," *The Good Book Blog*, Talbot School of Theology, accessed Oct. 1, 2021, https://www.biola.edu/blogs/good-book-blog/2017/building-board-unity
3. Richard J. Krejcir, Ph.D., "What is Going on with the Pastors in America?" *Francis A. Schaeffer Institute of Church Leadership Development* (survey of 1,050 pastors conducted at a pastor's conference in Pasadena, CA, 2005 and 2006), accessed Oct. 1, 2021, http://www.churchleadership.org/apps/articles/default.asp?articleid=42347
4. Wayman D. Miller, *The Role of Elders in the New Testament Church* (Tulsa: Plaza, 1980), 79, cited by Michael J. Anthony, *The Effective Church Board* (Grand Rapids, MI: Baker Books, 1993), 107.
5. Charles Willis, "Survey shows declining numbers in forced terminations of pastors," *Baptist Press*, Sept. 17, 1998, accessed Nov. 11, 2021, https://www.baptistpress.com/resource-library/news/survey-shows-declining-numbers-in-forced-terminations-of-pastors/

6. Charles Swindoll, *Swindoll's Living Insights New Testament Commentary: James, 1 and 2 Peter* (Carol Stream, IL: Tyndale House Publishers, Inc., database WordSearch: 2019), s.v. "1 Pet. 3:11."

Chapter Two

1. DeWitt Wallace, Lila Acheson Wallace, *Reader's Digest*, Vol. 199, 1981, 196.
2. Dave Beckwith, "Keys for Team Ministry," a training manual for staff and leadership, Jan. 1988, 4-8.
3. Franklin A. Gevurtz, The European Origins and the Spread of the Corporate Board of Directors, 931, accessed Oct. 1, 2021, https://www.stetson.edu/law/lawreview/media/the-european-origins-and-the-spread-of-the-corporate-board-of-directors.pdf
4. Robert H. Thune, *Gospel Eldership: Equipping a New Generation of Servant Leaders* (Greensboro, NC: New Growth Press, 2016), 28.
5. Charles Stanley, *The Source of My Strength* (Nashville, TN: Thomas Nelson Publishers, 1994), 224.
6. Charles R. Swindoll, "Take Heart, Insight for Today," April 3, 2020, accessed Oct. 1, 2021, https://insight.org/resources/daily-devotional/individual/take-heart1
7. Erwin W. Lutzer, "Who's in Charge Here?" *Moody Monthly*, July-August 1983, 69.
8. Bruce W. Jones, *Ministerial Leadership in a Managerial World* (Wheaton: Tyndale Press, 1988), 23.
9. A. W. Tozer, *God Tells the Man Who Cares* (Camp Hill, PA: Christian Publications, 1970), reprinted in *The Standard*, March 1985, 6-7.

Chapter Three

1. National Archives Store, accessed Oct. 15, 2021, hhttps://www.nationalarchivesstore.org/collections/

presidential/products/it-can-be-done-ronald-reagan-plaque
2. Bill Hybels, "Up to the Challenge," *Leadership*, Fall 1996, 61.
3. Charles Stone, "10 Signs You Might Be a Narcissistic Leader (and How to Change)," *ChurchJobFinder*, accessed Oct. 15, 2021, https://churchjobfinder.com/10-signs-you-might-be-narcissistic-leader-how-to-change-charles-stone/
4. Charles Stone citing Peter L. Steinke, "Clergy Affairs," *Journal of Psychology and Christianity*, Vol. 8, No. 4 (1989), 60-61.
5. Ray Stedman, "Should a Pastor Play Pope?" *Moody Monthly*, July-August 1976, 42.
6. Justin Barrett, "Does Your Pastor Need a Friend?" Christianity Today, Sept. 20, 2017, accessed Oct. 21, 2021, https://www.christianitytoday.com/ct/2017/october/does-your-pastor-need-friend.html

Chapter Four

1. *Reddit*, accessed Oct. 1, 2021, https://www.reddit.com/r/etymology/comments/bvjm5q/what_is_the_origin_of_board_in_board_of_directors/
2. John Morrish, "Where does the word board (of directors) come from?" *Management Today*, April 2, 2015, accessed Oct. 1, 2021, https://www.managementtoday.co.uk/does-word-board-of-directors-from/article/1340275
3. Gary C. Hoag, Wesley K. Willmer, Gregory J. Henson, *The Council: A Biblical Perspective on Board Governance* (ECFA Press, 2018), 61.
4. Kenneth L. Barker, Gen. Editor, *NIV Study Bible* (Grand Rapids, MI: Zondervan Publishing, 2002), 123.
5. Aubrey Malphurs, *Leading Leaders* (Grand Rapids, MI: Baker Books, 2005), 105.

6. Dan Busby, John Pearson, *Lessons from the Church Boardroom* (ECFA Press, 2018), 98-102.
7. Larry Osborne, *Sticky Teams* (Grand Rapids, MI: Zondervan Publishing, 2010), 38.
8. John Carver, *Boards That Make a Difference* (San Francisco: Jossey-Bass, 1997), 19.

Chapter Five

1. Richard K. Wallarab, "A Meeting of the Board: A Satire," *Christianity Today,* Jan. 19, 1979, accessed Oct. 21, 2021, https://www.christianitytoday.com/ct/1979/january-19/meeting-of-board-satire.html
2. John Carver, *Boards That Make a Difference* (San Francisco, CA: Jossey-Bass Publishers, 1997), xiv.
3. Peter F. Drucker, *Management: Tasks, Responsibilities, Practices* (New York: Harper-Collins, 1974), 628.
4. Aubrey Malphurs, *Leading Leaders* (Grand Rapids, MI: Baker Books, 2005), 15.
5. Dave and Joanne Beckwith, *Your Winning Edge: God's Power Perfected in Weakness* (Plymouth, MA: Elk Lake Publishing, 2019), 42.
6. *The State of Pastors: Barna Report, 2017* (Pepperdine University, 2017), 11, 20.
7. "The Results of Our 2016 Pastor Survey," accessed Oct. 21, 2021, www.expastors.com/2016-expastors-pastor-survey/
8. *The State of Pastors: Barna Report,* 2017, 11.
9. Richard J. Krejcir, "Statistics on Pastors: 2016 Update," *Francis A. Schaeffer Institute of Church Leadership Development, accessed Oct. 30, 2021,* http://www.churchleadership.org/apps/articles/default.asp?blogid=4545&view=post&articleid=Statistics-on-Pastors-2016-Update&link=1&fldKeywords=&fldAuthor=&fldTopic=0
10. C. H. Spurgeon, *Lectures to My Students, Vol. 1* (Pantianos Classics, 1875), 124.

11. Marshall Shelley, *Well-intentioned Dragons* (Minneapolis, MN: Bethany House Publishers, 1985), 42.
12. Busby and Pearson, *Lessons from the Church Boardroom* (Winchester, VA: ECFA Press, 2018), 205.

Chapter Six

1. Richard J. Foster, *Freedom of Simplicity: Finding Harmony in a Complex World* (New York: Harper Collins, 1981), 72.
2. Larry Osborne, *Sticky Teams* (Grand Rapids, MI: Zondervan, 2010), 140.
3. Busby and Pearson, *Lessons from the Church Board Room* (Winchester, VA: ECFA Press, 2018), 212-216.
4. Henry T. Blackaby and Claude V. King, *Experiencing God* (Nashville, TN: Lifeway Press, 1990), 64.
5. Busby and Pearson, *Lessons from the Church Boardroom* (Winchester, VA: ECFA Press, 2018), 205.
6. George Babbes and Michael Zigarelli, *The Minister's MBA: Essential Business Tools for Maximum Ministry Success* (Nashville: B&H, 2006), 127.
7. Chuck Smith, "The Tragic Mistake of the Modern Church," *Decision*, June 2021, 40, used with permission from *Living Water* by Chuck Smith (Santa Ana, CA: Word for Today. 2007).
8. Smith, 40.

Chapter Seven

1. Kenneth L. Barker, Gen. Editor, *NIV Study Bible* (Grand Rapids, MI: Zondervan Publishing, 1984), 1713.
2. Robert L. Saucy, *The Church in God's Program* (Chicago: Moody Press, 1972), 150.
3. Dave Beckwith, *New Testament Elders—Twentieth Century Pastors* (Grace Graduate School of Theology: Master of Biblical Studies Thesis, 1978), 28.
4. Timothy Z. Witmer, *The Shepherd Leader* (Phillipsburg, NJ: P&R Publishing, 2010), 35.

5. Witmer, 102.
6. William Barclay, ed., *The Gospel of John*, vol. 2, The Daily Study Bible Series (Philadelphia, PA: Westminster John Knox Press, 1975), 53.
7. William F. Arndt and Wilbur F. Gingrich, *A Greek-English Lexicon of the New Testament and Other Early Christian Literature* (Chicago: The University of Chicago, 1957), 436.
8. Trent C. Butler, Gen. Editor, *Holman Bible Dictionary* (Holman Bible Publishers, 1991), s.v. "Deacon, Deaconess."
9. Pliny the Younger, cited by Kenneth S. Wuest, *Romans in the Greek New Testament* (Grand Rapids, MI: Wm. B. Eerdmans Publishing Co., 1955), 257.
10. John MacArthur, *The New Testament Commentary: 1 Timothy* (Chicago: Moody Publishers, 1995), s.v. 1 Timothy 3:11.
11. John F. MacArthur Jr., *The MacArthur Study Bible: New American Standard Bible* (Nashville, TN: Thomas Nelson Publishers, 2006), s.v. Titus 1:6.
12. Patrick Lencioni, *The Advantage: Why Organizational Health Trumps Everything Else in Business* (San Francisco: Jossey-Bass, 2012), 21-23.
13. Sarah Eekhoff Zylstra, "Governing God's House: How 500 Churches Keep from Collapsing," *Christianity Today*, Aug. 2, 2016, accessed Oct. 30, 2021, https://www.christianitytoday.com/news/2016/august/how-500-churches-keep-from-collapsing-ecfa-board-governance.html
14. Phil Taylor, *Eldership Development: From Application to Affirmation* (Orlando, FL: Floodlight Press, 2017), 105.
15. Larry Osborne, *Sticky Teams* (Grand Rapids, MI: Zondervan, 2010), 42.

16. There are a number of versions of this all attributed to an unknown source.
17. Paul David Tripp, *Dangerous Calling* (Wheaton, IL: Crossway, 2012), 62.

Chapter Eight
1. Frederick Buechner, *Wishful Thinking: A Theological ABC* (New York: Harper & Row, 1973), 15.
2. Ruth Haley Barton, *Pursuing God's Will Together* (Downers Grove, IL: InterVarsity Press, 2012), 42-43.
3. Henry T. Blackaby and Claude V. King, *Experiencing God* (Nashville, TN: Lifeway Press, 1990), 64.

Chapter Nine
1. Michael Pritchard, "Quotable Quotes," *Goodreads*, accessed Oct. 22, 2021, https://www.goodreads.com/quotes/3689-fear-is-the-little-dark-room-where-negatives-are-developed
2. John McCormick, "You Snooze, You Lose: Montgomery Ward's woes began with a bad bet," *Newsweek*, July 21, 1997.
3. Kate Bowler, "I'm a scholar of the 'prosperity gospel.' It took cancer to show me I was in its grip," *Vox*, Mar 12, 2018, accessed Oct. 22, 2021, www.vox.com/first-person/2018/3/12/17109306/prosperity-gospel-good-evil-cancer-fate-theology-theodicy
4. Thom S. Rainer, "Ten Rules of Thumb for Healthy Churches in America," *Church Answers,* March 4, 2013, accessed Oct. 22, 2021, www.churchanswers.com/blog/ten-rules-of-thumb-for-healthy-churches/
5. Henry M. Morris, *The Defender's Study Bible*, (Nashville, TN: Thomas Nelson Publishing, 1995), s.v. Luke 14:28.
6. Blackaby and King, *Experiencing God* (Nashville, TN: Lifeway Press, 1990), 108, 170.

7. Rick Warren, "How God Grows You Through the 6 Phases of Faith," *Pastors.com*, Aug. 28, 2015, accessed Oct. 22, 2021, https://pastors.com/how-god-grows-you-through-the-6-phases-of-faith/

Chapter Ten

1. Claude V. King, "A Sacred Assembly," *Solemn Assembly, A Step-by-Step Guide*, accessed Oct. 21, 2021, https://downloads.frc.org/EF/EF09E08.pdf
2. King, *op. cit.*
3. Thom S. Rainer, "Is It Time to Rethink Church Business Meetings?" *Church Answers*, February 18, 2015, accessed Oct. 21, 2021, https://churchanswers.com/blog/time-rethink-church-business-meetings/
4. Thom S. Rainer, "10 Really Strange Things That Happened at Church Business Meetings," *Christian Post Contributor*, accessed Oct. 21, 2021, https://www.christianpost.com/news/10-really-strange-things-that-happened-at-church-business-meetings.html
5. Roy R. Roberts, *The Game of Life: Studies in James* (Winona Lake, IN: BMH Books, 1976), 116.
6. Henry T. Blackaby and Claude V. King, *Experiencing God*, (Nashville, TN: Lifeway Press, 1990), 169.

Section Two

1. Stephen W. Smith, "Leadership's Perfect Storm," *Outcomes Magazine*, accessed Oct. 31, 2021, www.outcomesmagazine.com/leaderships-perfect-storm/

Chapter Eleven

1. Thom Rainer, "The Pastor's Work Week," *Church Answers*, Podcast Episode #017, Aug. 9, 2013, accessed Oct. 21, 2021, www.churchanswers.com/podcasts/rainer-on-leadership/the-pastors-work-week-rainer-on-leadership-017/

2. George Barna, "A Profile of Protestant Pastors in Anticipation of Pastor Appreciation Month," *The Barna Group*, Sept. 25, 2001, 2.
3. George Barna, *The Habits of Highly Effective Churches* (Ventura, CA: Regal Books, 1999), 37.
4. "Statistics on Pastors: 2016 Update." *Francis A. Schaeffer Institute of Church Leadership Development.*
5. Steve Sjogren, "Tea with Drucker," *Church Planting*, accessed Oct. 21, 2021, www.churchplanting.com/tea-with-drucker/#.XGH
6. Ken Sande, "Strike the Shepherd," *The Desperate Pastor Blog*, accessed Oct. 21, 2021, www.desperatepastor.blogspot.com/search?q=stalin
7. "Statistics on Pastors: 2016 Update." *Francis A. Schaeffer Institute of Church Leadership Development.*
8. *The State of Pastors: Barna Report, 2017* (Pepperdine University, 2017), 11, 20.
9. "The Results of Our 2016 Pastor Survey," accessed Oct. 21, 2021, www.expastors.com/2016-expastors-pastor-survey/
10. "Statistics on Pastors: 2016 Update." *Francis A. Schaeffer Institute of Church Leadership Development.*
11. Charles R. Swindoll, "Leadership and Administration: The Pastor's Relationship with the Board," *Leadership Handbooks of Practical Theology, Volume 3*, 332-333, cited by *Christianity Today*, "The Pastor's Relationship with the Board: What a pastor can do to grow the relationship," accessed Oct. 21, 2021, *https://www.christianitytoday.com/pastors/2007/july-online-only/030822.html*
12. Miles J. Stanford, *The Green Letters: Principles of Spiritual Growth* (Grand Rapids, MI: Zondervan Publishing 17

Chapter Twelve

1. Perry Noble, *Overwhelmed* (Carol Stream, IL: Tyndale House Publishers, Inc., 2014), xii.
2. Noble, 49.
3. Leonardo Blair, "New Spring Named 'Jesus Christ' as Senior Pastor After Perry Noble Left, Church was $47M in Debt," *Christian Post*, Sept. 30, 2018, accessed Aug. 24, 2021, https://www.christianpost.com/news/newspring-named-jesus-christ-senior-pastor-perry-noble-church-47m-debt.html
4. Dallas Willard, quoted by John Ortberg, "Ruthlessly Eliminate Hurry," *CT Pastors*, 2002, accessed May 24, 2022, https://www.christianitytoday.com/pastors/2002/july-online-only/cln20704.html
5. Tim Stafford, "Imperfect Instrument," *Christianity Today* (March 2005, Vol. 49, No. 3), 50.
6. Benjamin E. Mays, quoted by Willie Jolley, *It Only Takes a Minute to Change Your Life* (New York: St. Martin's Paperbacks, 1997), 2-3.
7. Aesop, *Fables 536* (from Phaedrus 5.8) (trans. Gibbs) (Greek fable C6th B.C.), accessed Aug. 25, 2021, https://www.theoi.com/Daimon/Kairos.html
8. John D. Arnold, "The Chin-down Manager," *Fortune*, v. 90, no. 1 (July 1974), 98-99.
9. Richard A. Swenson, M.D., *Margin* (Colorado Springs, CO: Navpress, 2004), 69-70.
10. Robert H. Thune, *Gospel Eldership* (Greensboro, NC: New Growth Press, 2016), 92.
11. "Bo Peep' to Aid Shepherds," *The Vidette Digital Archives*, Vol. 89, Number 131, March 8, 1977 (Milner Library, Illinois State University).
12. Dan Graves, "Our Hearts are Restless," *Christian History Institute,* accessed Nov. 10, 2021, https://christianhistoryinstitute.org/incontext/article/augustine

13. "Sleep and Mental Health: Why Our Brains Need Sleep," *Primary Care Collaborative,* May 2019, accessed Oct. 15, 2021, https://www.pcpcc.org/resource/sleep-and-mental-health-why-our-brains-need-sleep
14. "Sleep Deprivation Increases Alzheimer's Protein," *National Institute of Health,* April 24, 2018, accessed Oct. 15, 2021, https://www.nih.gov/news-events/nih-research-matters/sleep-deprivation-increases-alzheimers-protein
15. Spiros Zodhiates, *The Complete Word Study Dictionary: New Testament* (Chattanooga, TN: AMG Publishers, 2000), s.v.4521 *sabbaton.*
16. "Why Protestant Pastors Need a Sabbath," *Christianity Today Gleanings: March 2015,* research by Baylor University sociologists, accessed Aug. 21, 2021, https://www.christianitytoday.com/ct/2015/march/gleanings-march-2015.html
17. Dr. Monica Johnson, "Seven Types of Rest You've Been Missing," Oct. 22, 2021, accessed Nov. 4, 2021, https://www.quickanddirtytips.com/health-fitness/mental-health/types-of-rest#:~:text=There%20are%207%20different%20kinds,social%2C%20sensory%2C%20and%20creative.
18. Butch Blume, "Billy Graham's pastor reflects on 'dear friend, mentor'" *Baptist Press,* March 1, 2018, accessed Aug. 21, 2019, https://www.baptistpress.com/resource-library/news/billy-grahams-pastor-reflects-on-dear-friend-mentor/
19. Stephen W. Smith, "Leadership's Perfect Storm: The Tempest Threatening Leaders' Souls," *Outcomes* (Christian Leadership Alliance), accessed Aug. 24, 2021, https://outcomesmagazine.com/leaderships-perfect-storm/

Chapter Thirteen

1. *Merriam-Webster Dictionary,* accessed Oct. 21, 2021, https://www.merriam-webster.com/dictionary/success

2. Cindy Adams, *Goodreads*, accessed Oct. 21, 2021, https://www.goodreads.com/quotes/65175-success-has-made-failures-of-many-men
3. William James, *GoodReads*, accessed Oct. 21, 2021, https://www.goodreads.com/quotes/168833-the-moral-flabbiness-born-of-the-exclusive-worship-of-the
4. Stephen W. Smith, "Leadership's Perfect Storm," *Outcomes Magazine*, accessed Oct. 31, 2021, www.outcomesmagazine.com/leaderships-perfect-storm/
5. "Church Hopping," *BeliefNet*, accessed Oct. 21, 2021, https://www.beliefnet.com/faiths/christianity/2000/10/church-hopping.aspx
6. Op. cit., *BeliefNet*.
7. Cited by Ray C. Stedman, *Body Life* (Ventura, CA: Regal Books, 1972), 155, 158.
8. Aaron Earls, Lifeway Research, "The Church Growth Gap: The Big Get Bigger While the Small Get Smaller," *Christianity Today*, March 6, 2019, accessed Nov. 6, 2021, https://www.christianitytoday.com/news/2019/march/lifeway-research-church-growth-attendance-size.html
9. Karl Vaters, *The Grasshopper Myth: Big Churches, Small Churches, and the Small Thinking that Divides Us* (Fountain Valley, CA: New Small Church, 2012), 41.
10. Vaters, 115-116.
11. Gene Getz, *Elders and Leaders* (Chicago: Moody Publications, 2003), 215.
12. Robert Stewart, MD, "Seeking to Understand the Rise, Fall, and Loss of Young Pastors," *Chuck DeGroat Blog* (May 20, 2020), accessed Nov. 6, 2021, https://chuckdegroat.net/2020/05/20/guest-post-seeking-to-understand-the-rise-fall-and-loss-of-young-pastors-by-robert-stewart/

13. Stephen W. Smith, "Leadership's Perfect Storm," *Outcomes Magazine*, accessed Nov. 6, 2021, www.outcomesmagazine.com/leaderships-perfect-storm//
14. Scott Thomas, *The Gospel Shaped Leader* (Greensboro, NC: New Growth Press, 2021), 8.
15. Scott Thomas, 1-2.
16. Scott Thomas, 3.
17. "Eleven Bible Verses about Comparison to Help You Stop Comparing Yourself to Others," *Undoubted Grace*, accessed Nov. 6, 2021, https://undoubtedgrace.com/bible-verses-about-comparison/#:~:text=1%20Corinthians%204%3A7,he%20has%20set%20before%20me
18. Jack McCullough, "The Psychopathic CEO," *Forbes*, Dec. 9, 2019, accessed Oct. 15, 2021, https://www.forbes.com/sites/jackmccullough/2019/12/09/the-psychopathic-ceo/?sh=68f9315d791e
19. Darvin Wallis, "The Modern Evangelical Church is Sick. Here's Where It Fell Apart," *The Christian Post*, Feb. 27, 2021, accessed Oct. 15, 2021, https://www.christianpost.com/voices/the-modern-evangelical-church-is-sick-where-it-fell-apart.html

Chapter Fourteen

1. Kathleen Hendrix, "Unlikely Saga of Great Peace March Nears Its Climax," *Los Angeles Times*, Nov. 9, 1986, accessed Nov. 7, 2021, www.latimes.com/archives/la-xpm-1986-11-09-vw-24076-story.html
2. Hendrix, "Unlikely Saga of Great Peace March Nears Its Climax," *Los Angeles Times*, Nov. 9, 1986.
3. Bernie May, President of Wycliffe USA, 11221 John Wycliffe Blvd., Orlando, FL 32832 in a letter to supporters.
4. Kathleen Hendrix, "Peace March: The Long Thin Line Gets Thinner," *Los Angeles Times*, March 14, 1986,

accessed Nov. 6, 2021, www.latimes.com/archives/la-xpm-1986-03-14-vw-20801-story.html
5. Hendrix, "Unlikely Saga of Great Peace March Nears Its Climax," *Los Angeles Times*, Nov. 9, 1986, accessed Nov. 6, 2021, https://www.latimes.com/archives/la-xpm-1986-11-09-vw-24076-story.html
6. Geroge Jarrett, Dept. of History, University of California, Davis, "The Great Peace March for Global Nuclear Disarmament: Popular Protest in the Reagan Era," *Academia Edu*, Presentation at the Pacific Coast Branch of the American Historical Association, Stanford University, August 5, 2006, 7.
7. William James, *BrainyQuote*, accessed Nov. 7, 2021, www.brainyquote.com/quotes/william_james
8. Ted Engstrom, *The Making of a Christian Leader* (Grand Rapids, MI: Zondervan Publishing, 1976), 104.
9. Charles R. Swindoll, *Living Insights New Testament Commentary: Galatians, Ephesians* (Carol Stream, IL: Tyndale House Publishers, 2015), s.v. Eph. 4:1-3.
10. *Life Application Bible Commentary* (Carol Stream, IL: Tyndale House Publishers, 2001), s.v. Eph. 4:3.
11. *Merriam-Webster Dictionary*, accessed on Nov. 7, 2021, https://www.merriam-webster.com/dictionary/ramrod
12. Jacob M. Braude, *Braude's Second Encyclopedia of Stories, Quotations, and Anecdotes* (Upper Saddle River, NJ: Prentice Hall, 1957), 35.
13. Charles R. Swindoll, 1 & 2 Timothy, Titus, vol. 11, Swindoll's Living Insights New Testament Commentary (Carol Stream, Il.: Tyndale House Publishers, Inc., 2014), 302.
14. *Discipleship Journal*, Issue 84, Nov/Dec 1994, 45.
15. https://www.brotherhoodmutual.com/resources/safety-library/risk-management-articles/children-and-youth/

abuse-prevention/prevent-child-sexual-abuse-in-the-church/, accessed January 4, 2022.
16. E. E. Hendricks quoted by Aquilla Webb, *One Thousand Evangelistic Illustrations* (New York: Harper and Brothers Publishers, 1921), 275-276.
17. Jack Doyle, "Reese & Robbie, 1945-2005," *PopHistoryDig.com*, June 29, 2011, accessed Nov. 6, 2021, https://www.pophistorydig.com/topics/pee-wee-and-jackie/
There is some debate as to whether it was 1947 or 1948.
18. Jonathan Bennett, "The Friendship of Jackie Robinson and Pee Wee Reese," *My Sports Column-Timeless Sport*, accessed Nov. 6, 2021, https://jibennett.com/2014/07/16/the-friendship-of-jackie-robinson-and-pee-wee-reese/
19. Jack Doyle, "Reese & Robbie, 1945-2005," *PopHistoryDig.com*, June 29, 2011, accessed Nov. 6, 2021, https://www.pophistorydig.com/topics/pee-wee-and-jackie/

Chapter Fifteen

1. "Eucalyptus Shallow Root Danger," *SFGate*, accessed Nov. 6, 2021, https://homeguides.sfgate.com/eucalyptus-shallow-root-danger-43715.html
2. Scott Sauls, *From Weakness to Strength* (Colorado Springs, CO: David C. Cook, 2017), 59.
3. Mary Oliver, "Where Are You?" *Red Bird* (Boston: Beacon Press, 2008), 73.
4. Miles J. Stanford, *Principles of Spiritual Growth* (Lincoln, NB: Back to the Bible, 1979), 28-29.
5. Neil T. Anderson, *Becoming a Disciple-making Church* (Bloomington, MN: Bethany House Publishing, 2016), 28.

SCRIPTURE INDEX

Genesis

32:39 62

Exodus

18:25-26 27
19:10 190
24:9-11 .... 31, 73
29:42-43 191
33:20 62

Leviticus

19:32 59
23:3-36 179

Numbers

10:33 58
11:16-17 59
11:16-25 27
11:24-25 60
12:1 297
12:1-15 27
12:1-2, 10 298
12:4 299
13:25-33 80
16:1-40 7
16:3, 19 61
16:31-32 61

Joshua
5:14 62

Judges
5:2 44
6:11-14 62
13:2-24 62

1 Samuel
3:10 142
16:7 134

1 Kings
19:12 142

1 Chronicles
22:19 .... 98, 109

2 Chronicles
20:1-30 180
34:14-35:19 180

Nehemiah
8-10 180

Psalms
1:4 316
5:3 I
19:13 163
19:14 .... 96, 351
20:4-5 .... 145, 196
39:4-5 232
46:10 .... 98, 151
46:11 195
50:10-12 329
51:1-2 143
56:4 144
80:18 XXV

92:4-5	151
127:2	229
133:1-3	11, 39
139:23-24	143
141:3	351
145:19	145

Proverbs

3:3	294
3:5-6	109, 158, 325
10:24	145, 153
11:11	178
11:13	294
11:23	145, 153
12:12	7
12:15	290
12:18	295
13:12	145
13:18	343
13:19	145, 153
13:2-3	290
14:34	178
15:1	297
15:22	27, 39, 175, 291
16:3	158, 175
16:9	175
16:21, 23	291
16:33	114
18:2, 13	294
18:21	103
22:29	343
24:6	39
26:20-22	295
27:5-6	299

28:12 178
28:13 143
28:26 219
29:2 179
29:18 178

Ecclesiastes
4:12 .... 39, 51, 249
7:10 89

Isaiah
6:5 95
6:6-7 96
6:8 96
8:12 126
41:10 195
58:8-9 .... 34, 79, 151
59:1-2 143

Jeremiah
17:7-8 .... 311, 321
45:5 275

Ezekiel
34:4 121

Daniel
10:2-3 115

Hosea
10:12 267

Joel
1:14 .... 178, 198
2:15-17 178

Amos
9:11-12 68

Jonah

3..180

Zephaniah

3:9..39

Zechariah

4:10..263

Matthew

6:3-4..330
6:19-20..329
6:20..256
6:21..329
6:33..256
8:15..122
9:36..146, 275
9:37-38..146
11:28-30...203, 275
15:18..96
16:18..269
19:29..329
20:25-27..30, 36, 57
20:26..XXIV
25:23...80, 282
25:26-28..161
25:34-44..122
26:39..187
26:59..60
28:19-20..101, 265

Mark

6:31..243
10:31..256
14:15..63
14:50..64
14:55..60

Luke

1:37	195
2:49	189
6:12	40
6:38	330
6:40	277
9:46	29, 46
9:54	64
10:39	228
10:40	122
10:41-42	228
10:42	238
11:46	203
14:25-30	275
14:28-30	165
19:36-40	276
22:24	29
22:31-32	315
23:18-25	276
24:33-36	63

John

1:12-13	331
2:12	42
2:23-24	275
3:16	331
6:35-36	85
6:67	256
10:3, 11	212
13:35	287
15:5	7
17:23	352
20:19	63
21:15-17	119, 212, 333

Acts

1:3	63

1:4-5 63
1:12-14 46
1:13-16 63
1:13-14 141
1:14 81
1:23-26 114
2:41 263
2:46 81
4:4 263
4:24 81
5:12 81
6:1 123
6:1-5 183
6:3 .... 124, 327, 328
6:4 .... 210, 333
6:7 264
13:1-3 .... 183, 190
14:23 .... 28, 38, 40, 115, 190
15:3 97
15:4-31 67
15:25 81
15:28 .... 48, 68
15:30 183
20:4 38
20:17 117
20:28 .... 48, 114, 117, 118, 136, 333
20:28-29 211
20:28-30 333
21:20 264

Romans

3:23 331
5:8 331
6:23 331

8:9 60
10:9 331
12:4-5 49
12:16 81
12:18 11
15:5-6 79
15:5-7 351
15:6 81
16:1 123
16:1-2 123

1 Corinthians

1:10 .... 81, 287
1:11 ....104, 295
3:6-7 269
5:4-5, 13 183
9:24-27 57
12:13 60
12:15-18 49
14:40 334
16:2 330
16:15 123

2 Corinthians

1:8-9 274
3:4-6 274
4:7 274
4:8-9 274
5:5 60
5:7 162
8:2 166
8:3 330
8:3-5 167
8:5 329
8:8-9 329

8:18-21 123
8:19 115
9:7 .... 167, 329
10:12 276
12:9 83
12:9-10 274
12:10 83

Galatians

5:20 186
5:22-23 .... 327, 327
6:10 234

Ephesians

1:13-14 60
3:16-19 318
4:1-6 288
4:2-3 307
4:3 289
4:11-12 211
4:12 .... 131, 333
4:15 294
4:16 270
4:29 32
4:30 60
4:30-32 106
5:15-16 .... 233, 253
5:18 235
5:21 28
6:12 314

Philippians

1:1 117
1:27 81
2:1-4 39
2:2 .... 51, 81

3:14 258
4:4 .... 105, 260
4:18-19 330

Colossians

1:15-18 .... 28, 32
1:18 186
1:27 331
2:7 .... 7, 15
2:10 247
3:12-13 40
3:12-15 54
3:23-24 .... 287, 335, 343
4:2 286

1 Thessalonians

2:3-5 92
2:3-6 86
2:4 86
5:12 .... 212, 243, 334, 343
5:16-18 102
5:16-19 343

1 Timothy

1:5 .... 211, 213
1:18 212
1:18-19 199
1:18-20 213
2:1-8 211
2:9 123
3:1-7 .... 40, 212, 327
3:4 .... 127, 212
3:8 123
3:8-13 327
4:7 213
4:12 212

4;13 .... 211, 334
4:14-15 213
4:16 213
5:17 .... 38, 118, 212, 334
6:9-11 213
6:11 212

2 Timothy

1:6 213
1:8 212
1:14 213
2:2 211
2:3 212
2:3-6 257
2:15 .... 211, 333
2:21-22 212
3:1-4 147
3:16 333
4:1-2 211
4:1-4 .... 223, 333
4:5 .... 211, 212, 334
4:7 .... 212, 257

Titus

1:5 38
1:5-7 117
1:5-9 .... 124, 212, 327, 333
2:3,6 123
3:10 87

Hebrews

3:13 301
4:1 251
4:9-11 247
4:11 247
4:13 31

4:16 31
11:6 162
12:2 95
12:14-15 13
13:17 .... 122, 212, 334

James

1:5 144
1:19 297
3:13-18 124
3:14-16 24
3:17-18 .... 126, 327, 328, 333
4:1 .... 25, 186
4:3 187
4:7-10 192
4:11 352
4:13-16 164
4:14 233
5:9 299

1 Peter

3:7 215
3:11 11
5:1-2 117
5:1-4 334
5:2 .... 118, 333
5:2-3 212
5:3 .... 120, 122
5:5 .... 44, 88
5:7 212

2 Peter

1:3 247
3:9 331

1 John

1:8-10 143

3 John

9-10 45

Revelation

3:15-16 85
3:20 182
4:8 191
5:11 264
19:6-7 191

SUBJECT INDEX

Accountability of leaders, 28, 44-45, 105, 122, 236, 291, 293, 353
Anthony, Michael, 21
Attitude, 38, 39, 61, 126, 131, 133, 259, 260, 268, 286, 329, 343
Augustine, 243
Authenticity, 30, 83, 84, 90, 319
Authority, 20, 28, 30, 32-33, 34, 44, 46, 48, 71, 106, 122, 128, 150, 184
Bakker, Jim and Tammy Faye, 163
Balance 21 Schedule, 235-243
Barclay, William, 119
Barna, George, 206, 208
Barna Group, 258
Barton, Ruth Haley, 144, 152
Blackaby, Henry, 102, 169
Board meetings
    Advantages, 22-23, 68-70
    Cancel board and replace, XXIII, 55-56, 77, 89
    Characteristics, 78-90, 217, 278
    Demonic influence, 24
    Divisiveness and infighting, XXIII, 37, 106, 187, 269, 302
    Dysfunction, XIII, 3-6, 23-24, 30-31, 56-57, 70-71, 93-94, 106
    Frustration for pastoral leaders, 8-11
    Frustration for volunteer leaders, 6-8, 55
    History, 21, 56

386 | Subject Index

    Self-centered bullies, 23, 24, 40, 46, 57, 69, 111-113, 116, 125, 160, 186, 273, 290

    Voting blocks, 23, 30

Board Policy Manual (BPM), 69

Budget types

    Challenge, 168-169

    Missions, 168

    Play-it-safe, 159-162

    Prayer and faith, 1686-169

    Presumptuous, 162-166

Buechner, Frederick, 144

Burnout, 83, 204, 217, 272, 310, 313

Busby, Dan, 69, 70, 88, 91, 103

Busyness, 8, 225, 230, 251, 268, 311

Carver, John, 77, 91

Casting lots, 113-114

Christianity Today, 87, 260, 262

Chronos-driven leader, 235

Church discipline, 300-301, 349

Church growth, 265-271

Church numerical size in the Bible, 263-265

Commissioning leaders, 119

Commitment to ministry integrity, 292-293, 341

Communication checkpoints, 294-295

Conflict, 17, 41, 55, 69, 106, 140, 150, 186, 187, 207, 235, 249, 285, 289, 297-299

Congregation business meetings, 157, 181-188

CoreStrengths, 40-41, 219

Core values, 289, 337

Damiani, Lou, 101

Dangers

    Catering to the crowd, 275

    Celebrity status, 272-273

Subject Index | 387

Comparison, 276, 312
Excessive drivenness to achieve, 274
Isolation, 9, 50, 210, 242, 274, 310, 312, 313, 314, 318
Power and greed, 276-278
Shallow relationships, 273-274
Deacon, deaconess, 9, 23, 28, 117, 122-124, 127, 129, 135, 141, 302, 327
Decision making, 19-20, 23, 28, 33, 45, 48, 69, 78-79, 80-82, 97, 101, 104, 114, 121, 125, 130, 149, 158, 184-185, 188, 289
Depression and discouragement, 4, 83, 84, 142, 147, 203, 226, 242, 245, 301, 311, 313, 314, 317
Dictatorial leaders, 9, 17-18, 19, 28, 45-47, 111-113, 133
Diotrephes, 45, 48, 52
Dragon breath, 140, 152
Drucker, Peter, 77, 216
Eichler, Ken, 219
Elders, 9, 10, 18, 22, 23, 27, 28, 31, 38, 40, 44, 48, 59, 60, 61, 65, 66, 73, 77, 97, 103, 105, 106, 114, 115, 116, 117-122, 123, 124, 125, 126, 129, 130, 135, 136, 141, 177, 178, 198, 209, 211, 212, 213, 302, 313, 327
Encouragement, 50, 102, 103, 214, 235, 301, 314, 351
Engstrom, Ted, 286
Equipping believers, 131, 270, 333, 337
Failure in the ministry, 279
Faithfulness and success in the ministry, 278-280
Fasting and prayer, 38, 40, 115, 116, 131, 134, 177, 178-180, 190, 195
Financial debt, 164-166, 169, 170-171
Forward-looking, 88-89
Franklin, Ben, 291
Goals, 40, 86, 145, 148-150, 167, 170, 180, 190-194, 271
God Meetings
    Biblical examples, 58-68

Subject Index

Biblical pattern, 96-98
Characteristics, 78-90
Heart preparation, 95-96
Laugh and have fun, 42, 105, 249, 262
Meeting location, 70
Planning, 98-106
Prayer partnerships or cohorts, 99, 218, 325
Presence and power of God, 60, 61, 62, 95, 96, 99, 144, 191, 211
Priority of God's Word, 78
Separate shepherds' meeting, 100, 101
Size of the leadership group, 128-129-131
Terms of service, 129
Why meet? 2, 70, 71

God's will, 27, 78, 94, 97, 103-104, 142, 144
Graham, Billy, 249, 275, 292
Haskins, Dale, 310
Holy Spirit and leaders, 11, 60, 63, 66, 68, 78, 79, 81, 82, 97, 98, 99, 106, 107, 114, 115, 117, 124, 126, 127, 134, 143, 144, 145, 150, 166, 167, 185, 194, 203, 225, 234, 240, 250, 257, 260, 276, 287
James, William, 286
Jolley, Willie, 233
Kesler, Jay, 235-236
King, Claude, 102, 179
Laundry love, 148
Leadership gift, 43-44
Leadership styles, 20
Lessons from the Church Board Room, 69, 88, 91, 101
Lifeway Christian Resources, 10
Lincoln, Abraham, 26
Listening, 60, 67, 68, 69, 70, 71, 80, 96, 97, 102, 103, 125, 134, 141, 143, 145, 149, 150, 151, 180, 188, 192, 195, 196, 290, 291, 297

Listening to God retreat, 141-145, 150-151
Lordship of Christ and sovereignty of God, 29-34, 89, 144, 158, 188, 191, 195
Lutzer, Erwin W., 28
McCullough, Jack, 277
Metcalfe, J.C., 316-317
Miller, Chuck, 7, 14
Ministry Position Description (MPD), 69, 213, 300, 333
Mobilization of every believer, 270
Models of governance
    Corporate model, 21-25
    Presidential model, 25-28-
    Team ministry model, 28-29
Moral failure, 47, 138, 204, 272, 277, 278, 311, 313
Morrish, John, 56
Moses, 27, 31, 43, 58, 59, 60, 61, 65, 66, 68, 73, 83, 118, 190, 297, 298, 299
Munger, Robert, 7
Narcissism, 31, 45-47
Natural Church Development (NCD), 271
Oliver, Mary, 312
Oneness and unity, 48, 79, 82, 287-289, 351
Osborne, Larry, 70, 100
Pastors
    Caring for, 50-51, 249-251, 311
    Confusion of role, 18-19, 156, 208
    Cost of replacing staff, 10
    Expectations of people, 202-210
    Family and marriage, 208, 250
    Fine-tuning expectations, 213-216
    God's expectations, 10-213, 257
    Like a quarterback, 48-51
    Major tasks, 206-207, 214

390 | Subject Index

    Pressure to succeed, 258-261, 265-269, 271-278
    Qualifications, 327-328
    Reasons pastors are quitting, 8-11, 216-217
    Relationship with the board, 8-11, 57
    Resentment and bitterness, 6, 58-59, 64, 80, 204, 210, 235
    Schedule, 231-243, 251
    Search for the super pastor, 132, 208-209
    Sifted by Satan, 315-317, 318
    Termination, 8, 31, 57

Pearson, John, 69, 70, 88, 91, 103
Perfect storm, 199-200
Pierce, Bob, 231-232
Politics and power plays, 29-30, 31, 125, 151
Powers, Avery, 317-318
Preventing child sexual abuse policy, 293
Prime responsibility chart, 69
Pursuing peace, 11
Rainer, Thom, 183-184, 205
Reagan, Ronald, 42, 52
Rebellion, 61
Reconciliation, 11-13
Revival, XXV, 106-107, 178, 189
Rhyme of the Ancient Mariner, 51
Ruling elder, 121
Sabbath rest, 246-249
Sacred assembly, 179-196
Sande, Ken, 216
Saucy, Robert, 115
Sauls, Scott, 311
Schaeffer, Francis, 287
Schaeffer, Francis A., Institute of Church Leadership, 9, 14, 214, 216

Schaller, Lyle, 258
Selecting leaders

Subject Index | 391

    Based on biblical responsibilities, 117-124
    Dangers and cautions, 127-131
    Deacon and deaconess, 122-124
    Elder, overseer, pastor, 117-122
    Fasting and prayer, 115
    Qualifications, 125-127, 327-328
    Selected by the Holy Spirit, 114-127
    Selecting a lead pastor, 131-134
Shallow roots and relationships, 225, 257, 267, 273-274, 309 310, 318
Shelley, Marshall, 87, 139, 140
Silence and solitude, 59, 67, 98, 99, 142, 143, 145, 151
Sjogren, Steve, 216
Sleep, 245-246
Smith, Bob, 261
Smith, Chuck, 106
Smith, Stephen W., 199, 251, 257
Soul care, 243-245
Spirit-filled desires, 144-146, 149, 170, 196
Spiritual gifts, 40, 43-44, 49, 204, 206, 211, 213, 267, 270, 337
Spurgeon, Charles, 83-84
Staff reviews, 299-300, 343-347
Standing Stone Ministry and retreats, 50, 249-250, 313
Stanford, Miles, 219
Stanley, Charles, 24
Statistics
    Board conflict and why pastors leave, 9-10
    Burnout, 83, 217
    Church numerical size in America, 262
    Conflicts related to the motivational drive, 41
    Declining spiritual life for volunteer leaders, 7
    Depression, 83
    Fear of inadequacy, 83

392 | Subject Index

    Financing and debt ratios, 165
    Insomnia and ADHD, 245
    Megachurches and small churches worldwide, 263
    Numbers game, 258-261
    Organization control issues, 9
    Pastors leaving the ministry, 9-10, 216-217
    Pastoral time in needless meetings, 214
    Sleep deprivation, anxiety, and depression, 245
    Unrealistic expectations and overworked, 217

Status Quo, 88
Stedman, Ray, 48, 261
Steinki, Peter, 47
Stories and illustrations
    Baseball ins and outs, 19
    Board meeting on the fly, 93-94
    Build it—they will come, 165
    Burn out, not rust out, 231-232
    Celebrity status, 272
    CEOs who crave power, 277
    Challenge budget, 169
    Color of carpet, 187
    Declining numbers, 260-261
    Dissension is a sin, all in favor, 19
    Distrust and division, 137-140
    Divided leaders, 106
    Don't despise small things, 263
    Flo, 181-182
    Forged documents for Stalin, 216
    Gloom in a budget meeting, 155-156
    Grasshopper myth, 262
    Great peace march, 283-285
    Greek god kairos, 233
    Hope for pastoral burn out, 313

Subject Index | 393

I hate going to board meetings, 3-6
I have only a minute, 233
I was wrong, 163
Jr. High pastor fired, 259
Life in the fast lane, 228-230
Locust invasion, 177-179
Meeting of the board, 75-76
Mind-numbing, monotonous meetings, 185
Ministry tanking, 255-256
Montgomery Ward, 161
Moses's meltdown, 58
Narcissus, 45-46
NPC syndrome, 209
Overwhelmed, 225-227
Painful report to the board, 103
Pastor fires the elders, 17-18
Pastor hit in the face, 24
Pastor threatened with a gun, 24
Perfect pastor, 132-133
Perfect storm, 199
Power and greed, 276-277
Professional worrier, 163-164
Redwood trees, 309-310
Reese and Robbie, 303-305
Sexual affair in the staff, 295-296
Shoe-banging Pastor, 24
Sifting, 315-317
Slaying Goliath, 169
Squeaky wheel, 86-87
Stage four cancer, 217
Ten-day sleepover, 62-64
The ayes have it, 26
The bully, 111-113

394 | Subject Index

    The devil's arsenal, 301-302
    Twenty-one units in a week, 235-236
    Why can't you get more done? 201-202
    Woodbridge faith journey, 170-173
    World Reconciliation Sunday, 12-13
Storms in the ministry, 10, 113, 151, 156, 199-200, 208, 234, 244, 257, 272, 309, 310, 312, 314, 318-319
Submission definition, 44
Success in the ministry, 278-280
Success-saturated culture, 256-257
Surrendered lives of leaders, 31, 32, 34, 44, 47, 60, 71, 78, 82, 94, 96, 98, 100, 101, 102, 105, 107, 108, 139, 140, 142, 144, 150, 188, 191, 195, 220, 247, 325
Swindoll, Chuck, 11, 24-25, 127, 139, 218, 287
Synergy, 37-38
Tangeman, Gary, 313
Team ministry
    Biblical ideal, 37
    Commitment to, 302, 351-352
    Teams in the Bible, 38
    Shaping a group into a team, 39-42
Thomas, Scott, 273, 275
Thune, Bob, 169
Thune, Robert H., 22, 240
Time invested wisely, 232-243
Time priorities, 241-243
Tozer, A. W., 32-33, 35
Tripp, Paul David, 133
Trivia trap, 77-78, 94, 100, 157, 190
Vaters, Karl, 262, 263
Vision and mission, 21, 26, 40, 43, 49, 87, 141, 146-148, 152, 155, 156, 167, 178, 180, 181, 190, 191, 206, 214, 270
Voting in the Bible, 80, 81, 184, 187, 188, 193

Wallis, Darvin, 278
Warren, Rick, 170, 216
Willard, Dallas, 230
Wilton, Don, 249
Wimber, John, 260
Winans, Frank, 142
Who's in charge? 7, 17-19, 29-31, 34
Wounds, woundedness, 4, 12, 31, 57, 84, 103, 106, 112, 121, 139, 147, 215, 244, 259, 271, 299, 312, 313, 317

TRAIN YOUR TEAM ... TRANSFORM YOUR MINISTRY

Leadership has an enormous impact on the health and future of your ministry. Unfortunately, few board leaders receive biblical and practical training for this awesome responsibility. Some churches spend more time training ushers, greeters, and parking attendants than their board leadership.

Reverse this trend with the *God Meeting* Video Series. Prevent problems by training the team and resolve potentially explosive issues before they arise. Your team will deepen in their biblical understanding of leadership as they grow in their spiritual walk with God. Combine the reading of the chapter and viewing a brief video by a recognized national leader with a lively discussion of the issues raised. Each video goes with the corresponding chapter in the book.

Training new board members? Have them complete the videos and read the book. They will join your team in step with the others and ready to serve.

Here are two options for training your team. Plan a **Board Breakfast** or a similar gathering to build relationships. This is the format I suggest as you cover one chapter each time you meet: 1) participants read the chapter in advance; 2) when you gather, view the video; and 3) discuss selected questions at the end of the chapter.

Or better yet, schedule a **Leadership Retreat**. Two suggested retreat formats follow. The first retreat, "Teamwork Makes the Dream Work," provides the basic training for the principles in *God Meetings* followed by advanced training in the second retreat, "Healthy Leadership for a Thriving Ministry."

Train your team and experience a spiritual awakening in the boardroom.

GOD MEETING VIDEO SERIES

15 INSPIRATIONAL, TRAINING VIDEOS FEATURING CHRISTIAN LEADERS

Video 1: Navigating a Moral Crisis (9:48)—Jim and Debbie Hogan—Founders and former President of Standing Stone Ministry

Video 2: Biblical Solutions for Resolving Conflict (14:36)—Ken Sande—President of Relational Wisdom 360 and founder of Peacemaker Ministries

Video 3: Teamwork Makes the Dream Work (11:43)—Willie Jolley—Award-winning speaker, consultant, and US Presidential Lifetime Achievement Award

Video 4: The Power of Meeting with God (9:04)—Ron Susek—Global TV ministry "Faith Walk" and President of the Susek Evangelistic Assoc.

Video 5: Building a Great Team (15:39)—Larry Osborne—Teaching Pastor and Kingdom Ambassador for N. Coast Church, Vista, Calif.

Video 6: Building Relationships at a Board Breakfast (5:28) —Larry Osborne

Video 7: Confronting Bully Behavior (9:59)—Scott Thomas—President of Church Planting Partners and former President of Acts 29

Video 8: Vision and Pursuing Dreams Together (11:24)—Bob Shank—Founder of the Masters Program and co-founder of the Barnabas Group

Video 9: Prayer and Planning that Prevents a Budget Blow-up (11:30)—Frank Winans—Sr. Pastor of Woodbridge Community Church, Irvine, Calif.

Video 10: Toxic or Life-giving Ministry (13:10)—John and Jacque Coulombe–Legacy Coalition and Former Sr. Adult Pastor at Evang. Free Church, Fullerton, Calif.

Video 11: Simplify Leading (9:21)—Rusty George—Lead Pastor of Real Life Church, a multi-site church in S. Calif.

Video 12: Preventing Burnout (9:23)—Matthew Cork—Sr. Pastor of Friends Church of Yorba Linda, Calif. and Lionsgate movie *Not Today*

Video 13: Reframing Biblical Success (11:03)—Karl Vaters—International leader for healthy medium and small-sized churches, Host of *The Church Lobby*

Video 14: A Playbook for God's Team (12:14)—Les Steckel—Veteran NFL Coach and former President of Fellowship of Christian Athletes

Video 15: Healthy Personal and Home Life (16:09—Jim Burns—Founder and President of the radio ministry *HomeWork*

Use the Code **GODMEETINGS** to access the entire course for **FREE**

https://standingstone.thinkific.com/courses/god-meetings

RETREAT #1

Teamwork Makes the Dream Work

- What makes for a great team?
- In what ways is serving on a church or ministry board different from a secular board? In what ways is it similar?
- How to have a God Meeting.
- How to identify the unique contribution each person brings to the team.
- What accelerates spiritual and professional growth while you serve together?
- How do you develop healthy personal and family life while serving?

Format: This is a suggested schedule for a training retreat with your leadership team or candidates for your team or ministry staff. Feel free to adapt as needed.

Advance preparation: if possible, encourage participants to read chapters 1 to 6 in *God Meetings* during the 30 days prior to the retreat.

Session One: Friday Evening
(Chpt. 1 "Frustration in the Board Room")

1. Interaction: Outside of your current church, describe an effective leader who has influenced your life and an

example of a leader who was a disappointment. What made the difference?

2. View **VIDEO #1 NAVIGATING A MORAL CRISIS** (11:35) with Jim and Debbie Hogan.

3. Select one or more "Reflection and Discussion" points to talk over (p. 14-15).

4. Self-examination and prayer: "Is there someone you need to contact to pursue peace and ask forgiveness?"

SESSION TWO: SATURDAY MORNING
(CHPT. 3 " TEAMWORK")

1. Personal quiet time: read 3 John 1:5-12 and make notes of the differences between Gaius, Diotrephes, and Demitrius. Following this, read or review chapter 3 "Teamwork."

2. Interaction: What was one of the greatest sports teams in your opinion? What made them great?

3. View **VIDEO #3 TEAMWORK MAKES THE DREAM WORK** (9:37) with Dr. Willey Jolley.

4. Identify the strengths each person brings to the group (make certain no one is left out). To some degree, these characteristics should identify each of us, but who in your group is particularly exemplary in one of these areas (or identify other character traits not listed)?

Helpful	Detailed
Visionary	Confident
Compassionate	Good Listener
Organized	Supportive
Encouraging	Analytical
Insightful	Flexible

- Optional: For fun, act out the football team lineup drama (see #4 on page 53).

BREAK

SESSION THREE: SATURDAY MORNING OR AFTERNOON
(CHPT. 5 "BOARD MEETINGS OR GOD MEETINGS" AND CHPT. 6 "A MEETING WITH GOD")

1. View **VIDEO #5 BUILDING A GREAT TEAM** (12:03) and **VIDEO #6 BUILDING RELATIONSHIPS AT A BOARD BREAKFAST** (6:07) with Dr. Larry Osborne.
2. Select one or more "Reflection and Discussion" points to talk over (p. 91-92 and 108-109).

SESSION FOUR: SATURDAY EVENING
(CHPT. 2 " WHO'S IN CHARGE?")

1. Select one or more "Reflection and Discussion" points to talk over (p. 34-35). Discuss the three models of governance in the chapter. What are the pros and cons for each?
2. View **VIDEO #2 BIBLICAL SOLUTIONS FOR RESOLVING CONFLICT** (15:35) with Ken Sande.
3. Before sharing communion together, meditate and pray through these verses: "Get rid of all bitterness, rage, anger, harsh words, and slander, as well as all types of evil behavior. Instead, be kind to each other, tenderhearted, forgiving one another, just as God through Christ has forgiven you" (Eph. 4:31-32 NLT).

Session Five: Sunday Morning
(Chpt. 4 "Biblical Meetings with God")

1. Personal quiet time: read Ps. 46:1-11. What are the storms on the horizon in your life? Pressures, disappointments, discouragements, threatening situations? Ps. 46:10 says, "Cease *striving* and know that I am God" (NASB). To "cease" means to "go limp, relax, take your hands off, stop trying to control everything, rest." This is translated or paraphrased in the following ways: *Be still* (NLT, NKJV, NIV, ESV), *cease striving* (NASB), *let go of your concerns* (GW), *stop fighting* (GNB), *let be and be still* (AMP), *stand silent* (TLB), *calm down* (CEV), *Step out of the traffic! Take a long, loving look at me, your High God, above politics, above everything* (MSG). What phrase from the various translations speaks most clearly to your life situation?

2. View **Video #4 The Power of Meeting with God** (10:35) with Dr. Ron Susek. When you meet as a group, how will you apply the 4 dimensions of a God Meeting? 1) *Surrender* before God; 2) *Report* what God is doing; 3) *Discover* the Will of God; and 4) *Do* the work of God (see Appendix 1 on page 325).

3. Conclude with a **"Letting Go" Service.** Hand out slips of paper to everyone. Have them write down one or more pressures in their personal life, family, work, or the church. They may choose to keep these confidential or share them with the group. Have a time of prayer focused on releasing these concerns to God.

4. Conclude with one of the great classic hymns based on Ps. 46:10 like "Be Still My Soul" or one of several newer songs.

RETREAT #2

HEALTHY LEADERSHIP FOR A THRIVING MINISTRY

- Identify and prevent the three storms that threaten healthy ministry.
- Apply the principles to develop balance in personal, family, and ministry life.
- Understand why so many ministries suffer shipwrecks even when things appear to be going great.
- Overcome the danger of shallow spiritual roots and relationships.
- Establish a firm commitment to one another on the team.

Format: This is a suggested schedule for a training retreat with your leadership team or ministry staff. Feel free to adapt as needed.

Advance preparation: if possible, encourage participants to read chapters 7 to 15 in *God Meetings* during the 30 days prior to the retreat.

SESSION ONE: FRIDAY EVENING
(CHPT. 15 "STORMS AND STANDING STRONG")

1. Interaction: How many have experienced a nerve-racking, even life-threatening storm (hurricane,

tornado, blizzard, earthquake, tsunami, or another event)? Share your story.

2. View **Video #15 Healthy Personal and Home Life** (16:09) with Dr. Jim Burns.

3. Select one or more "Reflection and Discussion" points to talk over (page 320-321).

4. Do you have an agreed on "Commitment to Ministry Integrity" statement? Duplicate the statement on page 341 Appendix 8 and suggest revisions or additions for your ministry. When finalized have each person sign this.

Session Two: Saturday Morning
(Chpt. 11 "Unrealistic Expectations")

1. Personal quiet time: suggest each person spends time alone focused on the words of Jesus from Mt. 11:28-30. Read or review chapter 11 "Unrealistic Expectations."

2. View **Video #11 Simplify Leading** (9:21) with Rusty George.

3. Select one or more "Reflection and Discussion" points to talk over (page 221-223).

BREAK

1. Discussion: What are the five things God expects of a pastor? How about the expectations for volunteer leaders? What adjustments need to be made? Too often, we overcomplicate the ministry. Effective leadership teams purposefully stay out of meddling and micromanaging.

2. Discuss steps to protect and prioritize spiritual growth and family health.

3. Do you have clear written "Ministry Position Descriptions" for all members of the staff and volunteer leaders as well? (see Appendix 5 on page 333-335 for a sample of an MPD for a senior or lead pastor). Do you have a "Prime Responsibility Chart" indicating the assigned roles for the pastor, board, and staff? How about a "Board Policy Manual" of established policies and past decisions? The retreat is not the time to write these but assign a team to begin work on them. These are tools to simplify the ministry.

Session Three: Saturday Evening
(Chpt. 12 "An Unrealistic Schedule")

1. View **Video #12 Preventing Burnout** (9:23) with Matthew Cork.

2. Select one or more "Reflection and Discussion" points to talk over (page 252-253).

3. Optional: pastors and staff share the general flow of their weekly schedule using the pattern on page 237 and 239. Talk through the pressure points in the schedule along with the challenges. Does the schedule have margin built-in to respond to the unexpected crisis?

Session Four: Sunday Morning
(Chpt. 13 "Unrealistic Pressure to Succeed")

1. Quiet time: read Numbers 12:1-4. What was the surface issue dividing the team of Moses, Aaron, and Miriam? What was the real issue? How did God deal with the issue?

2. View **Video #13 Reframing Biblical Success** (11:03) with Karl Vaters.

3. Select one or more "Reflection and Discussion" points to talk over (page 281-282).
4. Discuss "what matters most" in life and ministry.
5. Prepare copies of "My Commitment to the Team" (Appendix 11 page 351-352) for each retreat participant. Read and talk this through. In a prayer of commitment, invite each person to sign this renewing their commitment to the Lord and their commitment to each other.

www.ingramcontent.com/pod-product-compliance
Lightning Source LLC
Chambersburg PA
CBHW060103170426
43198CB00010B/757